IMAGES
of America

NOCKAMIXON TOWNSHIP

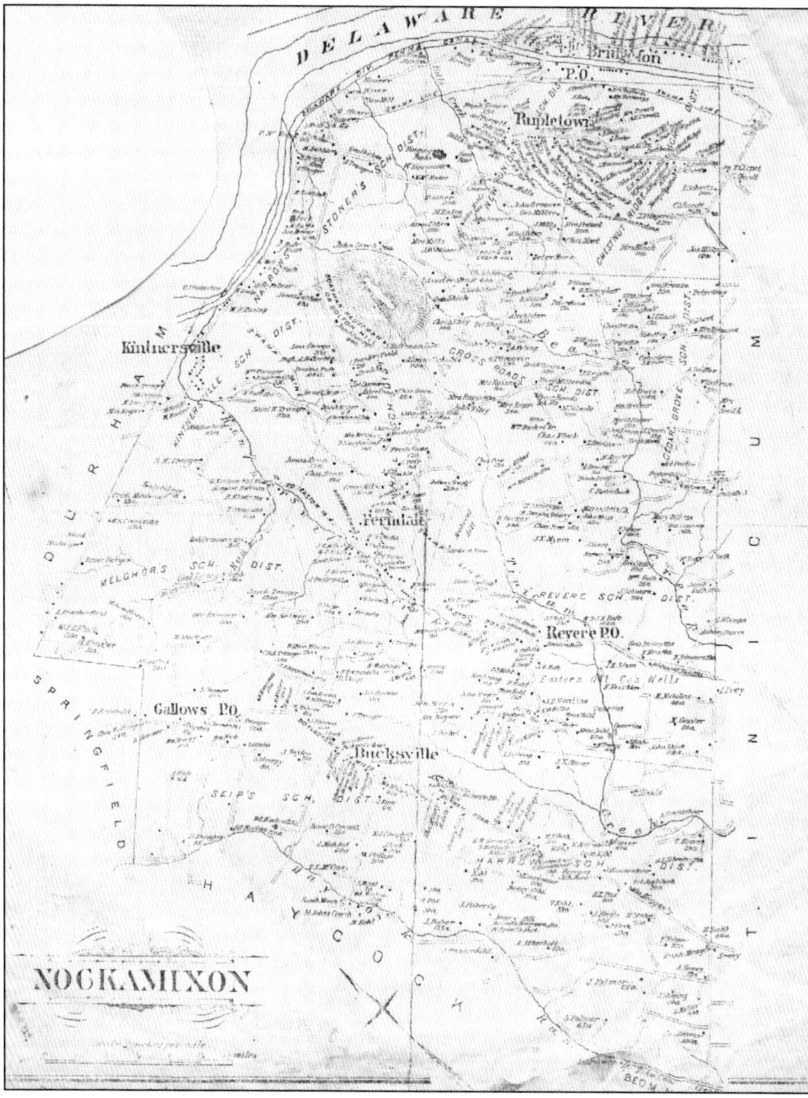

Nockamixon Township's villages, covering 22.09 square miles, are shown on an 1876 map. Durham and Easton Roads are main thoroughfares through the township, emanating at the village of Harrow in the southern corner. Following Durham Road north are the villages of Bucksville and Kintnersville. Traveling Easton Road north are the villages of Revere, Ferndale, and Kintnersville. The hamlet of Narrowsville, located at the township's eastern point, is on River Road, which intersects Easton Road. Bridgeton, located in the southeast, seceded in 1890. (NHS.)

ON THE COVER: Villagers relax in front of the Narrows Hotel in this turn-of-the-century canal scene. For more information, see page 46. (NHS.)

IMAGES
of America

NOCKAMIXON TOWNSHIP

Christine de Socarras and Roger de Socarras
for the Nockamixon Historical Society

ARCADIA
PUBLISHING

ISBN 978-0-7385-7392-2

Published by Arcadia Publishing
Charleston, South Carolina

Printed in the United States of America

Library of Congress Control Number: 2010929510

For all general information, please contact Arcadia Publishing:
Telephone 843-853-2070
Fax 843-853-0044
E-mail sales@arcadiapublishing.com
For customer service and orders:
Toll-Free 1-888-313-2665

Visit us on the Internet at www.arcadiapublishing.com

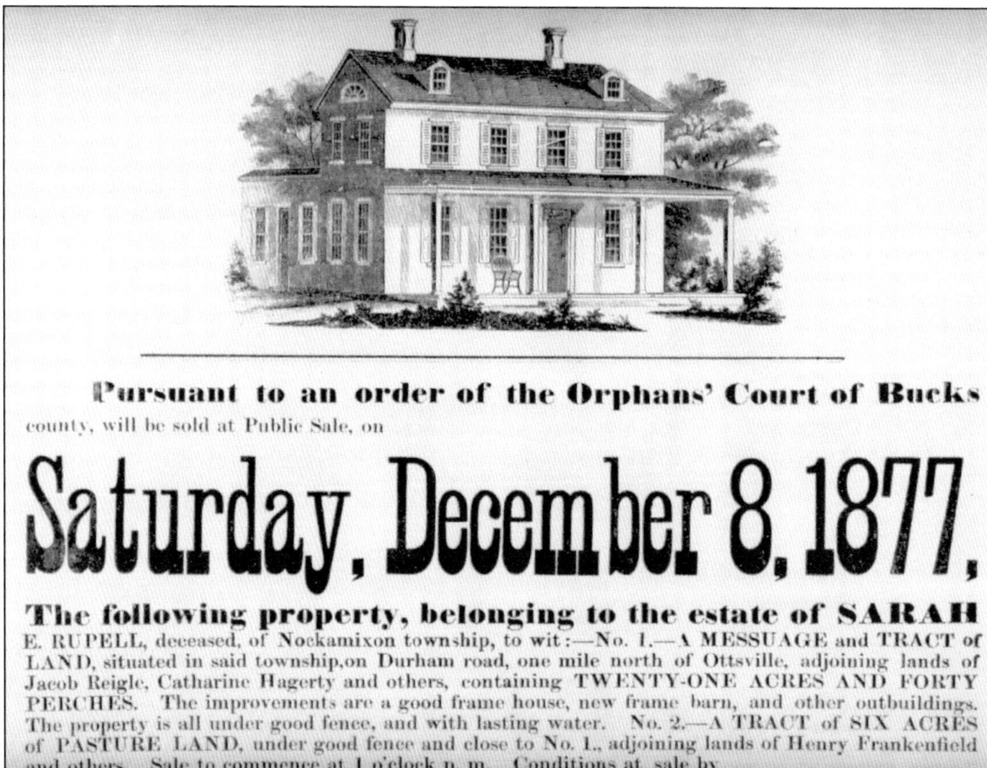

This original 1877 executor's sale of real estate poster advertises land to be sold in Nockamixon. Josiah N. Stover, the executor, posted this notice for the estate of Sarah E. Rupell. Two separate parcels of real estate are listed to be sold at public auction on Saturday, December 8, 1877. These tracts of land are located on the 1876 Nockamixon map on page 2. (NHS.)

Contents

Acknowledgments

We want to thank everyone who graciously provided photographs and information to assist with the writing of the history of Nockamixon Township. Thanks to Salome Trouts Zheltonoga for her memories of growing up in Harrow. She also provided great sources of township and county information published late 1800s to mid-1900s. Rosanne McCarty, a ninth-generation Bucksville resident, shared many albums full of wonderful photographs of the McCarty family and other relatives. Joe and Betty Jane Shuman were helpful providing additional information about the village. Our thanks to Jim Freeh and Bob de Groot for supplying answers to questions about Revere. Blanche Wehrung shared her memories of growing up in Ferndale and contacted friends for additional photographs. Kintnersville was well covered with Carl Lehr's knowledge of the village and post office, and lifelong resident Clarence Berger reminisced about farming in the township. Mildred Williams shared her Kintnersville memories and was also helpful with Narrowsville village and the Delaware River and Canal. Thanks to Ben Naska for memorabilia on the Boy Scouts and leisure activities and contacting residents. For their chronicled information on Nockamixon, the memoirs of Mabel Foellner, Ray Stover, and Mary Shively were extremely helpful.

Photographs are courtesy of the following: American Legion Palisades Post No. 399 (ALP), Clarence Berger (CMB), Gary Bickel (GBG), Robert Butterfoss (RBK), Lillian de Groot Crum (LDC), Roger and Christine de Socarras (RCD), Norma Michener Fox (NMF), Jim and Arlene Freeh (JAF), Michael Gallagher (MGS), Carrie Gamble (CGG), Carol Jones (CJF), Lloyd Keller (LHK), Carl Lehr (CLK), Carol Rufe Lehr (CRL), Loretta Lutz (LLR), Rosanne McCarty (RMC), Elsie McHale (EMH), Benjamin and Barbara Naska (BNB), Nockamixon Historical Society (NHS), Edith and Robert Rapp (ERR), Donna Sciacca (DSB), Joseph and Mary Jane Shuman (JSB), Larry and Janie Stangil (LJS), Martin von Dyck (MVD), Blanche Bartman Wehrung (BBW), Priscilla Lewis Whitman (PLW), Mildred Williams (MRW), Edward Wismer (EWK), and Salome and Alex Zheltonoga (STZ).

We hope that this book will bring back pleasant memories to longtime residents and start an interest in Nockamixon's history within the younger generation.

INTRODUCTION

The Penn family issued the first patent for a tract of land in Nockamixon to Jeremiah Langhorne and John Chapman in 1717. The earliest white settlers, who were English, arrived in 1735, while the Irish came in 1738. Other nationalities, primarily Germans, arrived later and settled in the township. The Shawnee and Lenni Lenape Indians were already inhabitants along the Delaware. The Shawnee left in 1730, probably as a result of the Grasshopper War. The Lenape tribe was forced to move west in 1742 as a result of the terms of the Walking Purchase Treaty of 1737. Nockamixon was able to petition Bucks County to form a township in 1742. The names of 25 English landowners appeared on the document—quite a respectable population for a frontier district. Taking its name from the Native American word *nocka-miks-ing*, meaning "at the place of soft soil" or "at the place of three huts," Nockamixon is one of two townships in Bucks County with an Indian name.

Bucksville was a recruiting post for Revolutionary War soldiers. Thomas McCarty (fourth generation), a member of the commander-in-chief's guard, enlisted in 1776 and was assigned to the cavalry. He stayed in a Valley Forge log cabin next to George Washington's headquarters. Capt. Nicholas Buck (second generation) founded the Washington Light Horse Cavalry in 1807, responding to British attacks on the frigate *Chesapeake*. Capt. Jacob Sassaman and Jacob Buck were members of the Bucks County Rifle Company. Annual training of neighboring townships' companies took place in the village.

Throughout the years, this rural area thrived due to residents who were industrious, imaginative, and persistent. The routes of stagecoach, trolley, and canal that traversed the township also helped to accomplish goals of bringing in more industry and business. Nockamixon's villages—Harrow, Bucksville, Revere, Ferndale, and Kintnersville—each had a general store, hotel or tavern, and a post office.

The primary business in Nockamixon for years was farming, and several farms remain in the township. A close second was the redware pottery industry, beginning in the 1740s, which found that using clay from the township could be manufactured. Products included plates, jugs, pots, crocks, and a variety of other articles used on the farm. When first manufactured, a pie plate sold for 4¢ to 8¢. By 1936, the price had risen to $1.50 each. Mabel Foellner recounts a story about Henry Chapman Mercer. As an addition to the historical and educational work of the Bucks County Historical Society, Mercer looked into resuscitating one of the old potteries and visited Harstine (Herstine) Pottery near Kintnersville in 1897. The Moravian Pottery and Tile Works was built the next year.

By the early 1900s, Easton and Durham Roads were home to many businesses: general stores, automotive garages, egg farms, car dealerships, eateries, sawmills, grist mills, shoe factories, ice cream shops, barber, shoe store, nurseries, fruit and produce stands, paper mill, blacksmith shops, pottery shops, excavators, appliance store, creamery, butcher shops, harness shop, feed mill, funeral home, small department stores, dairy, shoemaker, hotels, and post offices. The milk and bread men would deliver door to door, and the tax collector would stop by and visit while collecting taxes. There were also four doctors in the area. Dr. F. Harvey Grim had an office in Revere.

With the advent of the automobile, Nockamixon improved Easton Road to a cement-surfaced highway in 1921. Reportedly, the first township to do so, the modern highway was an improvement since the automobile made traveling more convenient. An early-1930s *Eastern Tours* book gives travel instructions and maps through the township. Stating that roads were concrete and macadam, the Philadelphia to Scranton route via Easton gave the following directions: "From Ottsville, curve left with concrete; Revere, fork, bend left with trolley; Ferndale; Kintnersville, turn left (sharp) across bridge."

Metropolitan Edison provided electricity to residents living along Easton Road in the mid-1920s, and power lines were strung on trolley-line poles. The Ferndale Telephone Company housed its center of communications in private homes located in Ferndale, Kintnersville, and Harrow. When the telephone exchange started, a typical telephone number was "11R22." It was common for people to listen in on other calls, and the story then traveled throughout the area.

A smallpox epidemic in Kintnersville in 1882 was obviously a sad time with the deaths of so many residents. A glimpse of this time was revealed in letter received by Augusta (Trauger) Frankenfield, Carl Lehr's grandmother, from her sister Catherine Ann Trauger. A young Bethlehem girl visiting the Greer family was carrying the disease. Christopher Greer later covered his sick child with his overcoat. He then wore the coat when a group of neighbors traveled together to dig a grave in cemetery and also serve as pallbearers. The disease apparently passed from one to another in the families exposed to the overcoat.

Music has always been an important part of community life. The Bucksville Coronet Band was organized by John T. Buck in 1890, and it traveled throughout the state in a bandwagon. Members performed at the Bucksville centennial in June 1893, held to honor ancestors of the early-township families. The program took place on five acres of wooded land off Durham Road, where it was reported 1,000 to 1,500 people attended. It has been said that the first piano and voice lessons in Bucks County were given in Bucksville.

Many residents born and raised in the township are descendants of original settlers. They all enjoyed growing up here, relishing outdoor activities with friends and extended families. Social organizations were popular in the community, and meetings were held at the local country store. The Pokanoket Tribe No. 178, International Order of Red Men members would attend their Saturday night lodge meeting in the hall on the second floor. They would then gather later in the store for refreshments.

For entertainment, families went to Ottsville on Friday evenings to watch movies shown on the back of a barn. Lake Warren, built by the Works Progress Administration (WPA) in 1936, was a popular community gathering place. During winter, residents congregated for ice-hockey games, skating, and sleigh riding. In the summer, everyone would get together to swim and enjoy hot dogs and drinks from the refreshment stand. Families always looked forward to attending the biggest celebration around, the St. Joseph's Society Carnival on Marienstein Road. Everyone in the area attended, where people could learn to square dance, play bingo, sample a variety of food, and try their hand at games.

The Nockamixon area is very scenic, whether it is traveling along the canal or climbing the Palisades. The township remains rural, and driving through the village of Kintnersville takes a person back in time.

The history of this community is well preserved in the many buildings that have survived centuries and through vintage postcards, photographs, and memories chronicled by longtime residents.

One

VILLAGES

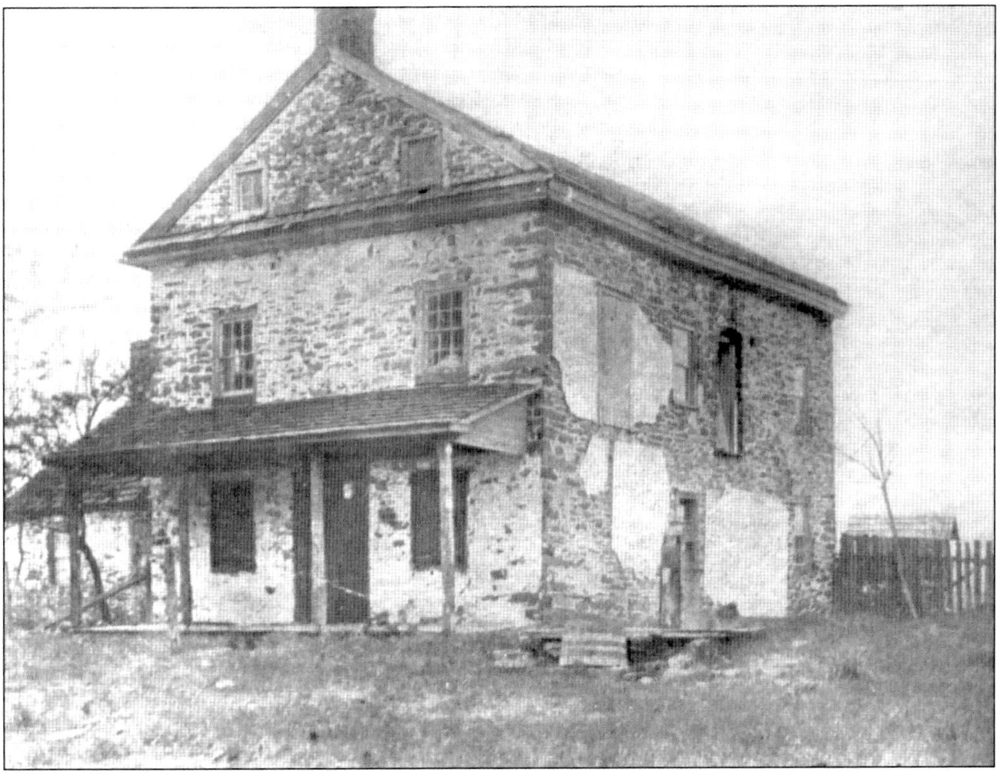

Old Red Hill Inn, built before the Revolution, once stood on Easton Road across from Landmark Inn. The stone shaft to the right of the building marks where participants stopped during the Walking Purchase in 1737. The purchase measured an area a man could walk in a day and a half, pitting three English walkers chosen by William Penn's sons to travel as far as possible in that time. The area covered by the walkers (some could say "runners") was then the land the Lenni Lenape had to vacate. Walking Purchase markers are now located across the highway by Landmark Inn, now an apartment building. (NHS.)

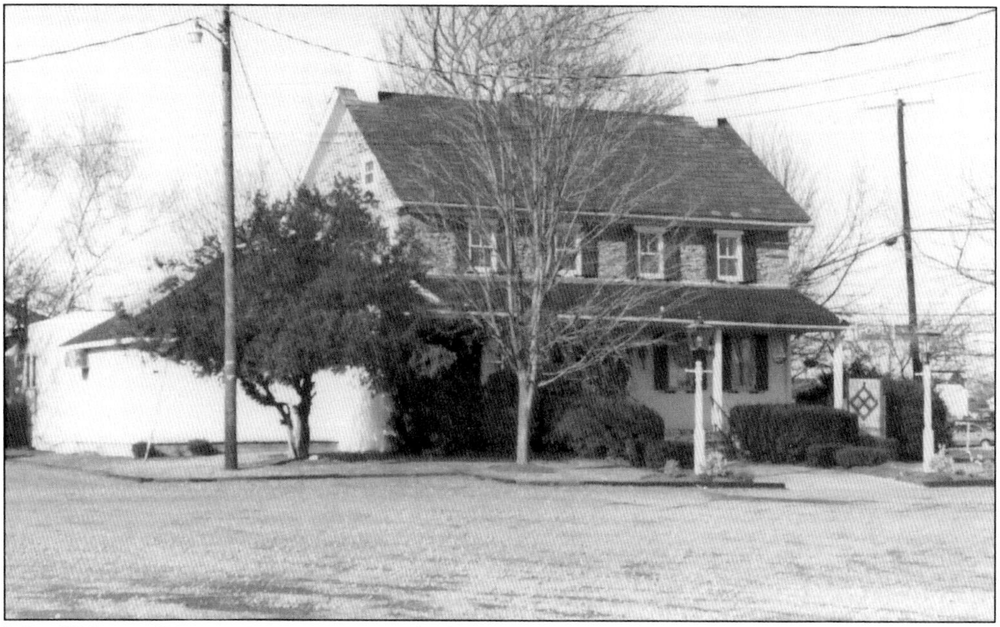

John Wilson of Harrow Inne was granted a license in 1744 "to keep house of public entertainment and retail strong liquors by small measure at the house in which he now dwelleth." He and grandfather Ralph Wilson, renowned trader with the Lenni Lenape, were among petitioners for the establishment of Nockamixon Township. George Shaw arrived in 1784 to keep a tavern. During days of the Philadelphia and Easton stagecoach, the Harrow was regular stopping place. (NHS.)

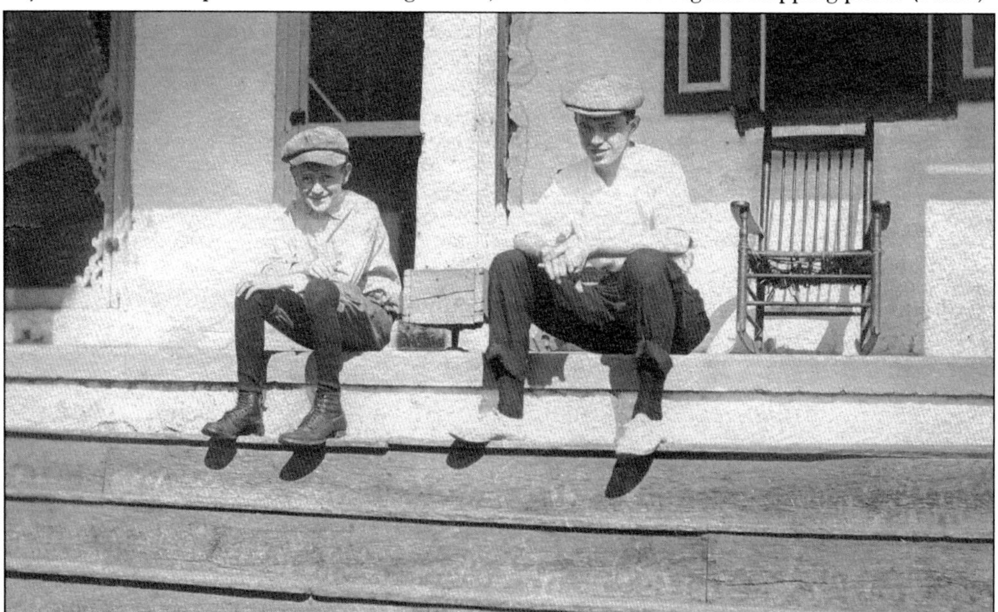

Teenage friends Burt Kohl (left) and Howard Butterfoss sit on the Harrow Inne porch in the early 1900s. Burt followed his father, Abel Kohl, and ran a Ferndale Telephone Company central office in their home at the corner of Quarry and Easton Roads. Howard, son of George and Mary Butterfoss, enjoyed growing up in Nockamixon. Returning in 1932 with wife and children, he purchased a farm on Rock Ridge Road in Revere. (RBK.)

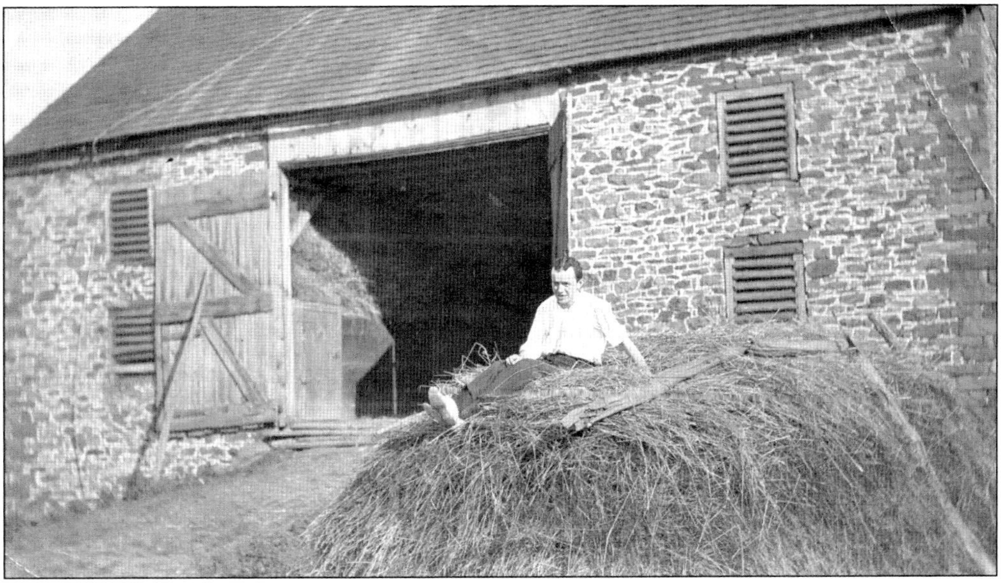

Howard Butterfoss relaxes on a hayloft outside Harrow Inne's barn in the early 1900s. Returning to Nockamixon, the family had to get acclimated to country living. Sons Robert and Howard Jr. were not accustomed to walking such a long distance to school; Howard learned to drive, commuting to work at Philadelphia Electric. Robert remembers Marienstein as a dirt road that the WPA improved and paved. He and his wife reside at their home built on the family farm. (RBK.)

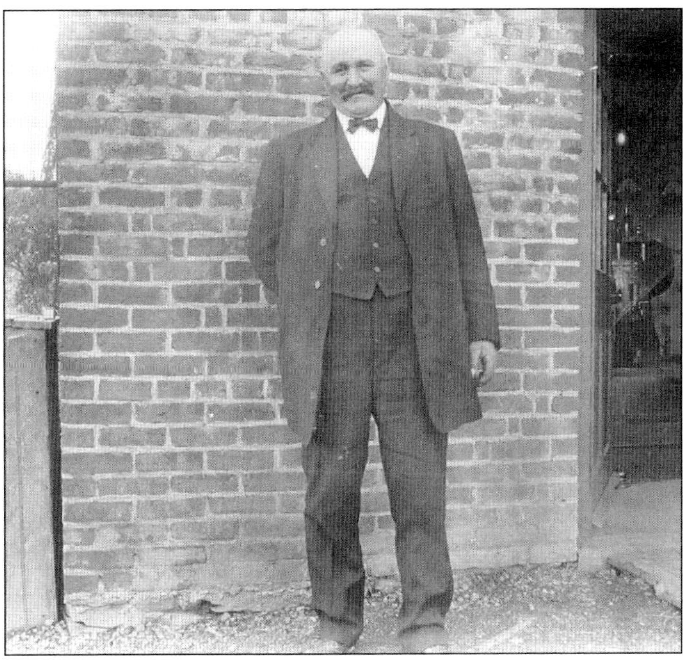

William Scott Schwar, a canal boat operator, stands in front of a Doylestown and Easton Railway trolley power substation that was located in a triangular-shaped area at the Harrow intersection of Durham and Easton Roads. The line, completed in 1904, was busy hauling both passengers, mail, and freight. Oliver S. Kimenhour operated the substation for the trolley line. A switch allowing north- and south-bound cars to pass was located in Revere across the road from Nockamixon Consolidated School. (MGS.)

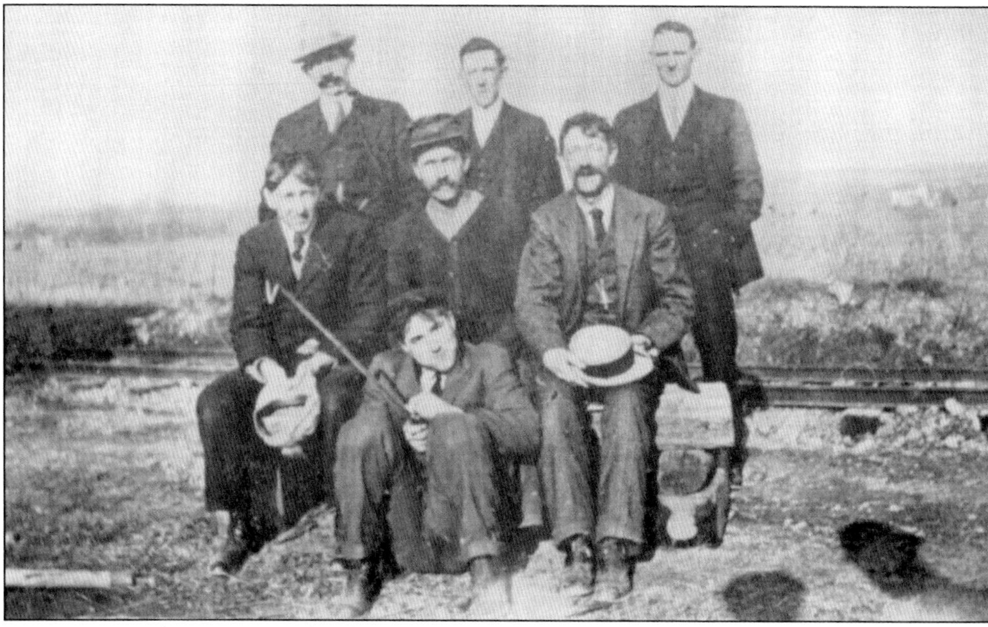

Passengers are shown waiting for the trolley at the Harrow substation. The conveyance sometimes was used to move stones from the village quarry. Wagonloads would be brought up by mules. The stone—red, blue, and gray—was then loaded on the trolley and transported to a destination where it would be used for curbing. Operations were suspended in late 1926 due to the popularity of the automobile. (NHS.)

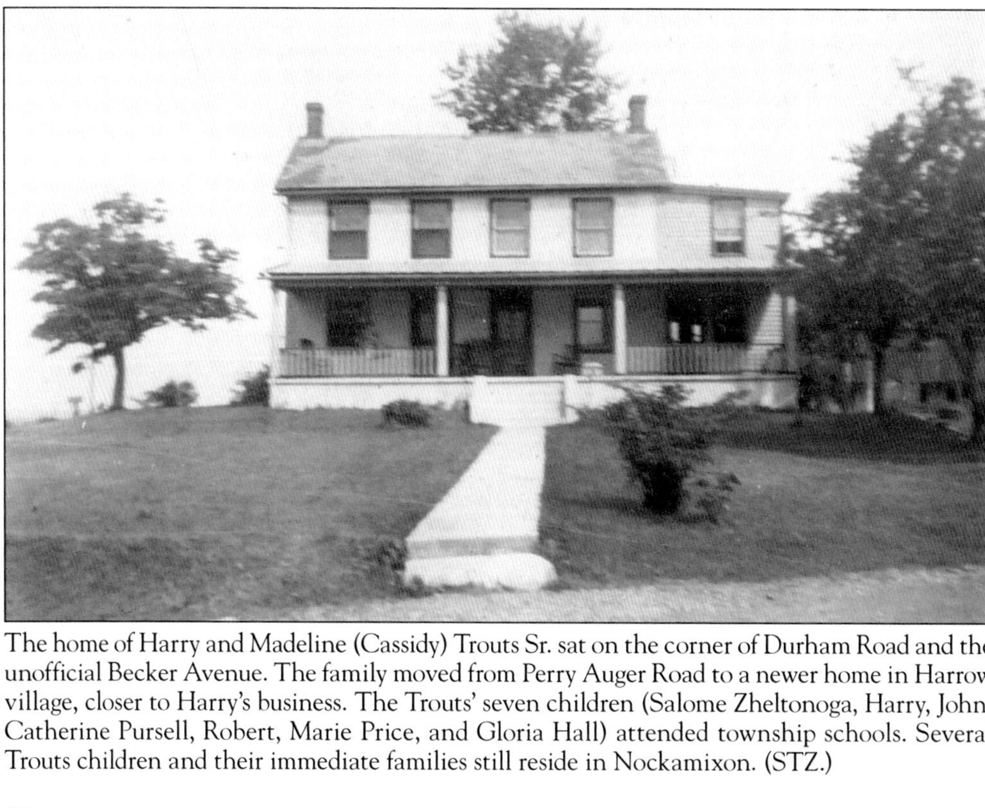

The home of Harry and Madeline (Cassidy) Trouts Sr. sat on the corner of Durham Road and the unofficial Becker Avenue. The family moved from Perry Auger Road to a newer home in Harrow village, closer to Harry's business. The Trouts' seven children (Salome Zheltonoga, Harry, John, Catherine Pursell, Robert, Marie Price, and Gloria Hall) attended township schools. Several Trouts children and their immediate families still reside in Nockamixon. (STZ.)

Trouts Garage in Harrow, shown in this 1948 photograph, was owned by Harry Trouts Sr. A blacksmith by trade, he also built wagons. Harry often was called to the battleship *New Jersey* for repairs at Philadelphia Naval Shipyard. The increase in automobiles brought a demand for repair facilities, so he and his sons were kept busy servicing vehicles. As road master, he also hauled large amounts of stone out of the local quarry. (STZ.)

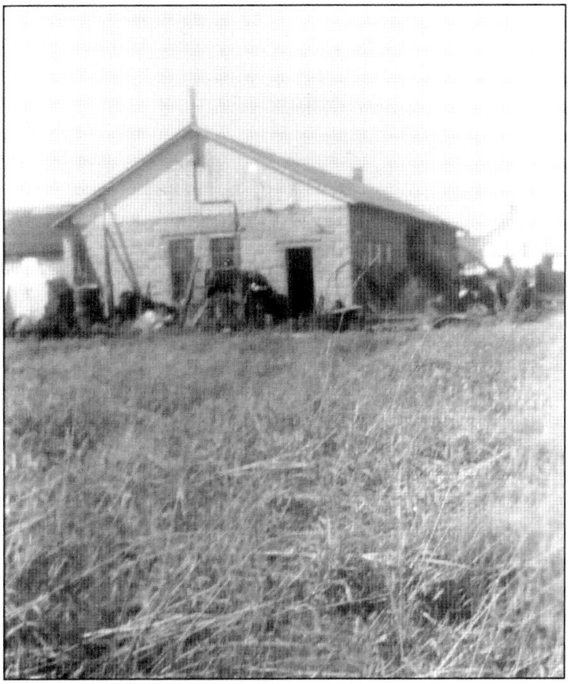

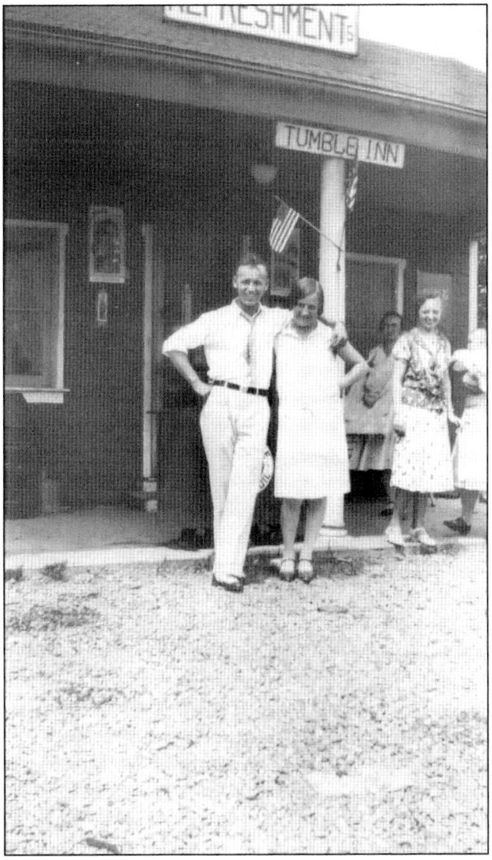

Tumble Inn, seen here in 1931, was owned by Andrew and Ottilia Balbirer and was located at the intersection of Durham Road and Mountain View Drive in Bucksville. It was a busy spot due to its location, with roads leading to Quakertown and Doylestown. The luncheonette served food and drinks and sold general-store items and gasoline. Standing in front are, from left to right, Eugene Loeffelman, Anna Balbirer, Stephanie (Loeffelman) Denning, and Ottilia Balbirer holding granddaughter Eleanor Snyder; in back is Regina (Balbirer) Snyder. (RMC.)

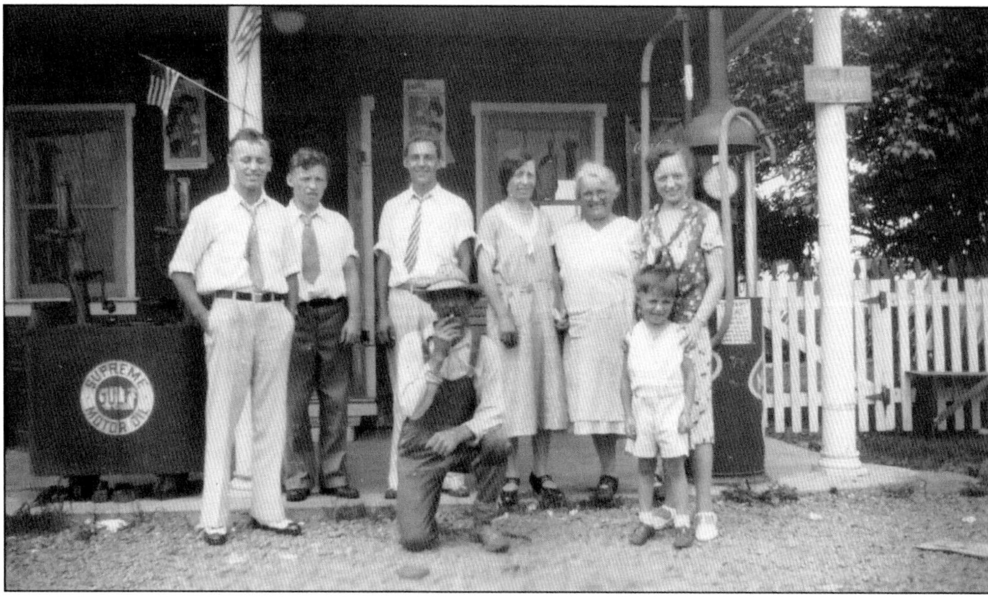

Andrew and Ottilia Balbirer had difficulty dealing with salesmen coming to their store since they did not understand English. Daughter Anna Balbirer realized this and left school to manage the luncheonette. She enjoyed helping her parents, and business prospered. Family and friends gather here in 1931 at the Tumble Inn. Seen from left to right are (front) Andrew Balbirer and Andrew Snyder Jr.; (back) Eugene Loeffelman, Leopold Loeffelman, Jack Foltz, Josephine Loeffelman, Ottilia Balbirer, and Stephanie (Loeffelman) Denning. (RMC.)

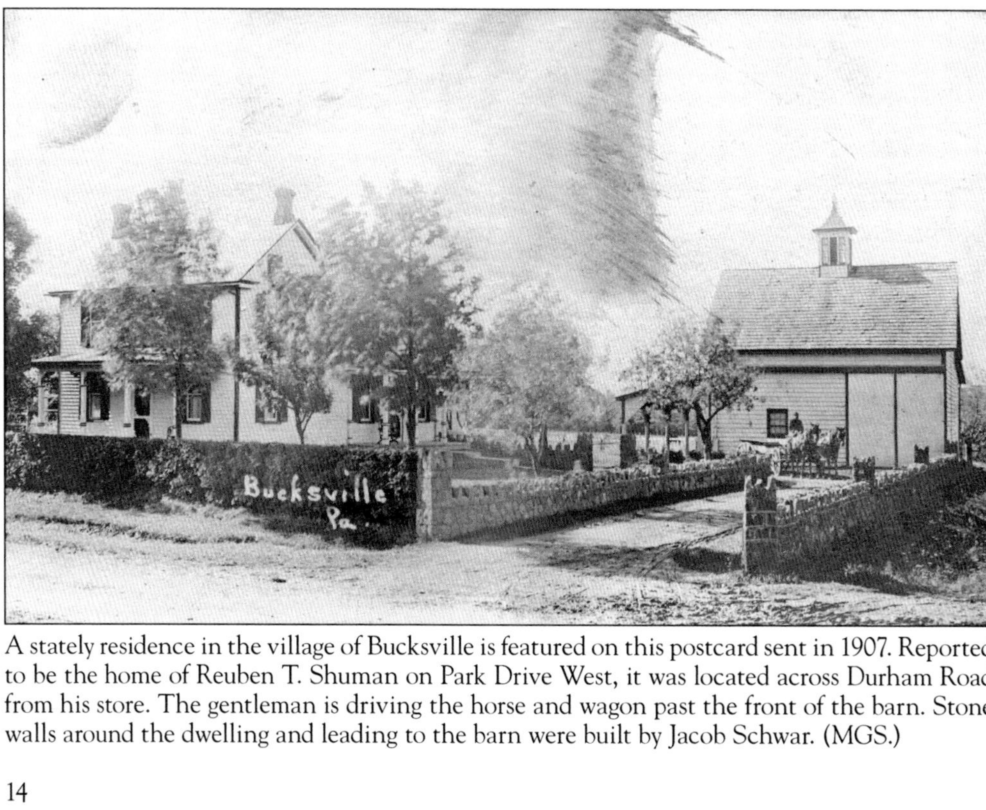

A stately residence in the village of Bucksville is featured on this postcard sent in 1907. Reported to be the home of Reuben T. Shuman on Park Drive West, it was located across Durham Road from his store. The gentleman is driving the horse and wagon past the front of the barn. Stone walls around the dwelling and leading to the barn were built by Jacob Schwar. (MGS.)

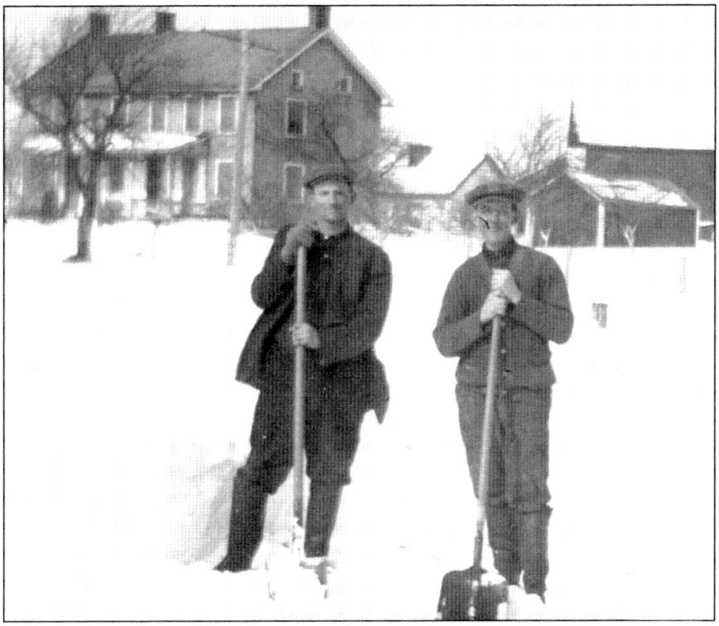

This early-1900s winter scene shows two gentlemen taking a break from shoveling snow to pose for a photograph. The early-1800s stone house with outbuildings is located on Durham Road in Bucksville. Christian Traugher Jr. is documented as the owner of this parcel at one time. The 1798 Federal Direct Tax Record shows buildings on the property included a 20-foot-by-20-foot log house of two stories, a log kitchen, and a stable. (DSB.)

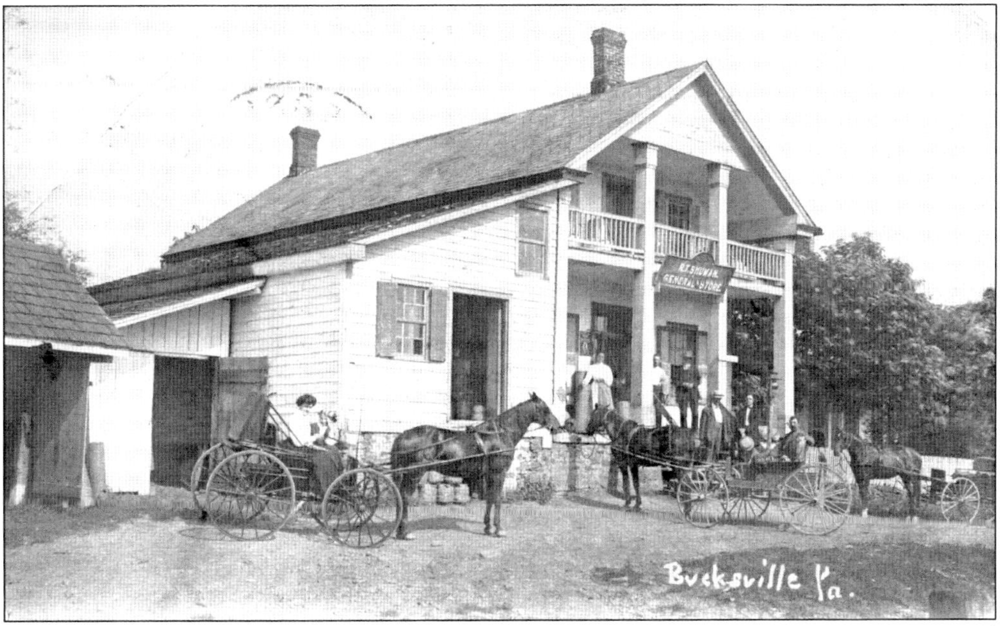

Reuben T. Shuman ran the general store on Durham Road in Bucksville. The farmer's store sold feed and grain, while a two-story section housed the grocery store and post office. The Fox family built it in 1856, later selling it to Thomas Y. McCarty before Reuben purchased the store in 1890. Sold in 1922 to Erwin Anders, Reuben repurchased it in 1924, retaining ownership until his death. Reuben's daughter May Raub ran the store and sold it to Paul Freeh in 1954 for an antique shop, which was destroyed by a fire in 1964. (JSB.)

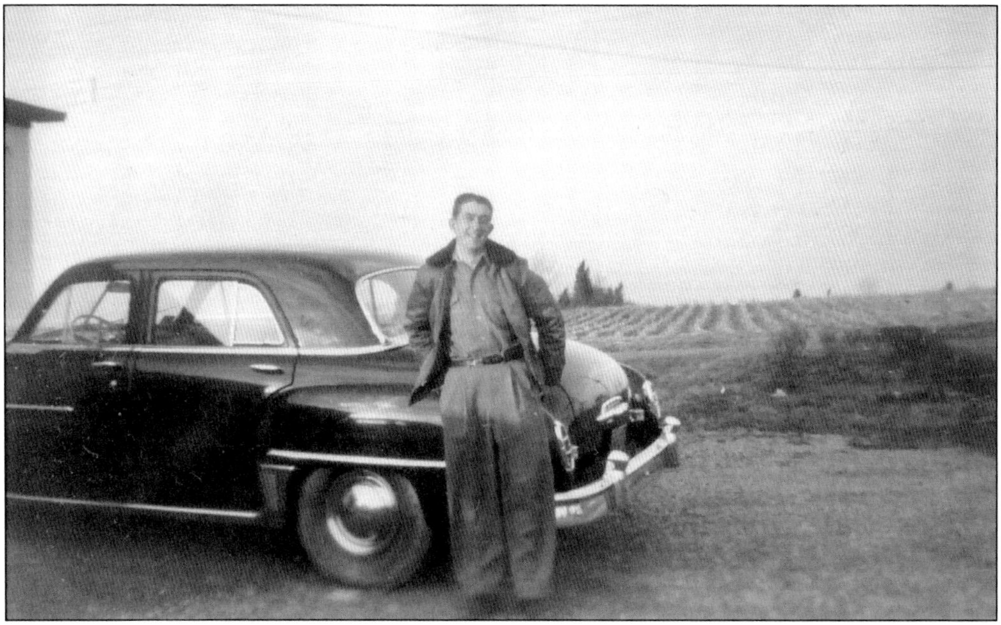

Joseph Shuman, son of Winfield and Laura (Mitch) Shuman, owned and operated Mountain View Dairy on Church Road in Bucksville from 1939 to 1953, selling pasteurized and homogenized Guernsey milk and cream on the family farm. At only 17 years old, he started his business milking 53 cows, hand-bottling the milk, and then making deliveries with one truck. The dairy progressed to automatic bottling and three trucks as its delivery area went beyond the Nockamixon area to Plumsteadville. (JSB.)

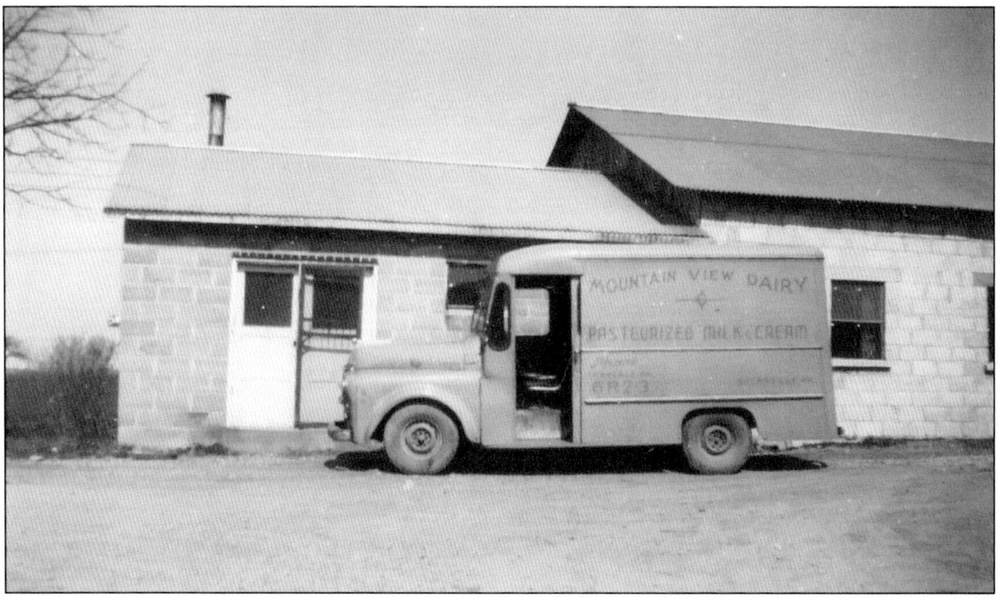

Joseph Shuman's six siblings assisted with milking the cows, running the dairy store, and making deliveries. Local schoolchildren looked forward to the small bottles of milk with paper caps on top, which they enjoyed for lunch. To supply his many customers with regular and chocolate milk and other products, raw milk was purchased from other dairies and then pasteurized and homogenized. Joseph also bought butter, cheese, and sour cream from Ottsville Creamery. (JSB.)

After 14 years, Joseph Shuman sold his business to Rosenberger Dairy and went to work as a cabinetmaker, following his father, Winfield. He and his wife, Mary Jane (Beck) Shuman, have Mountain View Dairy milk bottles with the slogan, "Fresh from the Farm," and a special commemorative china plate issued in 1953. Many of these dairy items have become collectible and often seen at area auctions. (JSB.)

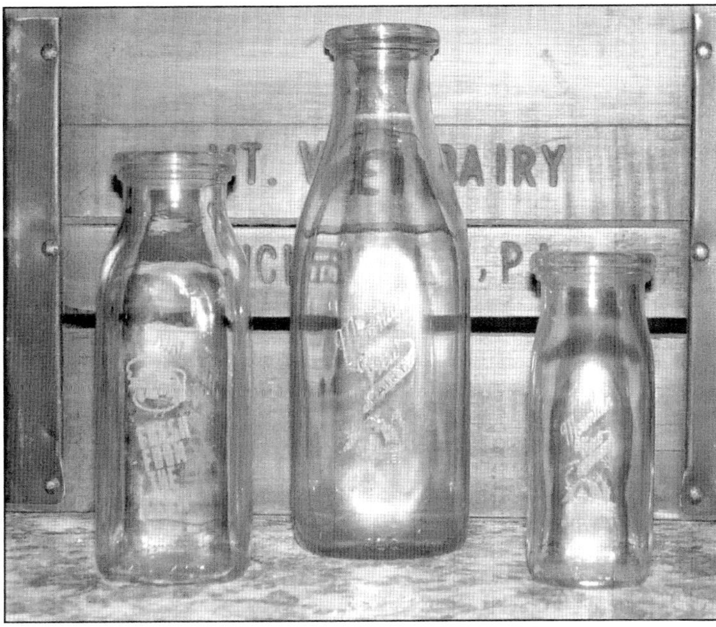

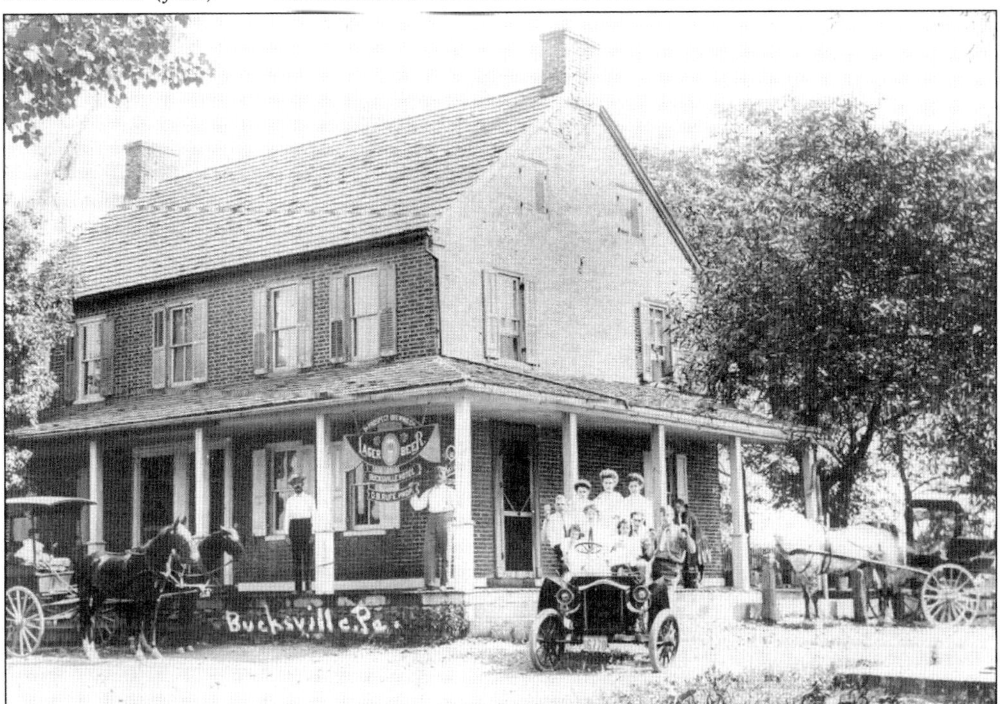

The Bucksville Hotel on Durham Road is shown here in the early 1900s, with O.B. Rufe as the proprietor. Originally known as the White Horse Tavern, the structure includes sections of the original 1795 stone building constructed by Bucksville founder Capt. Nicholas Buck, with an 1840 expansion by son Nicholas Buck Jr. Ferndale's John H. Nickel rented the hotel from Buck's estate and became Bucksville Hotel's proprietor in 1899. Sheridan Matlack was later the owner in 1914. Supposedly a speakeasy during Prohibition, the Bucksville House is now a bed-and-breakfast. (NHS.)

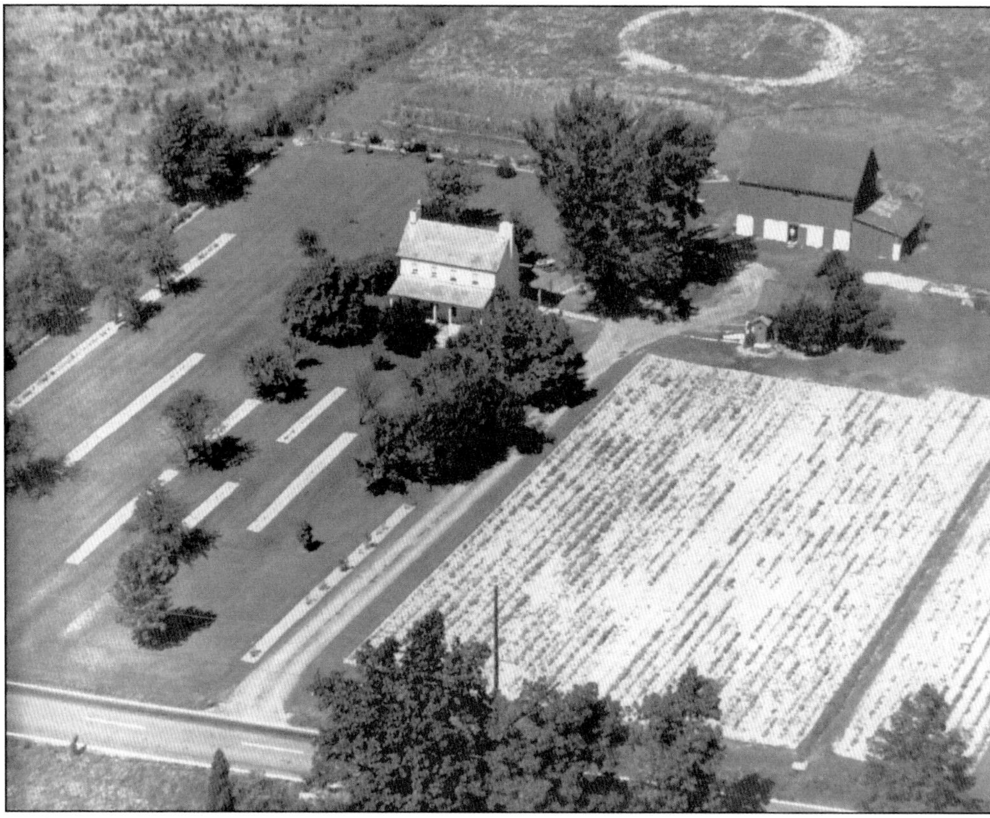

Paul W. and Gladys M. Lewis moved in 1947 to the Durham Road farm in Bucksville, believed to have been Frank Buck's home. The Lewises used the property in the early 1950s to raise over 2,000 chickens for production of eggs, which were crated and sold at the Doylestown auction. The front porch of the house was once enclosed. It was destroyed along with other buildings when Hurricane Diane hit in 1955. (PLW.)

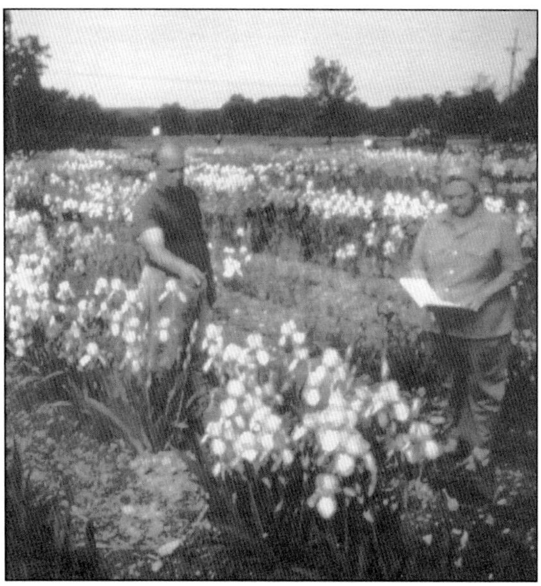

The Lewises raised seven children: three boys and four girls. Paul Lewis farmed the property and surrounding area, including a nearby housing development and land where the high school is now located. In 1954, he was a foreman overseeing work when Palisades High School was built. Daughter Priscilla Whitman reminisces that some of the best memories of her life were experienced on the farm, even though it was a lot of hard work. (PLW.)

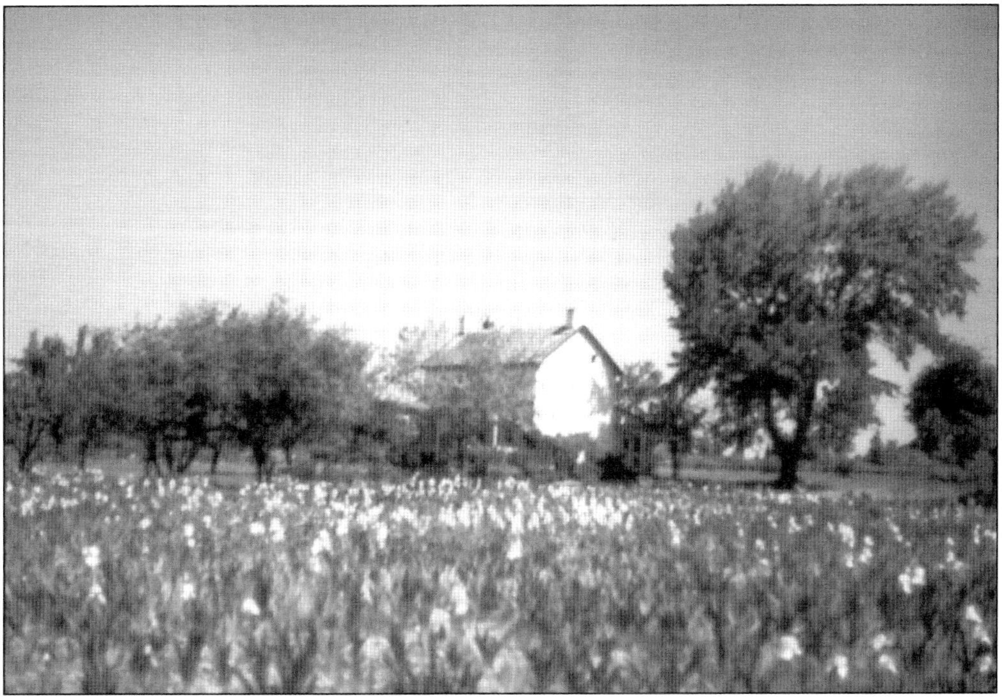

In the early 1960s, what started as a hobby of raising German bearded irises turned into a family business: the Old Orchard Iris Garden. Memorial Day was the most beautiful and busiest day of the selling season, which only lasted two weeks. The fields were blooming with hundreds of different colors, and people from all over would come to buy the plants. Paul and Gladys Lewis sold the business in late 1970s. (PLW.)

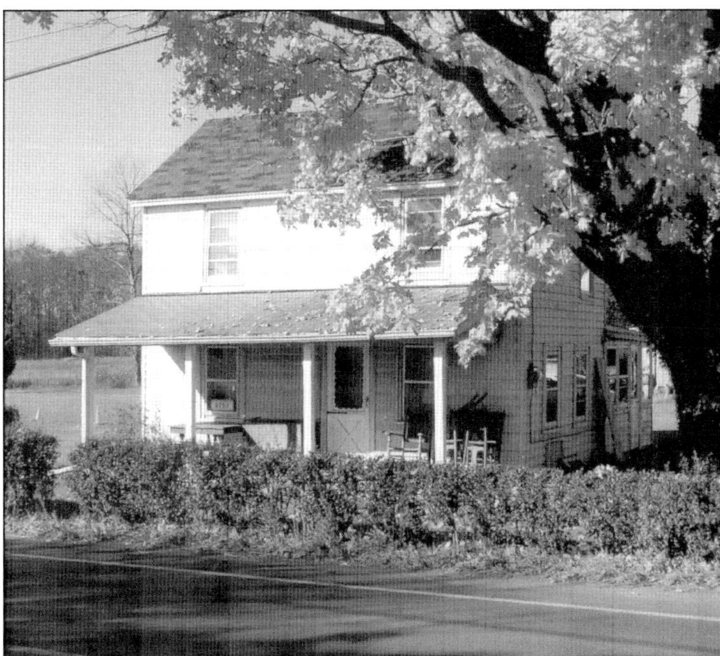

The Easton Road land in Revere where Wayne and Mary Shively's home was built has a long history. It was originally purchased by I.M. Keller in 1857, along with neighbors Christian Trumbower, Abraham Christian, Wyker Hager, John Rufe, and David Wilson. The enclosed porch housed the Revere Post Office in the late 1800s and tax collector's office in 1916. The Shivelys ran a postal delivery route for many years. (NHS.)

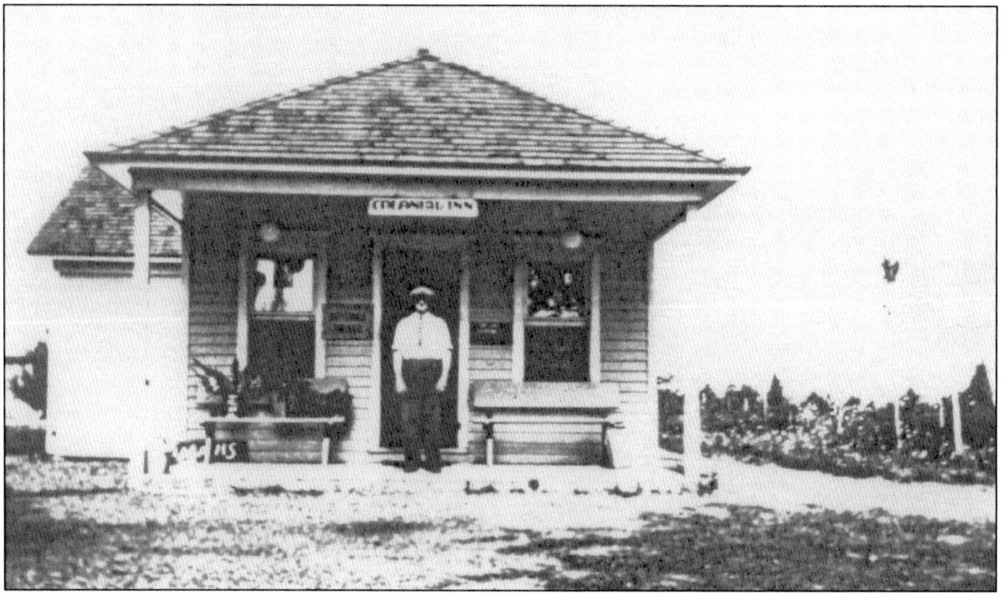

The Colonial Inn, seen here in 1920, was owned by Austin and Addie (Trauger) Shively and was a popular place to stop for a bite to eat. A new kitchen, actually a converted shed, was added to the left rear of the original building. In the 1930s, refreshment stands opened, supplying food for hungry travelers. Popular stops along Easton Road were Shively's stand as well as one run by Alvin Esser. Later, Przyuski's Country Drive-In and Four Winds Tavern became popular places to dine. (NHS.)

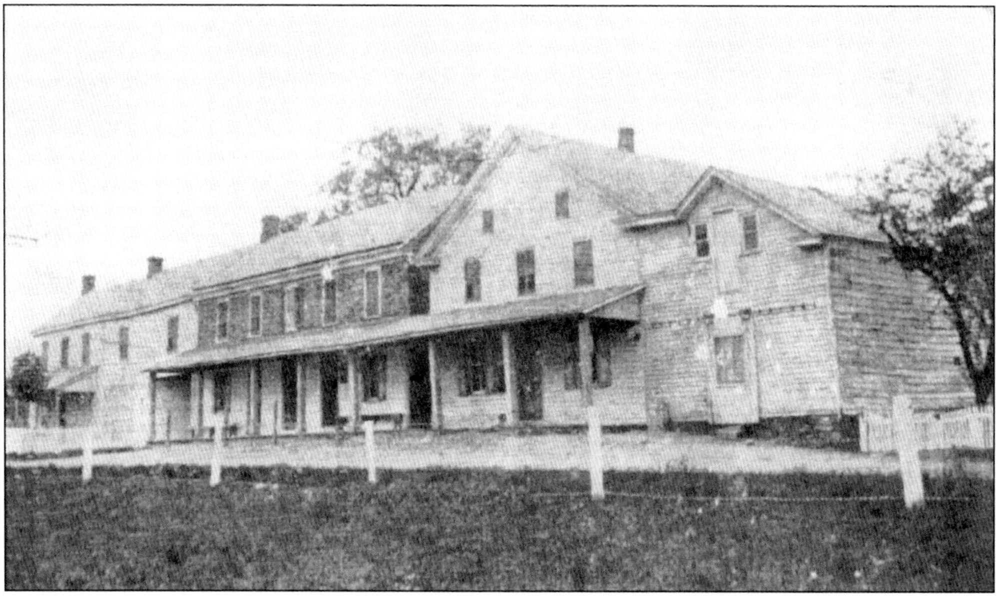

Jacob Buck established Sorrel Horse Inn around 1800; he sold it to his brother John in 1818. The log inn was then replaced with a stone structure. John Rufe later owned Rufe's Tavern there. The building burned in 1850. Son William Rufe rebuilt the structure and ran a store in a frame addition in Rufe's Corner in the early 1900s. The post office was named Revere in 1894. The landlord was Jacob Black, and Harry Kiefer was the store owner when the building was destroyed by fire 1918. The Hotel Paul Revere was later rebuilt. (NHS.)

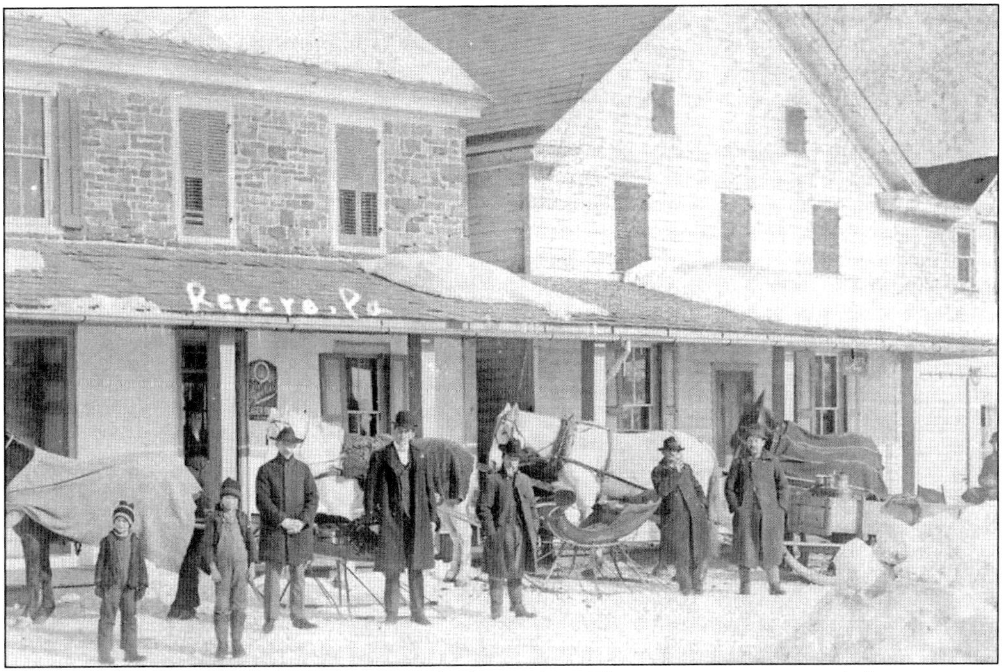

Residents gather by Sorrel Horse Inn in the late 1890s. This interesting postcard shows various sleighs used for transporting people and freight in Nockamixon's harsh winter weather. Harry Kiefer moved his store to the first floor of the Knights of Golden Eagle building across highway. A tornado tore off the roof and third story in 1923; Harry Kiefer was killed. The hotel was a Doylestown-Easton trolley stop in early 1900s. Fire again destroyed the building in 1959, and it was never rebuilt. (NHS.)

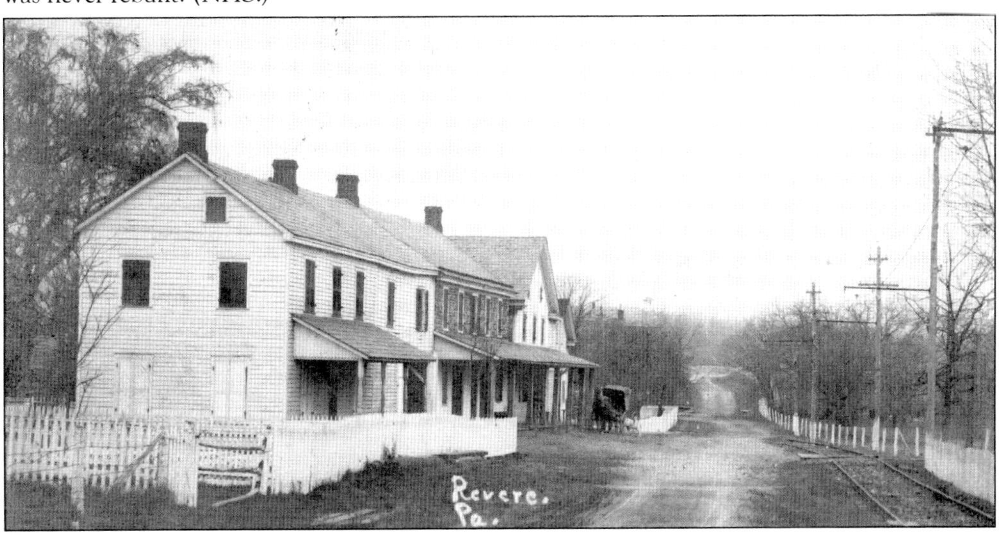

Revere Hotel stands beside Revere-Upper Black Eddy Road in this postcard with a May 21, 1907, cancellation. Joseph Wismer addressed the card to his girlfriend, Minnie Moninghoff, of Upper Black Eddy with a note on the front of the postcard stating, "Not lost. All o.k." Grandson Edward Wismer confirms everything was fine and that Wilhelmina Moninghoff married Joseph. Looking toward Marienstein Road, Revere School's belfry can be seen on the left surrounded by trees. (EWK.)

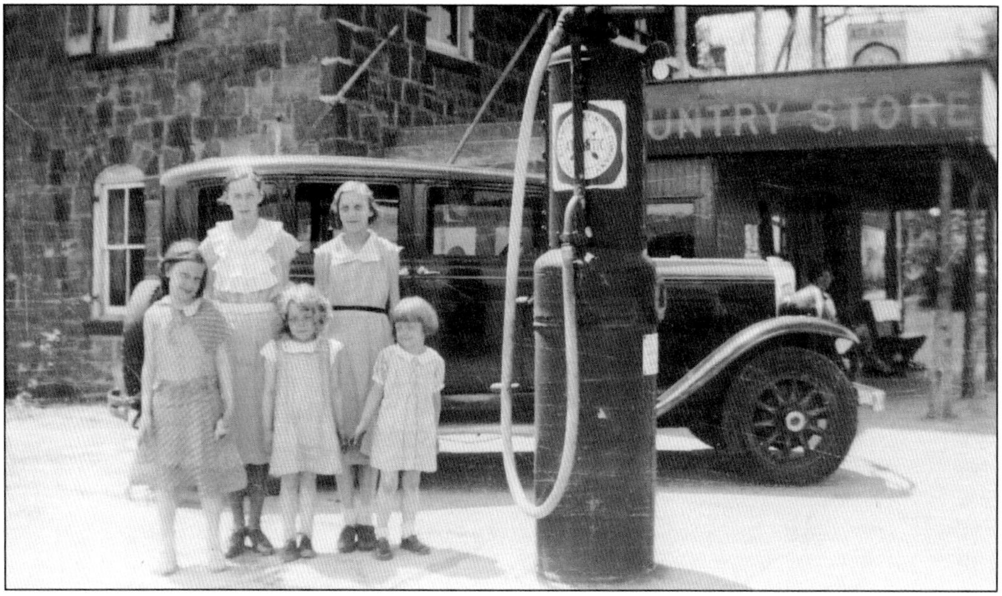

Sylvester Moninghoff and Florence (Heller) Moninghoff, Jim Freeh's grandparents, purchased the Revere Store from widow Mrs. Kiefer around 1929 after Harry Kiefer was killed when a tornado tore off the roof and the building's third story. Five Moninghoff daughters pose by their father's automobile. From left to right are Florence (Betty) Allshouse, Mary (Agnes) Freeh, Edith Hoffman, Margaret (Gladys) Proca, and Catherine Litschauer. (JAF.)

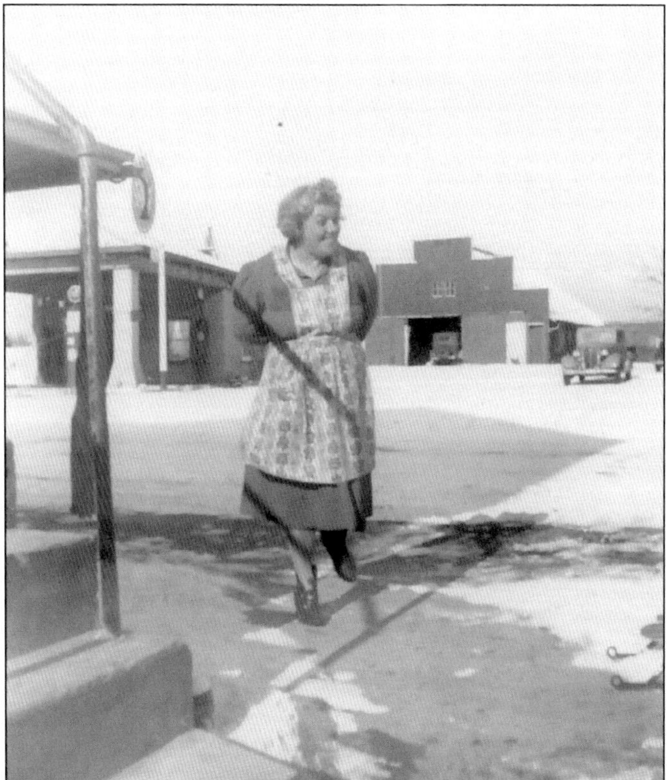

Florence Moninghoff stands outside the Revere Store during winter, with snow on the ground and children's sleds ready to go. With Florence's assistance, her husband Sylvester took on postmaster duties and ran the Revere Store. He delivered groceries and feed twice weekly to customers until 1945, when he sold the store to Cornelius de Groot. In the background across Easton Road, the gas station owned by Charles Chevalier was busy servicing vehicles and selling gasoline. (JAF.)

Helene de Groot served as Revere postmaster for 31 and a half years, from 1945 to 1975. The post office inside the general store grew from 30 to 148 boxes during her tenure. Brass post office boxes were available to patrons who purchased use of one to pick up mail anytime the store was open. Penny postcards cost just that, and 3¢ carried a letter anywhere in the country. (LDC.)

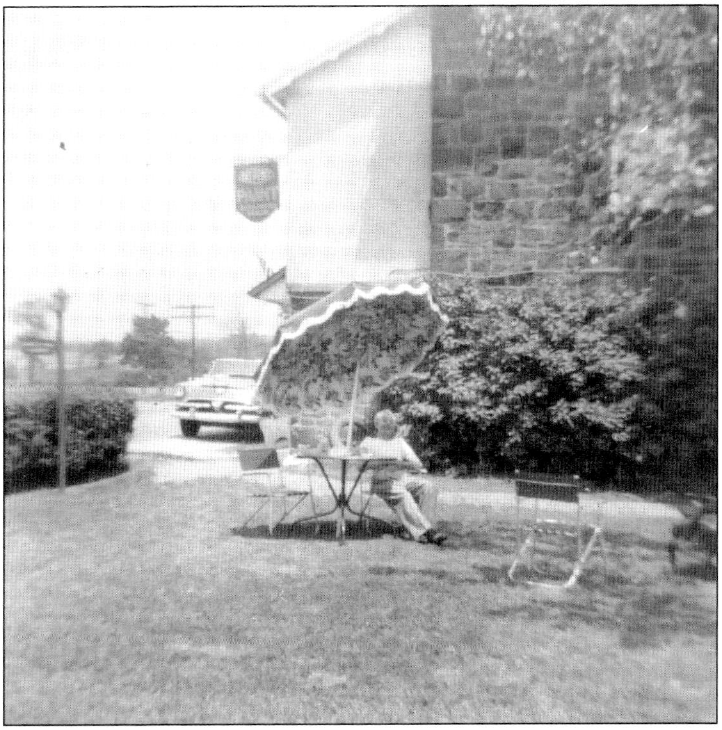

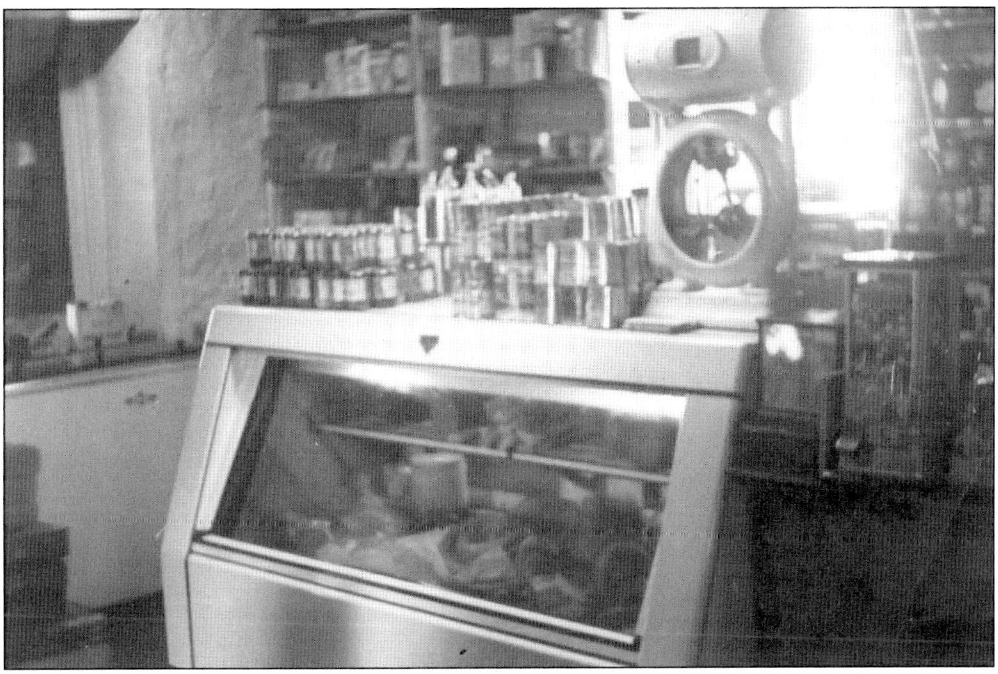

Concerns for their family's future brought Helene and Cornelius de Groot to Bucks County in 1945 during World War II. They moved from a modern Long Island, New York, apartment with every convenience to come to Revere with their three children. Two other children were born later. Their new home, which included the general store and post office, featured bare lightbulbs with pull strings, an old kerosene stove, and an outhouse. (LDC.)

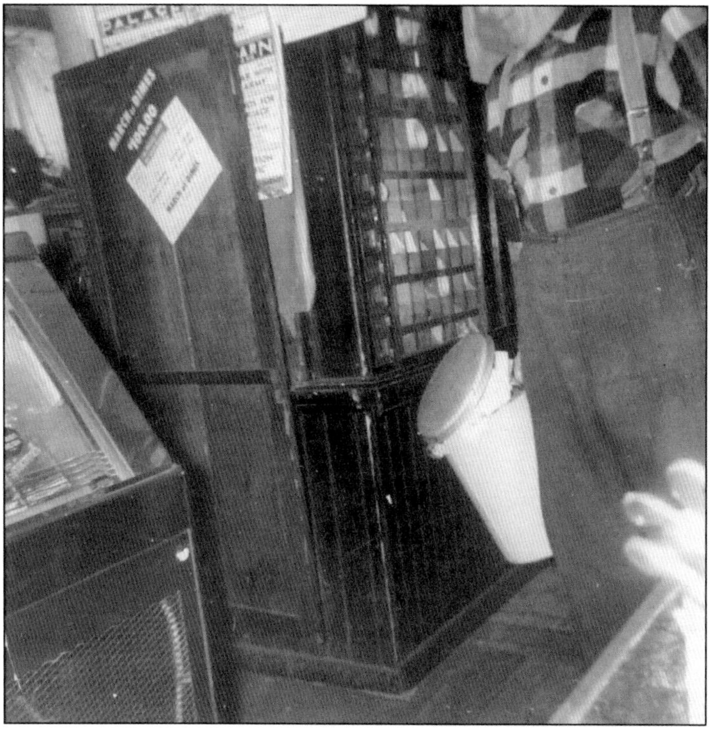

Cornelius de Groot purchased the Revere Store from Sylvester Moninghoff and continued the merchandising business until 1970. Serving as justice of the peace, he was always there to serve as his wife's replacement as postmaster. The de Groot legacy continues with son Robert managing the complex, and he has made many improvements as store owner. Daughter Lillian (de Groot) Crum operates the Revere Deli on the second floor, and Robert's wife, Christine, manages the Revere Video Store. (LDC.)

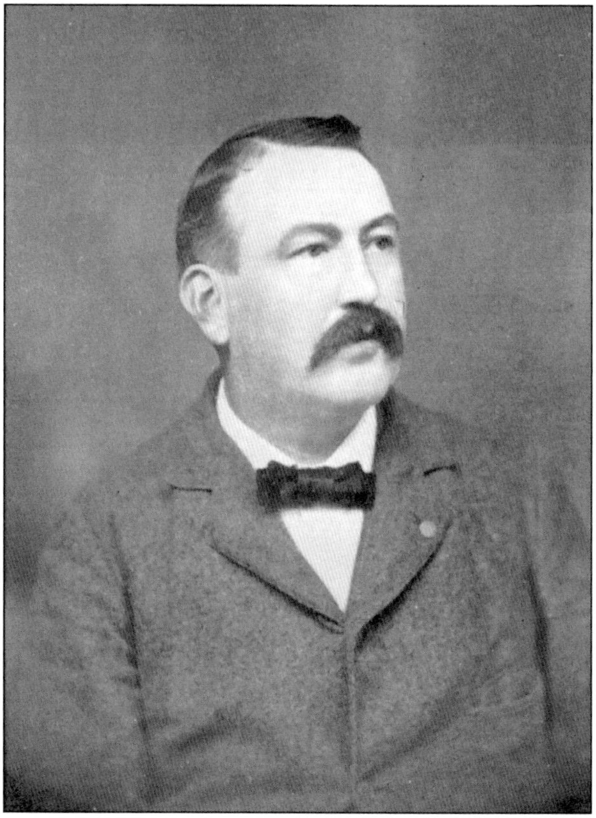

Dr. F. Harvey Grim, an esteemed physician/surgeon in Revere, was born in Nockamixon in 1859. Practicing with his father, Dr. George W. Grim, he acquired a large practice on his own and gained community confidence. F. Harvey and wife, Ella (Rufe) Grim, parents of seven children, owned all the property from Easton Road back to Nockamixon School. Sold many years ago, the doctor's office was intact, including apothecary jars filled with medicinals. The home is now Country Town Store. (STZ.)

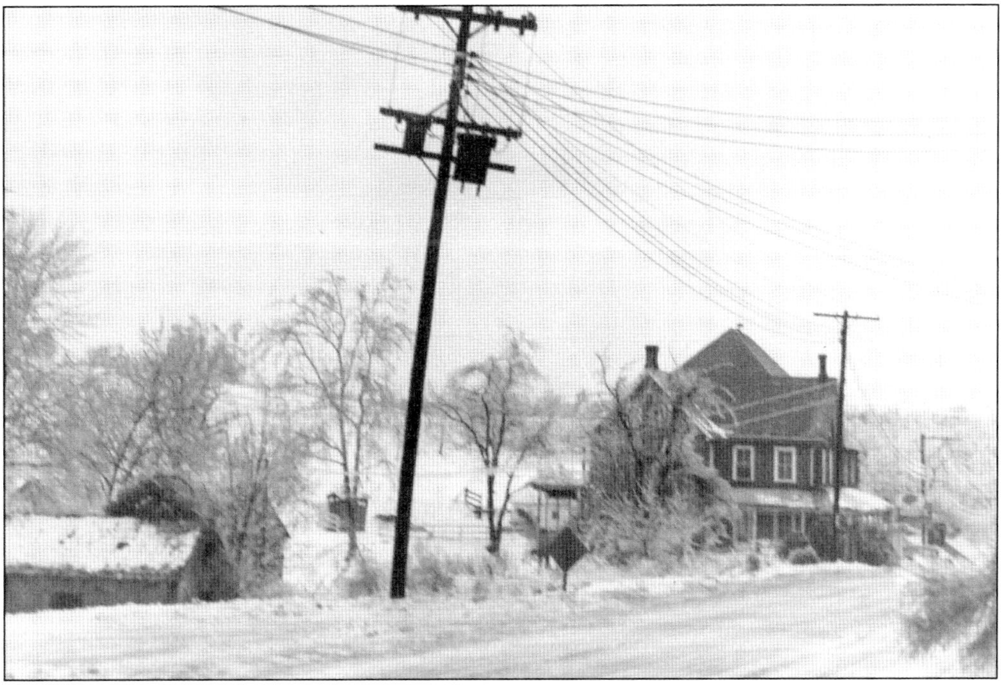

Mabel Foellner took this January 1948 photograph during a snowstorm. The winter scene shows ice coating trees and the highway in Ferndale. Theodore M. Moyer's house, built in 1895 of swamp stones by Schwar Brothers, is shown on the left. An addition built several years later became known as Moyer's Store. Theodore Moyer also served as justice of the peace. At the time of his death in 1944, he had served more years consecutively than any other justice in the state. (NHS.)

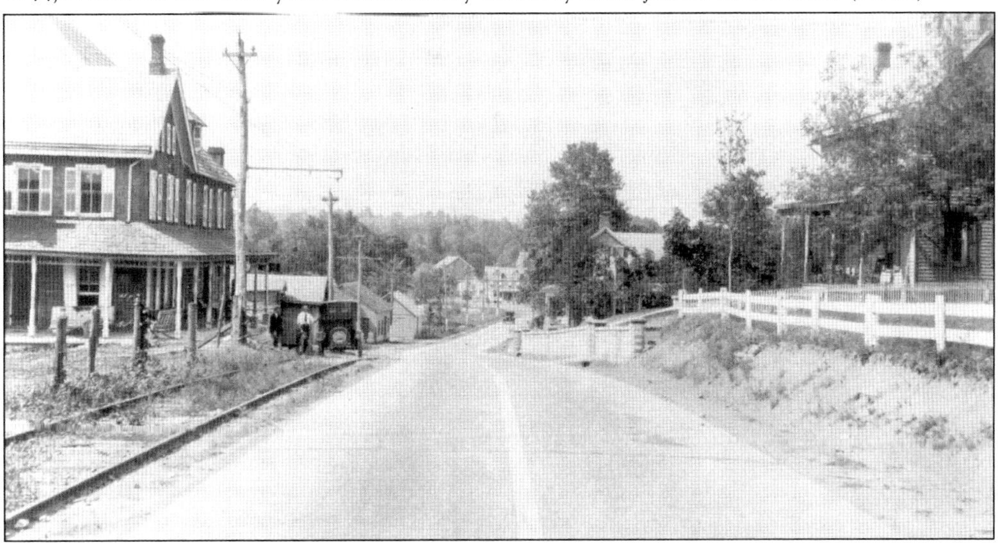

This view looks north on Easton Road in Ferndale around 1925. Originally known as Rum's Corner because of an area distillery, the first post office named Nockamixon opened in 1873, which was later changed to Ferndale. The Moyer Store was the post office site from 1903 to 1958 before moving to the creamery, which had stopped operations in 1939. Two gentlemen stand by an early vehicle near the building. The trolley tracks to the left of the road are seen passing many buildings that still stand today, and the Ferndale Inn is in the distance. (NHS.)

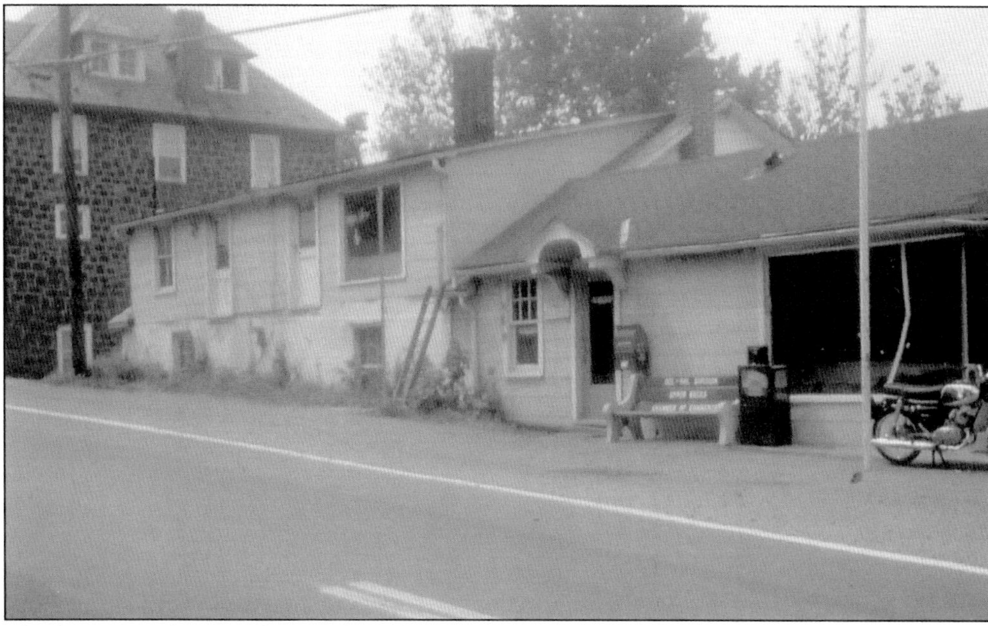

This late-1960s photograph was taken when Larry Stangil first purchased the old Ferndale creamery. Previously a home center selling building supplies, he completely remodeled the facility. Larry's Auto Body continued in business on Easton Road for many years as an automobile body shop specializing in collision repair and auto-glass replacement. The property is currently owned by Swamp's Auto Body. (LJS.)

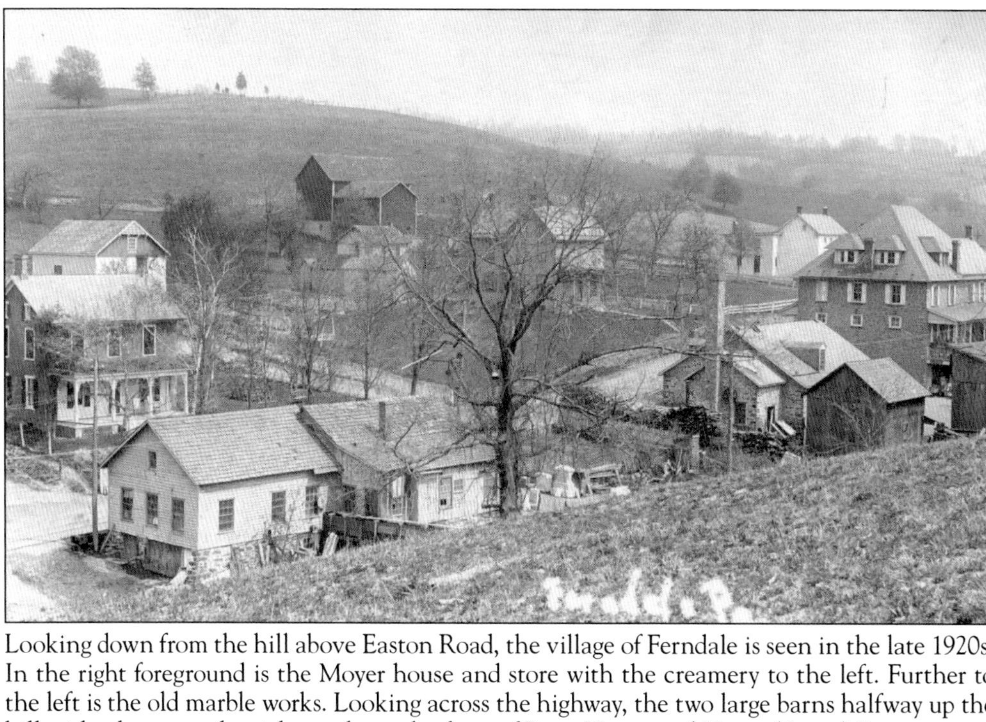

Looking down from the hill above Easton Road, the village of Ferndale is seen in the late 1920s. In the right foreground is the Moyer house and store with the creamery to the left. Further to the left is the old marble works. Looking across the highway, the two large barns halfway up the hill with a house to the right made up the farm of Peter Henry and Verna (Stone) Bartman and their three daughters: Doris, Blanche, and Rowena. (BBW.)

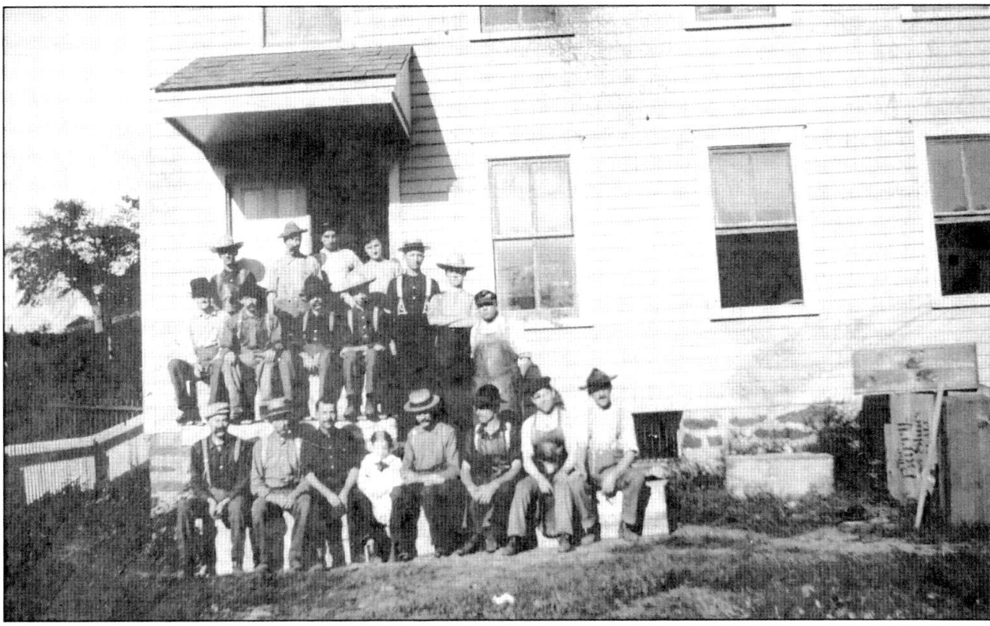

William Shick, born in 1847 in Ferndale, learned to make shoes working in his father's shop. The chief organizer of Ferndale Boot and Shoe Manufacturing on Easton Road in 1884 with Dr. F.H. Grim, S.F. Mann, and T.M. Moyer, he went on to become the sole owner. William used the latest and most improved machinery in manufacturing miners' boots before Wilson or C. Harvey Bean. In this 1904 photograph with his employees, he is seated in the first row, fifth from left. (BBW.)

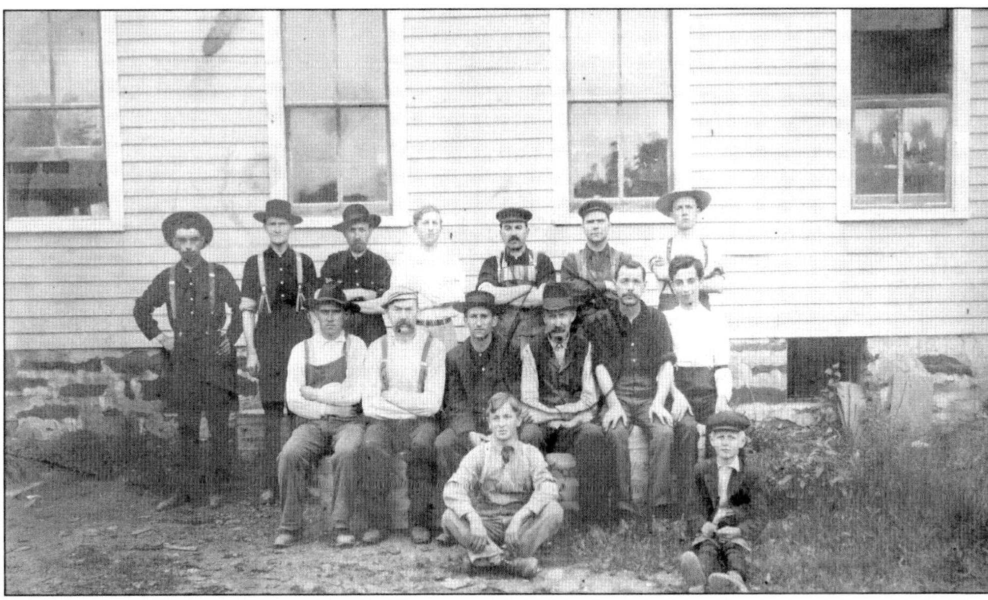

Twenty skilled workmen were employed and constantly working in William Shick's Ferndale two-story, 50-foot-by-30-foot brick building. Success of the enterprise was due to Shick's untiring efforts. The firm established a large patronage that continually increased, and enlarging the plant was possible in 1899. Daily output was 100 pairs of shoes, with principal shoe, first-grade union brogans being the majority of that production. Seen here in 1904, William Shick, Blanche Wehrung's great grandfather, is seated in the second row, fourth from left. (BBW.)

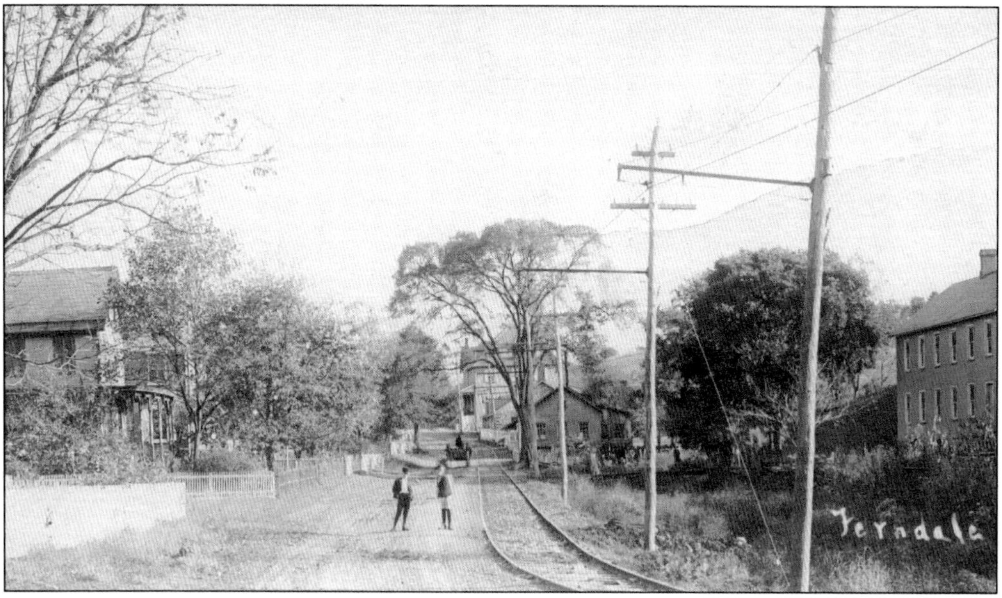

This south-facing photograph from the early 1900s shows trolley tracks on the right, a short distance from the Ferndale Hotel. Rev. Charles Weaver's factory, in the right foreground, specialized in children's shoes in the early 1900s. Ferndale Glove made canvas work gloves there in the 1920s, and Grace Stone operated an antique shop until 1948. Also on the right are the creamery and Moyer's store in the distance. Mabel Foellner's home is the first home on the left. William Nickel, the original owner and wheelwright, had the house built and made the iron fence in front. (LHK.)

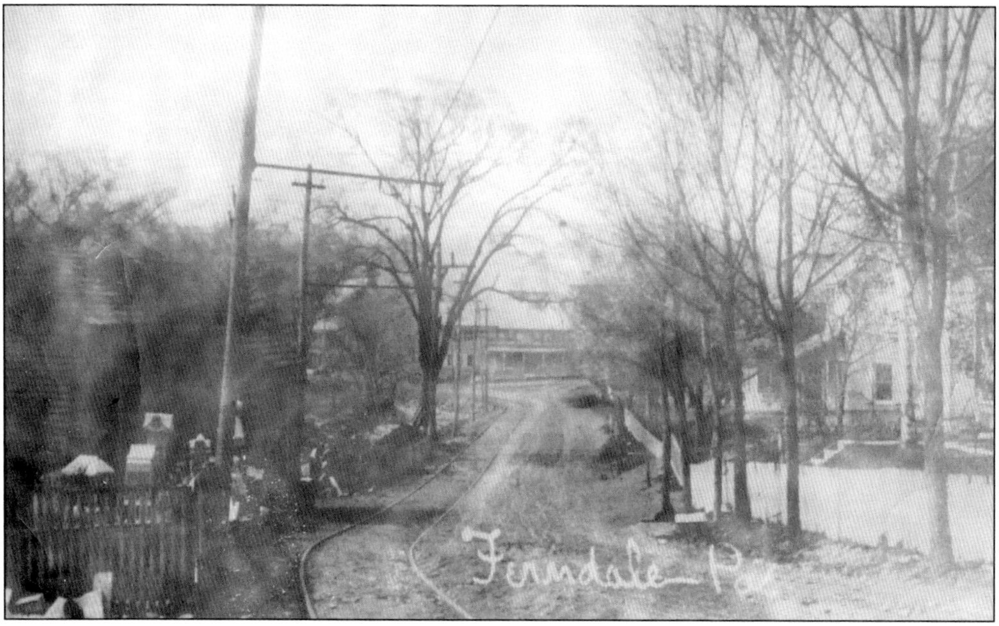

Looking north from Moyer's store, trolley tracks pass local Ferndale businesses. Freight and passenger cars of Doylestown & Easton Trolley Company used the tracks from 1904 until late 1926. On the left is evidence of Samuel Mann's Tombstone Works, and a small portion of Mann's house is on the right. Beyond is Rev. Charles Weaver's home, pastor of St. Luke's Reformed Church for many years. Ferndale Hotel is in the center of the photograph. (NHS.)

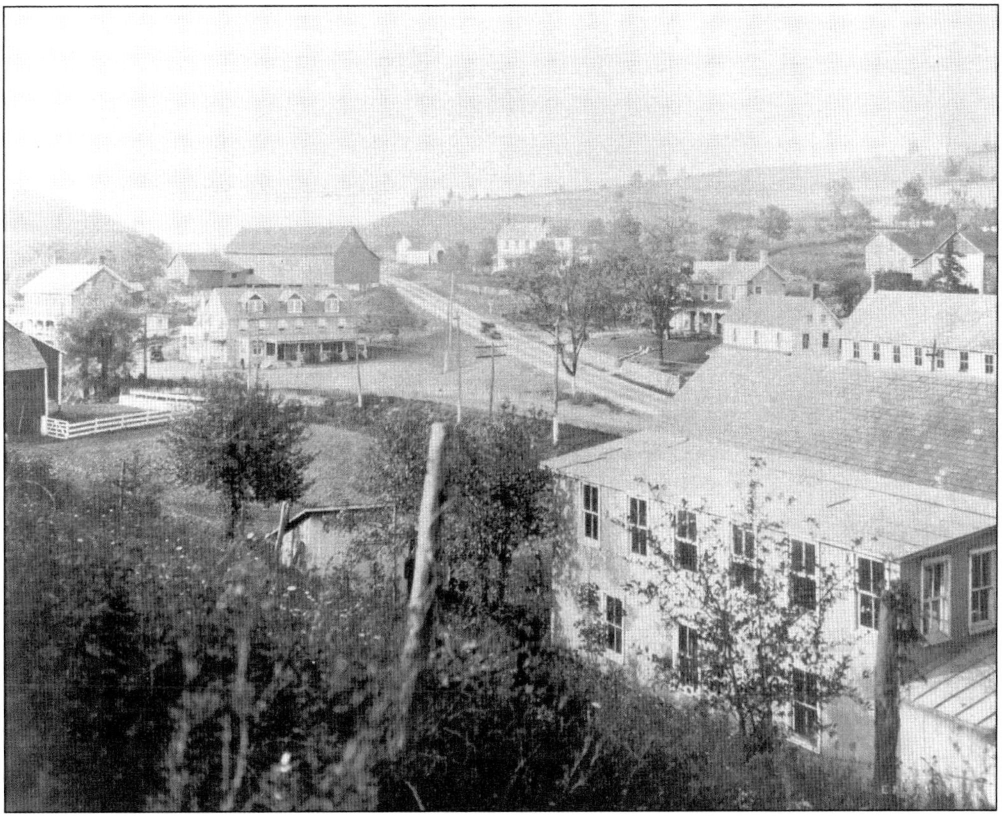

This 1910 photograph overlooking Easton Road shows many businesses. Ferndale was thriving in late 1800s to early 1900s. The village had a general store, butcher, blacksmith, wheelwright, glove factory, cider mill, creamery, marble yard, post office, and antique and gift shop. Also, four shoe factories made miner's shoes and boots that were sold to many mining towns throughout Pennsylvania. (GBG.)

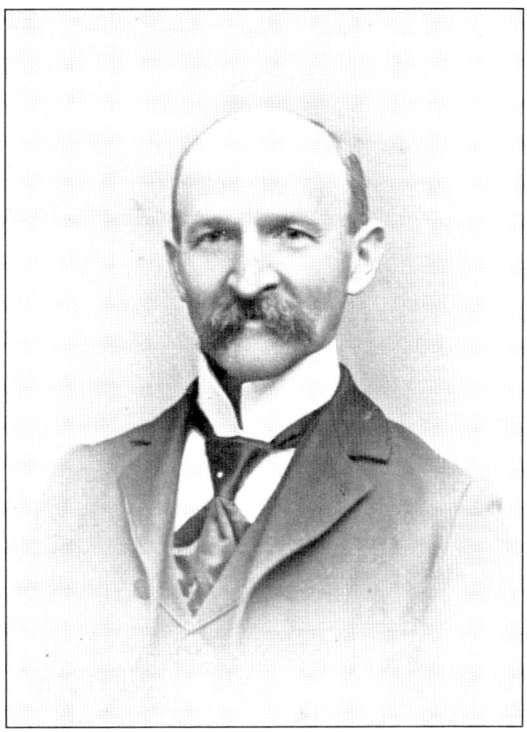

Wilson W. Bean, born 1853 in Ferndale, worked with father, Henry Bean, starting at age 15 learning the shoemaker trade. Continuing the occupation, he succeeded his father in 1871 and became general manager of Bean Boot and Shoe Manufacturers on Easton Road in 1895. Wilson and Ida C. (Rufe) Bean were parents of four children. Wilson embarked in business for himself in 1899, occupying the building opposite his dwelling. Hiring 15 men, he increased his force as required. (STZ.)

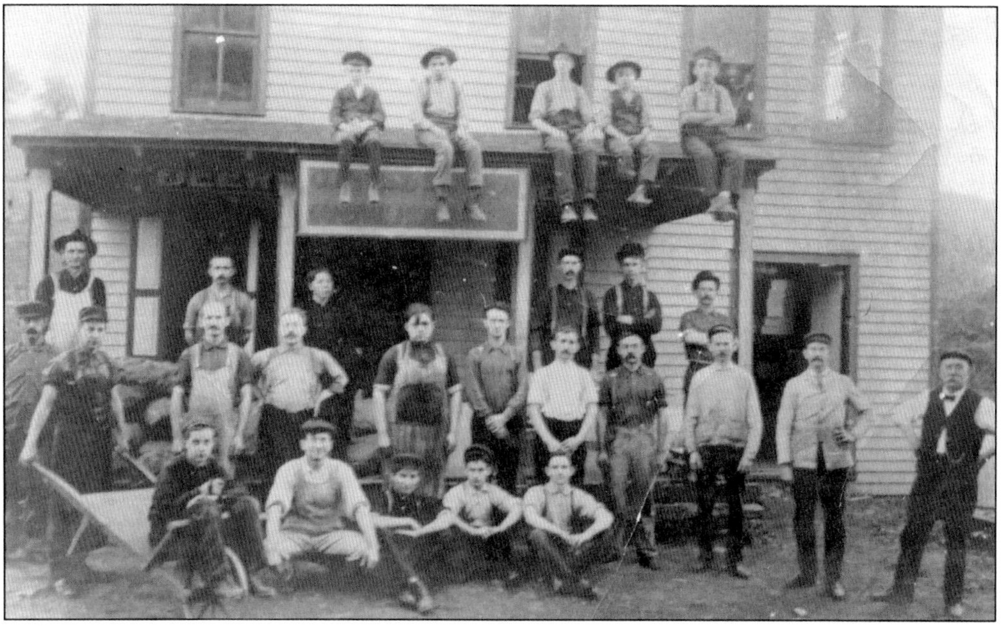

Wilson Bean's company made high-grade miners' brogans and employed 18 workers. Business increased in 1880, and a two-and-a-half story building was erected. Business was lucrative since the life of boots was from one payday to the next (at that time about one month) due to strong acids in mines. Some workers during the busiest years were Harry Heller, Jess Haring, Edward Kohl, and Asa Trauger. (NHS.)

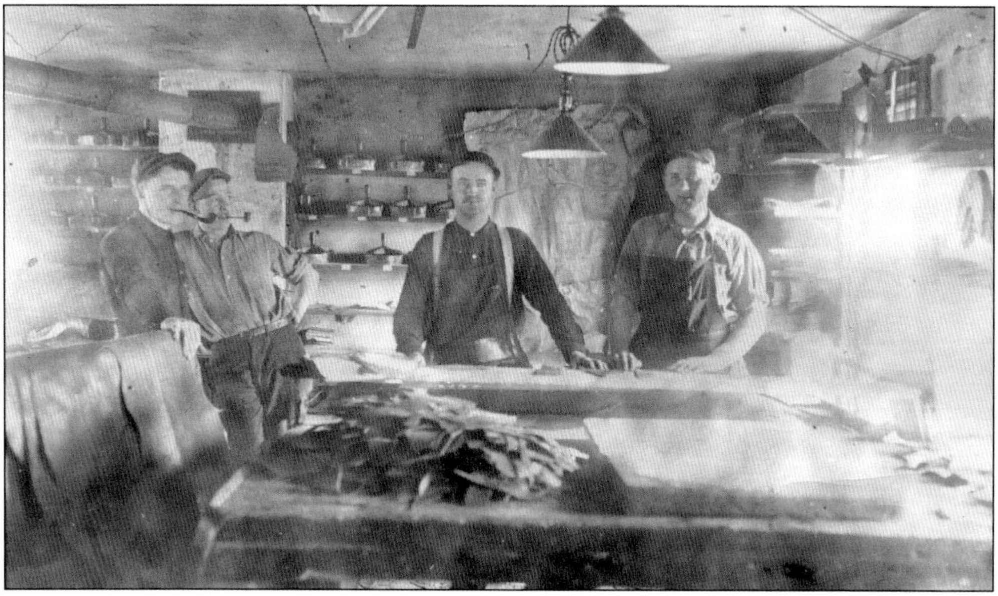

This photograph shows an interior view of Wilson Bean's shoe factory, built in 1899. Only three shoe manufacturers remained in Ferndale by 1914: C.H. Bean, W.W. Bean, and William Shick. Wilson ran the factory until 1920, when his youngest son Roy continued in the shop repairing shoes, harnesses, and clocks until around 1940. The shoe factory owned by Charles Harvey Bean, Henry Bean's younger son, is the only one still standing and is now the Ferndale Antique Store. (NHS.)

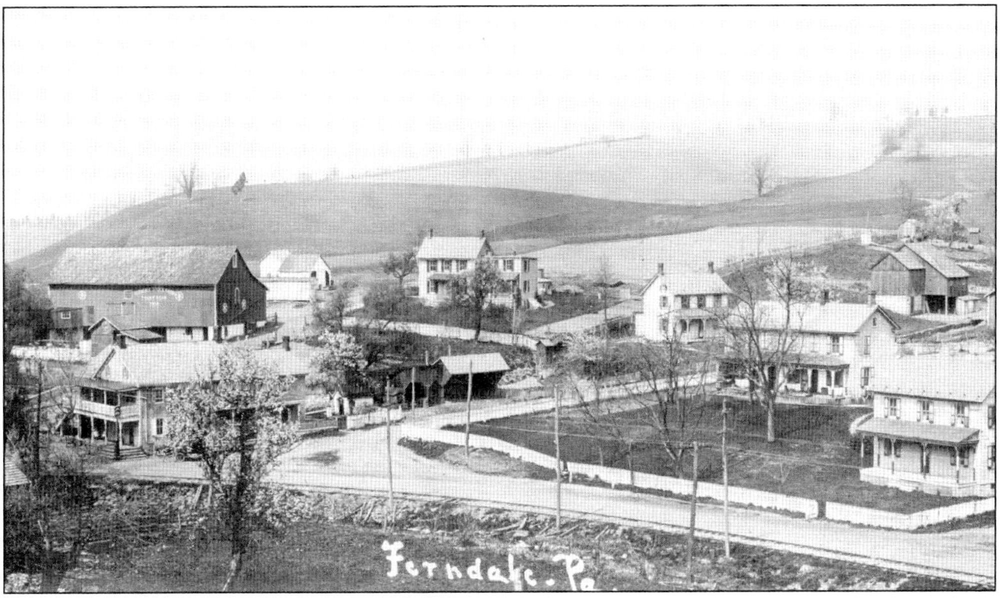

This view of Ferndale is from the field below Union Cemetery. Frank Bean remodeled his father's old home into a fine hotel in 1892 that was run by J.H. Rufe. Ferndale Hotel's covered-wagon shed was used to shelter horses and carriages belonging to patrons. Frank Bean's Ferndale Stock Farm barn was built in 1908 on top of a hill behind the hotel. No longer standing, it provided storage for large inventory of items sold in his store. (GBG.)

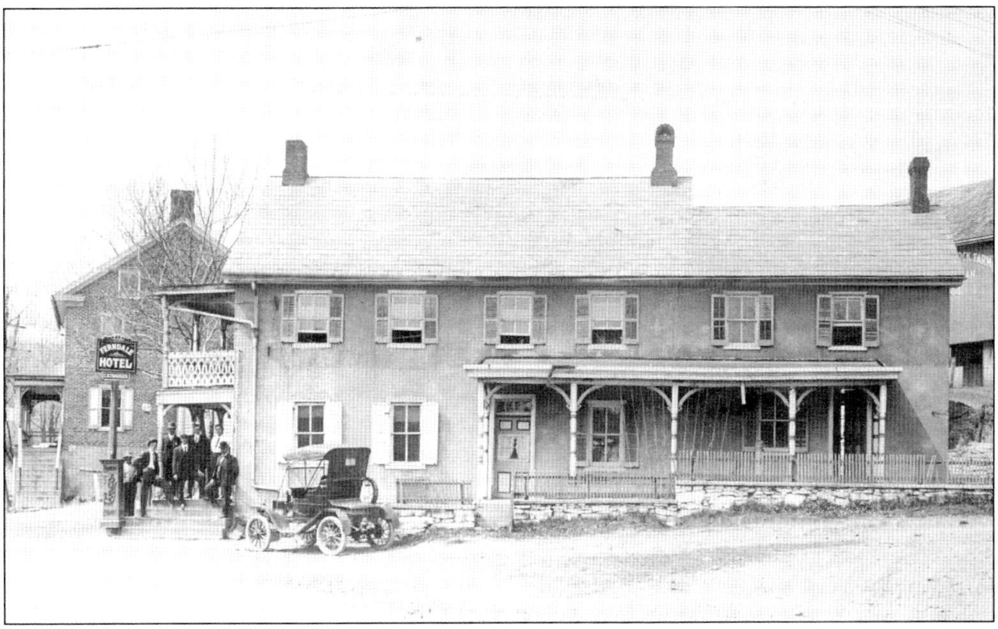

Seen here in 1862, the Ferndale Hotel on Church Hill Road first operated as an inn around 1830 and was sold for $1,275. The present building dates back to pre-1827 as part of Michael Meisser's estate. Patrons never knew who owned the automobile that was always parked in front of the hotel. It was reportedly first Ford Model T in Ferndale. The brick building to the left of the hotel was owned by Frank Bean. His mercantile store, established in 1870, carried large stock to supply customer's needs. (GBG.)

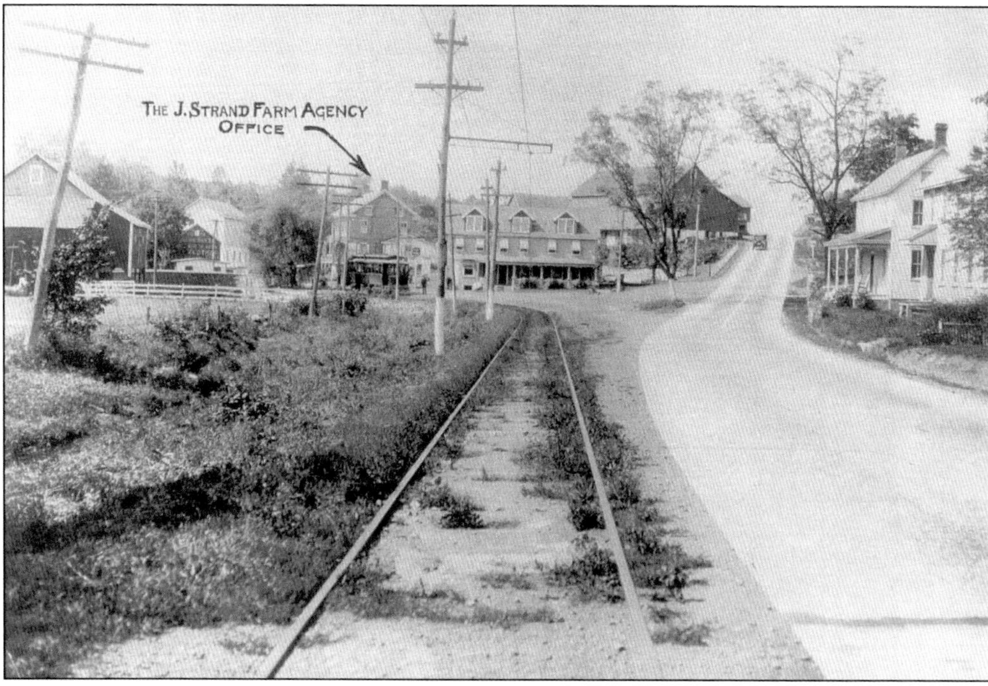

Seen here in the 1920s, a Doylestown and Easton trolley car has stopped at Ferndale Hotel on Church Hill Road. It was a busy intersection; an automobile is parked in front while another drives south down Easton Road. The J. Strand Farm Agency was located in Frank Bean's store. On the left, across from the store, a barn advertises Jacob Mayer clothes. William Shick's shoe company is on Easton Road, seen on the right side, the first building (partial) with a small porch. (GBG.)

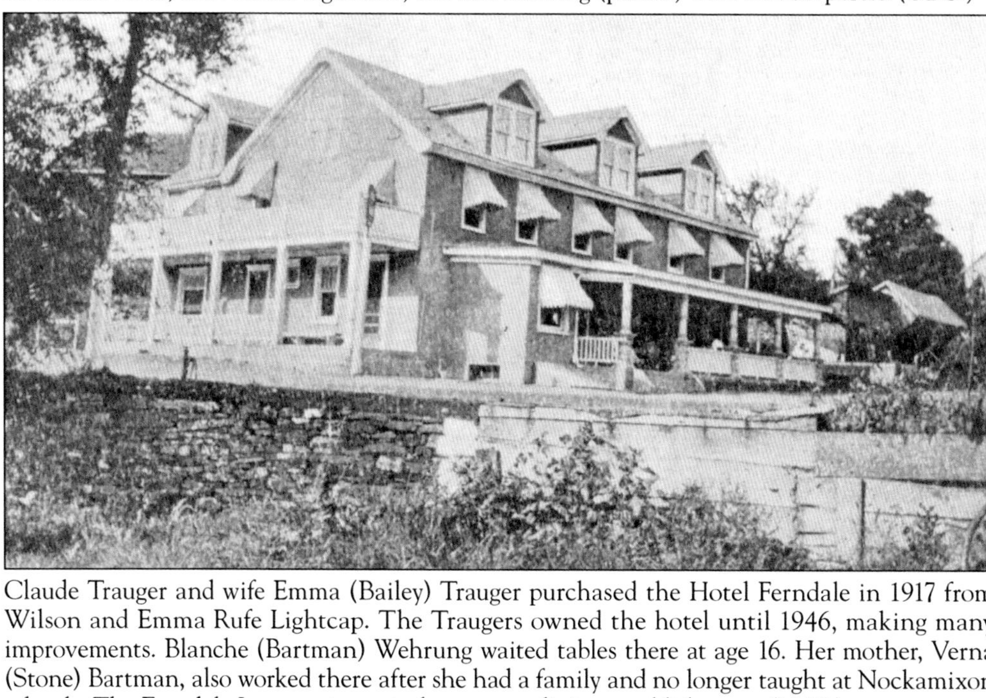

Claude Trauger and wife Emma (Bailey) Trauger purchased the Hotel Ferndale in 1917 from Wilson and Emma Rufe Lightcap. The Traugers owned the hotel until 1946, making many improvements. Blanche (Bartman) Wehrung waited tables there at age 16. Her mother, Verna (Stone) Bartman, also worked there after she had a family and no longer taught at Nockamixon schools. The Ferndale Inn continues its legacy as a dining establishment. (LHK.)

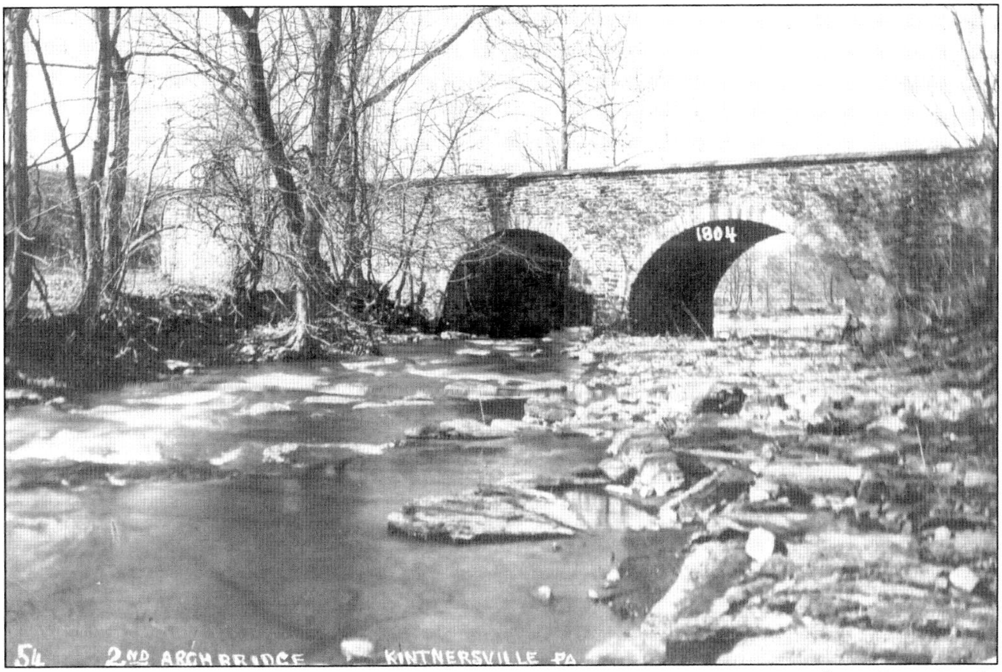

Two Ahler's double-barreled stone arch bridges in Nockamixon cross over Gallows Run Creek. The bridge pictured was the first one built, in 1804, and was on Old Easton Road south of Ealer Hill Road. The second bridge, constructed in 1826, was north of Ealer Hill Road on Old Easton Road. Due to the historic significance of these two bridges, rehabilitation restoration was the chosen method of recent renovations, allowing for structural repairs while maintaining the bridge's appearance. (CLK.)

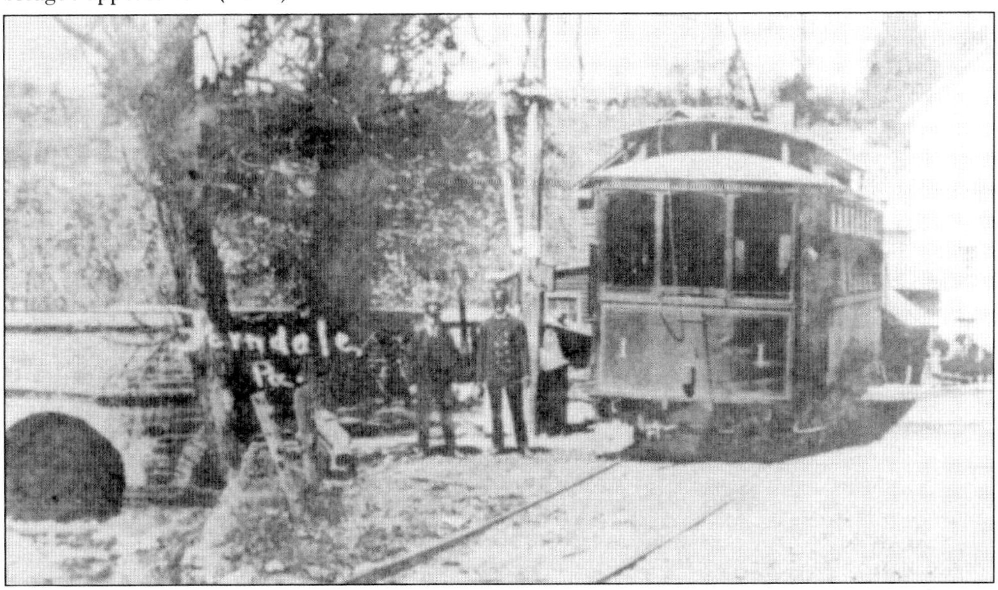

Trolley car No. 1 heads to Easton on the right-of-way at Ferndale in this c. 1905 photograph. Two conductors stand near one of the stone arch bridges. The Doylestown and Easton Railway Company trolley line was completed in 1904. The line hauled both passengers and freight. Operations were suspended in 1926 due to the popularity of the automobile. (NHS.)

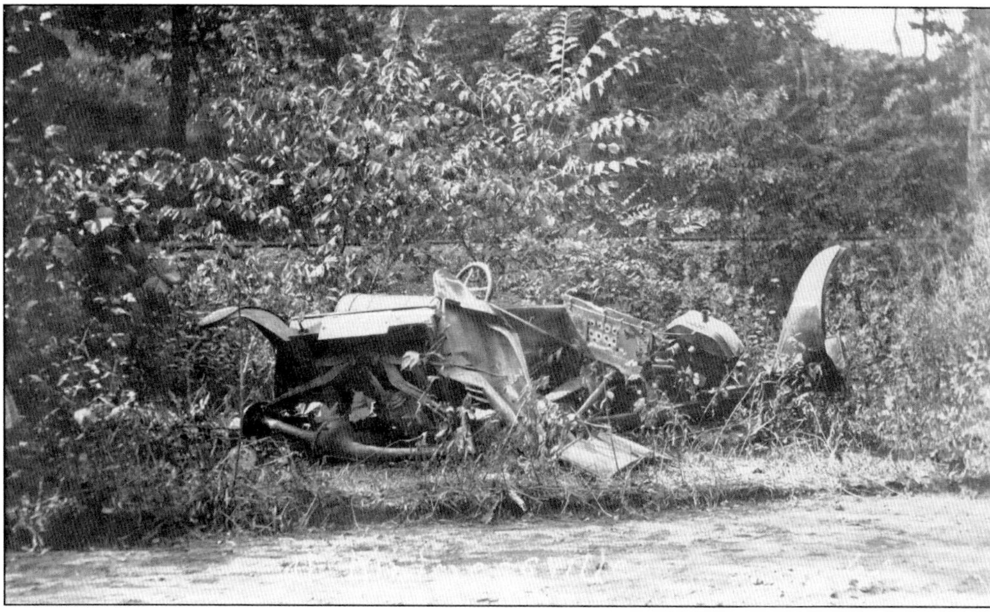

Under the influence of alcohol, Titus Trauger of Kintnersville was driving his Model T Ford erratically through the fields toward home. As he drove over the stone arch bridge leaving Ferndale, the Model T was hit by the Doylestown and Easton trolley when the car crossed its path. As can be seen, the automobile was completely demolished from the accident. Titus was lucky, however, and did not receive a scratch. (LHK.)

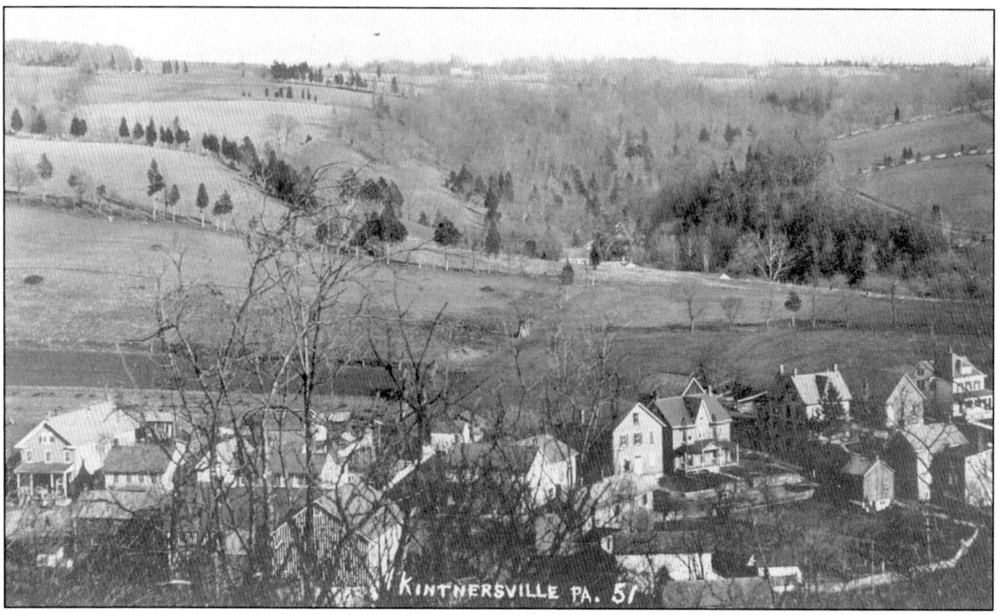

Overlooking Kintnersville, many original Easton Road buildings remain. Jacob Froelich, the first landowner in 1743, purchased 101 acres from the Penns. George Gintner (Kintner) arrived in 1749 and started a pottery business, selling supplies to Durham Iron Furnace until it blew up 1792. Originally called Pleasant Valley, the village renamed itself to honor George Kintner's son, Maj. Jacob Kintner, who was a resident and sheriff of Bucks County. By 1860, Nockamixon's largest village had 20 dwellings, a hotel, a store, a lumberyard, and saw and gristmills. (CLK.)

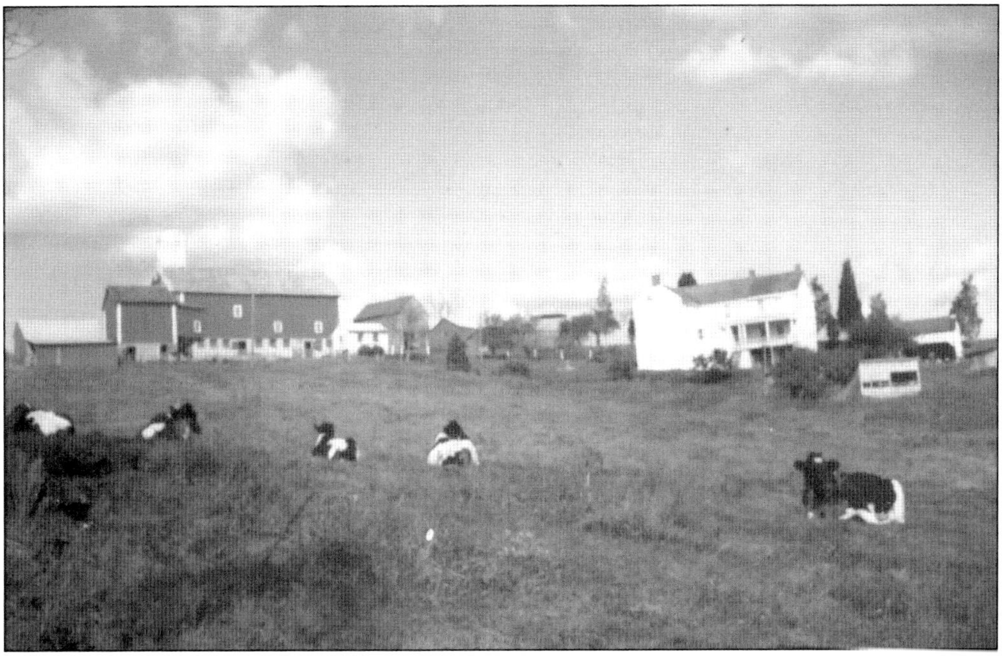

The Berger family members were longtime farmers in Nockamixon. The Harold Berger farm pictured on Berger Road in Kintnersville is no longer owned by the family. Originally, the farm belonged to Harold's grandfather Jerome Berger. His parents, Oliver and Anna (Haney) Berger, then ran the farm before Harold and his family took over. Oliver's brother Oscar had a farm down the road, which later was run by his sons Paul and Clarence Berger. (CMB.)

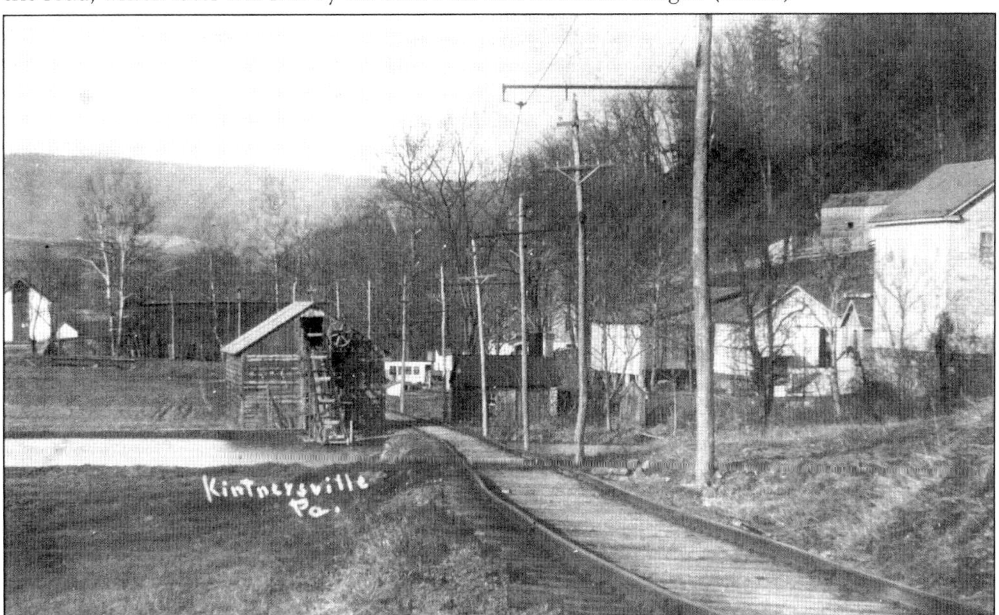

Cyrus Stover erected a large building to store natural ice. The ice was harvested in the winter from a large pond behind his mill and then stored until summertime. He had an extensive ice route in the nearby towns until his retirement. In this 1905 photograph are the old covered bridge in the background and Doylestown and Easton trolley tracks running beside the icehouse. (GBG.)

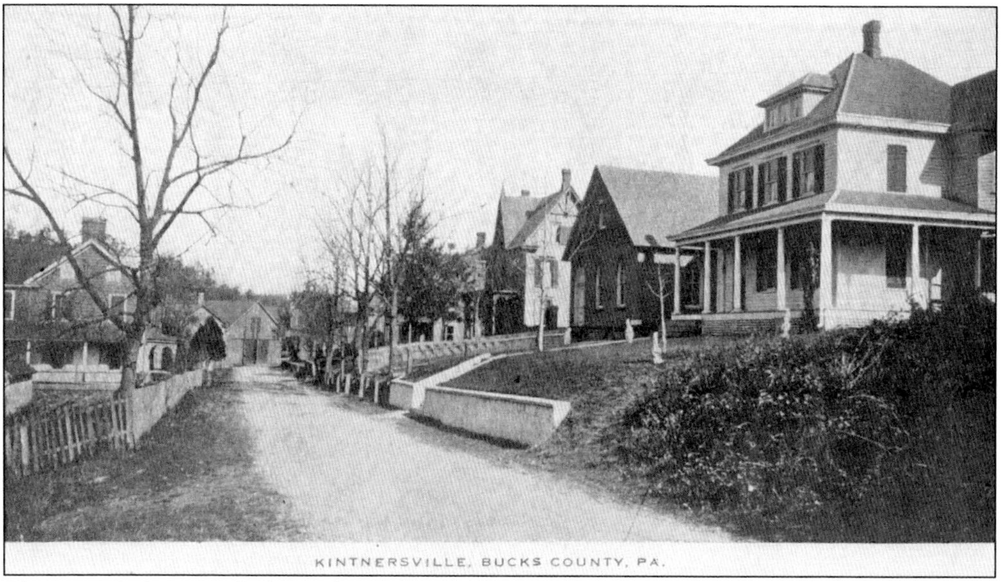

This c. 1893 photograph shows the view entering the village of Kintnersville traveling on Easton Road. Union Chapel, a private residence, is the second building on the right. Kintnersville Hotel stands on a slight rise on the far right as the road bends behind buildings. Although it is not visible, the hotel remained on a sharp curve until it was torn down when the road was improved into a highway. The large red barn seen in the distance on left belonged to the hotel. (CLK.)

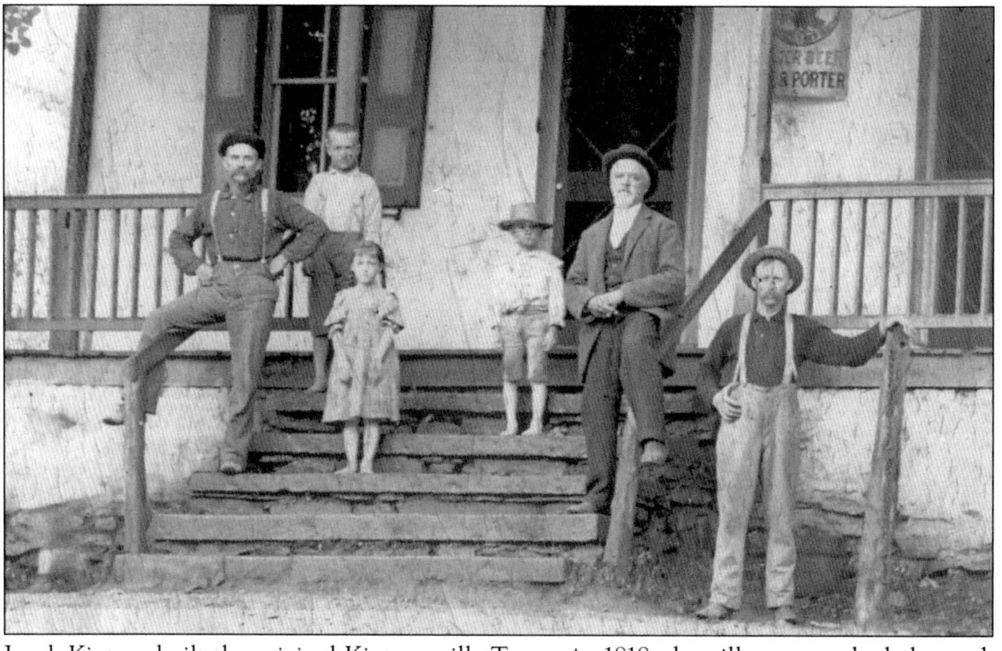

Jacob Kintner built the original Kintnersville Tavern in 1818; the village name had changed, honoring Kintner. By 1828, Lewis Algard owned the Town Tavern and Hotel, a two-story stone building on a small piece of Easton Road land on a sharp curve. William Hillman and Abraham Youngkin later owned the Kintnersville Hotel in 1914. The building was demolished in the 1920s when Easton Road improved. A federal government certificate, found behind the bar, forbid the establishment from selling firewater to Native Americans. (CMB.)

This large red barn across from the hotel was used to board horses and carriages for people staying overnight. After the hotel was torn down, the barn had other uses. In the 1960s, Pick and Poke Antiques sold furniture there. The barn still stands and is often used as a reference point when providing directions. In this 1984 photograph, a portion of the barn is shown next to remains of Leidy Morris's blacksmith shop, which had been destroyed by fire. (MRW.)

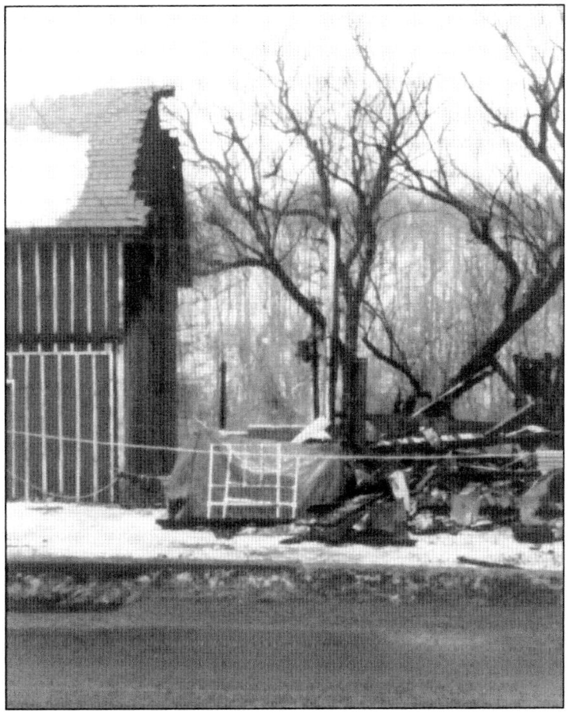

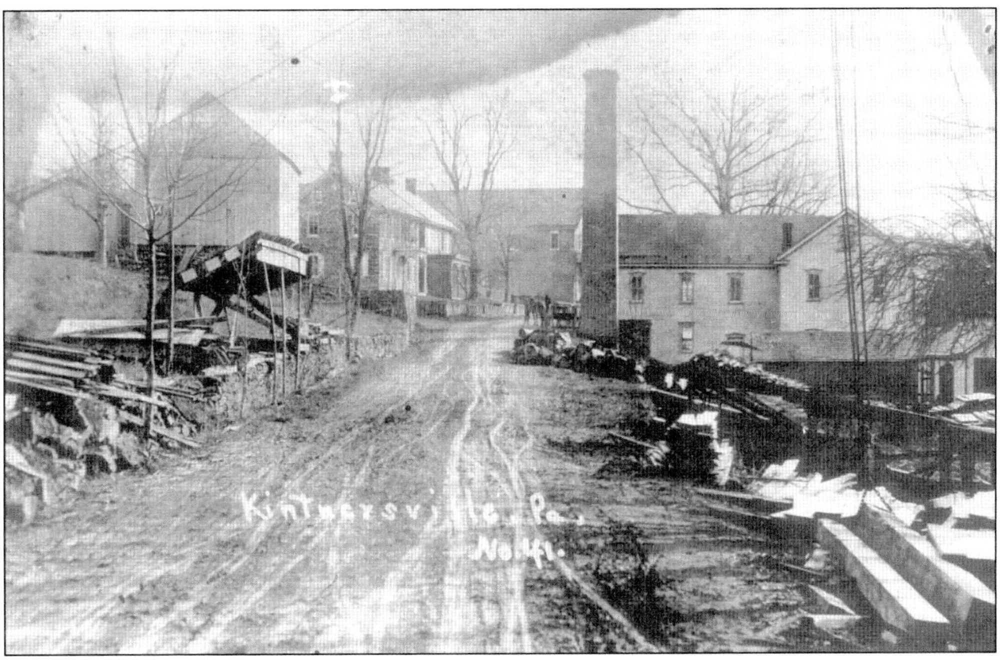

Jacob Froelich Sr. built this mill around 1772. Son Jacob Froelich Jr. inherited it in 1796 and sold it to Jacob Kintner in 1812. Changing hands again, it was sold to John Garis, then back to Jacob Kintner 1817, and then William Long and David Treichler in 1823. Treichler's son William inherited it in 1832 and began cutting woodland trees. During the height of lumber business, 40 huge log rafts floated downriver after spring rains. William built a large gristmill and two sawmills in 1848. (GBG.)

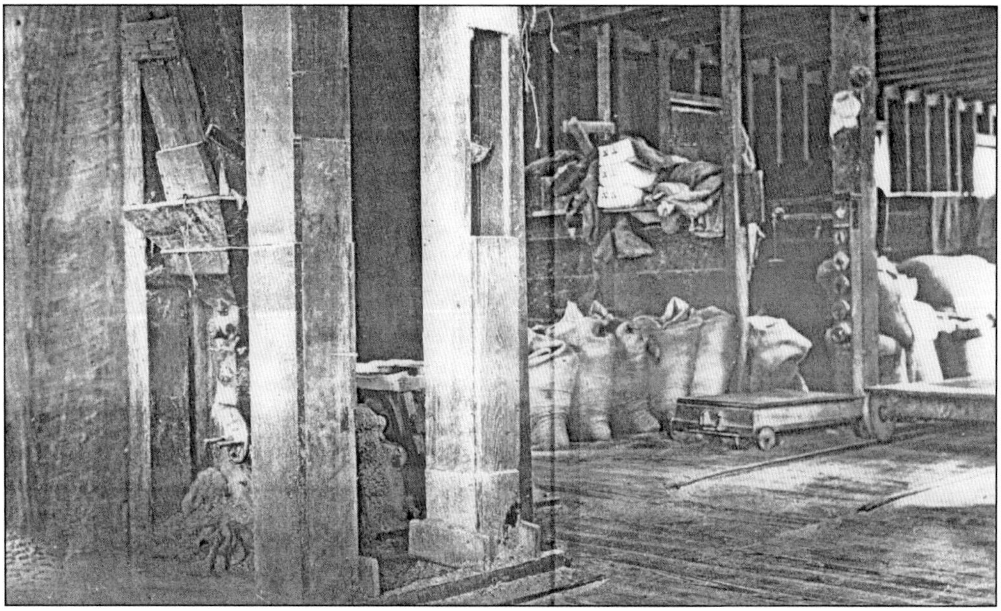

William Treichler died in 1866, and his property was transferred to Phoebe Williams, who sold the mills to Albert Stover in 1869. Fire destroyed saw, grist, and planing mills in 1887. Two sawmills were rebuilt in 1887–1888 that were run by steam; the gristmill was rebuilt in 1888 and ran on waterpower. Albert operated the flour mill and gristmill until 1903, when Cyrus Stover came to village. He learned the milling trade serving as an apprentice and was qualified to operate them. (NHS.)

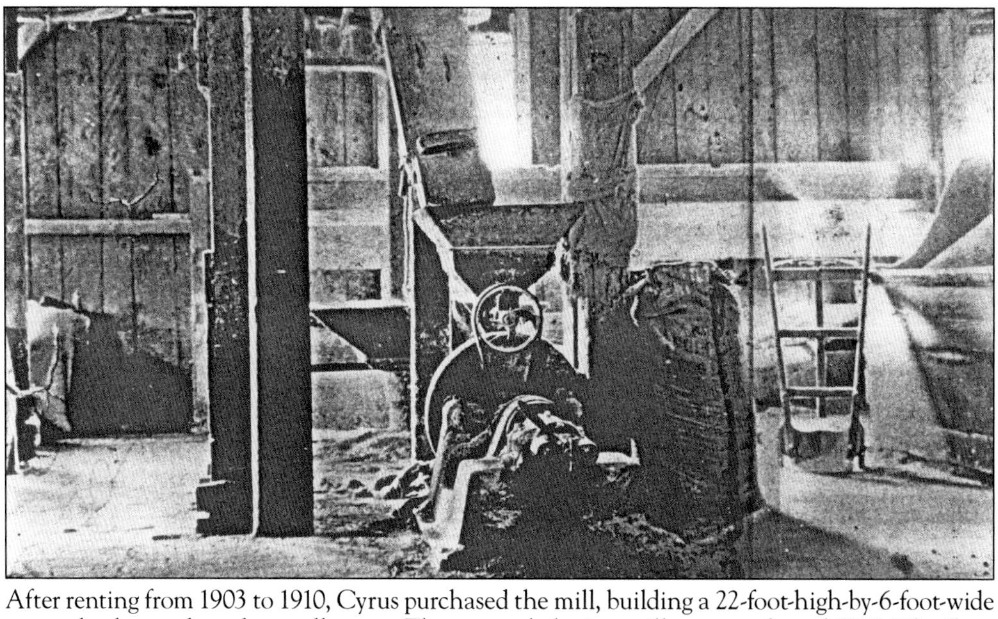

After renting from 1903 to 1910, Cyrus purchased the mill, building a 22-foot-high-by-6-foot-wide waterwheel to replace the smaller one. The saw and planing mills operated until 1926. The flour and gristmill closed in the 1930s, when portable hammer mills ground and mixed feed at farms. Earlier millers tolled feed, taking the amount of chop after the grain was ground as compensation; no money was exchanged. Now home to an antique shop, the mill retains a 45-foot-high smokestack and waterwheel. (NHS.)

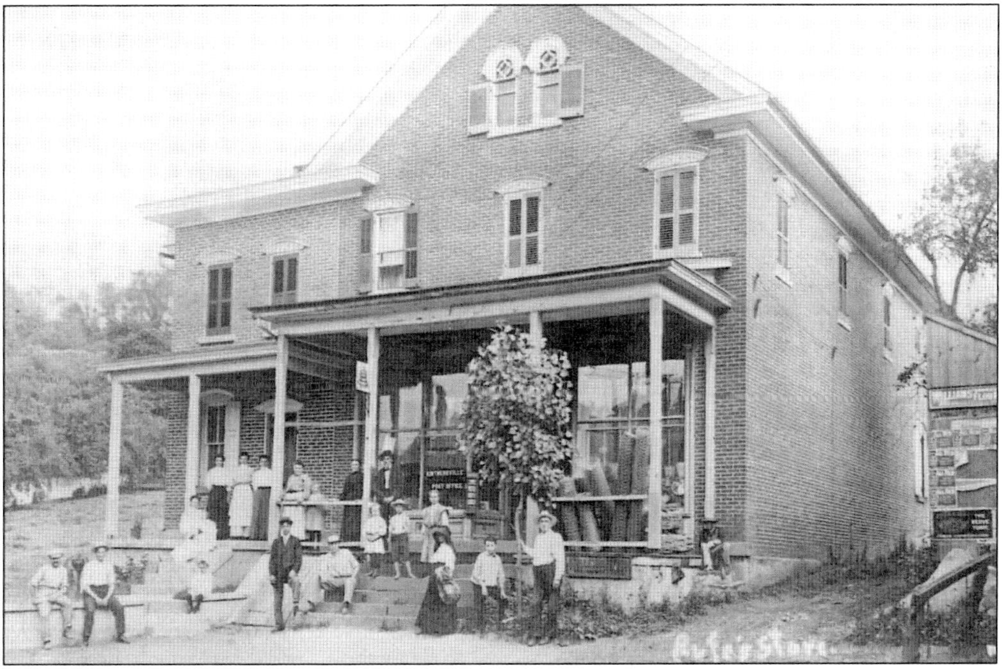

Daniel F. Rufe, Kintnersville postmaster from 1915 to 1917, was the proprietor of Rufe's Store until 1918. Daniel's parents, Preston and Rose Rufe, and his five children stand on the porch in 1916. One of Daniel's sisters was A. Della Rufe, a millinery operator. Young son Woodrow W. Rufe, Carol (Rufe) Lehr's father, is sitting on the left wall wearing a straw hat and rolled-up pants. The store sold a variety of goods, medicinals, groceries, and clothing. In 1879, Levi Althouse constructed the two-story brick building, which is now a private dwelling. (CRL.)

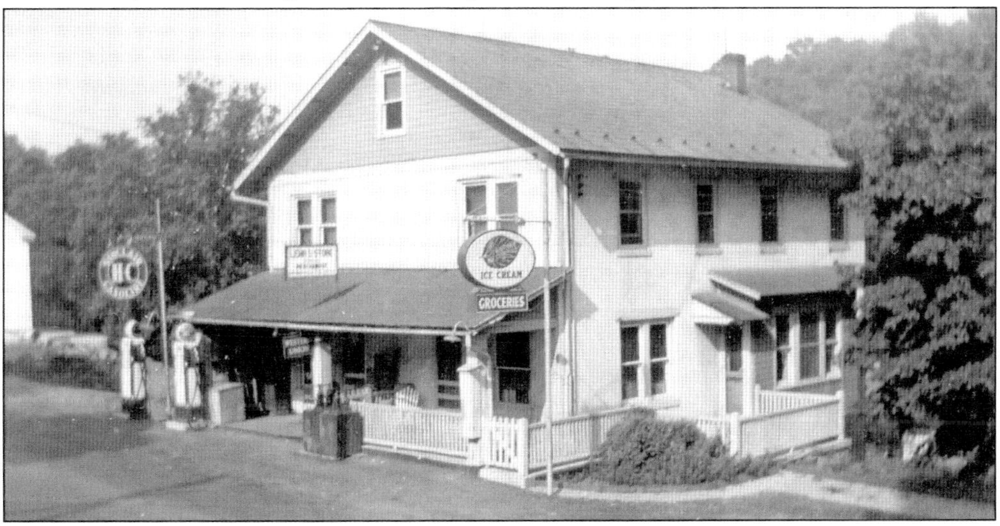

Frank Gutekunst, village postmaster from 1917 to 1947, spent the early years in the Althouse building. He built the post office in 1927 and his wife, Bertha, operated the store. George M. Lehr purchased the Gutekunst building in 1947, serving as postmaster from 1947 to 1968. His family lived in the residence, and wife Margaret operated Lehr's Store until its closing in 1964. Son Carl Lehr remembers that the general store supplied everything anyone needed. The space was converted into a large modern post office. George continued as postmaster, retiring in 1968. (CLK.)

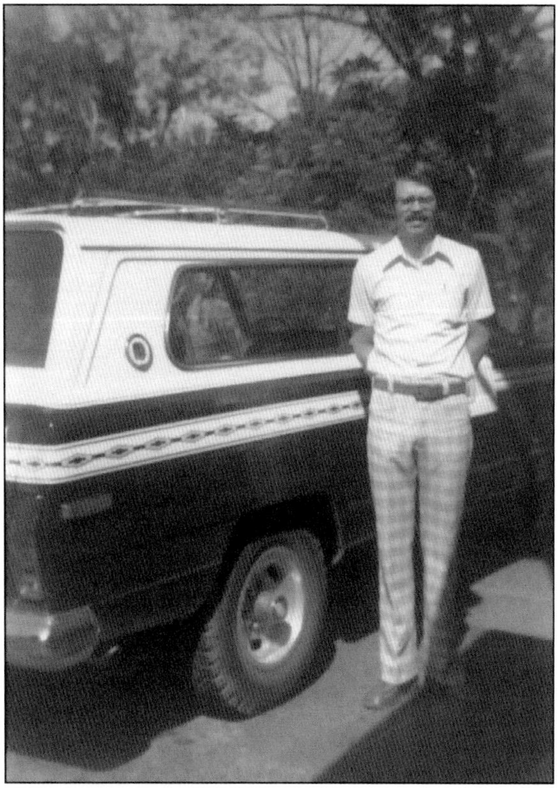

After serving in the US Army, Carl E. Lehr (George Lehr's son) worked at the Doylestown postal center. He transferred to Kintnersville in December 1968, serving as postmaster until 1999. The post office remains on Easton Road. As a youngster, Carl remembers the hall upstairs was used for Red Men Lodge and Pocahontas Women's Auxiliary meetings. When the women met, the men and children would congregate at the store, eat ice cream, and catch up on the news. (MRW.)

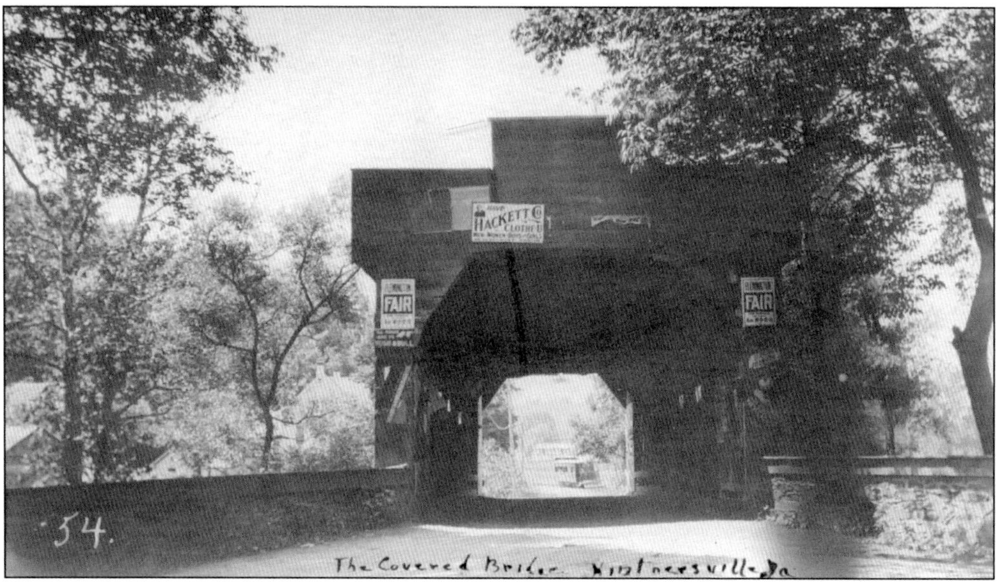

A Doylestown Easton trolley is about to travel through the covered bridge over the Gallow's Run, Easton and River Road intersection, in 1911. The covered bridge, often a shelter from a summer shower, was sometimes full of horses and wagons until the rains ceased. The Kintnersville covered bridge was removed in 1921 since emergency vehicles could not get to destinations in time. This postcard was sent to Verna (Stone) Bartman (Blanche Wehrung's mother) in November 1916 before she was married. (BBW.)

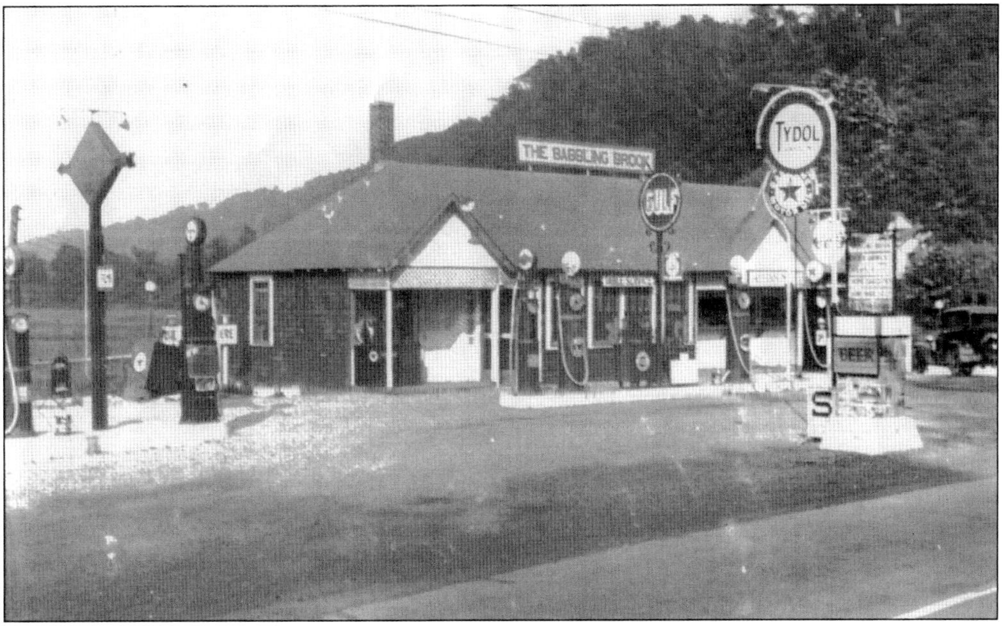

Throughout the years, the Babbling Brook has been mentioned as the site of the first gas station in Upper Bucks County. The Easton Road location made it a busy place with people traveling north to Lehigh Valley and the Poconos, south to Philadelphia or the New Jersey shore, or just a scenic drive down River Road. A varied selection of different brands of gasoline was available during the 1930s. (NHS.)

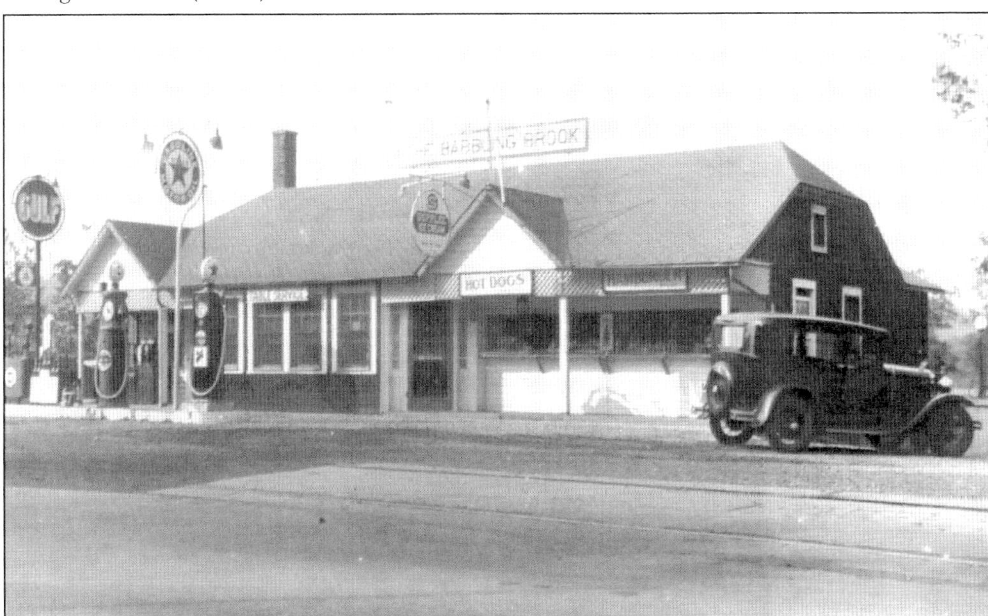

Andrew Rezzonico built Babbling Brook restaurant on Easton Road in Kintnersville in 1927. He and his wife lived in a Victorian house across the highway. Known for good food, the restaurant also had a takeout counter. A 1931 Ford Model A is seen here. In later years, the establishment had some colorful times. The popular Great American Grill evolved in the 1980s with casual 1950s décor and a New York–style menu. The restaurant is now John's American Grill. (NHS.)

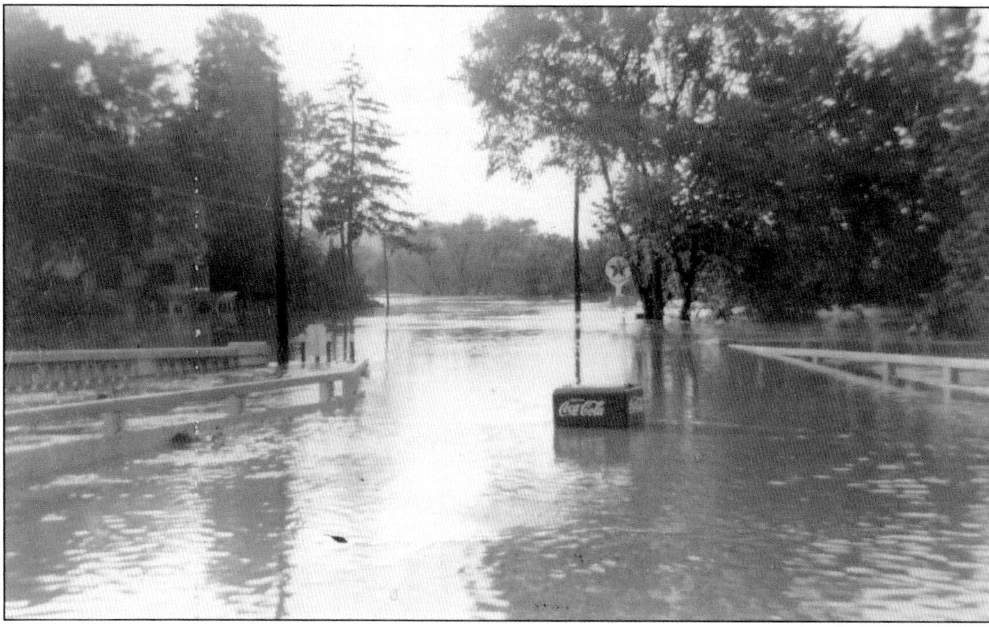

The Babbling Brook restaurant and gas station is shown through the trees with water rising during the August 1955 flood that devastated the area. Road signs on the right side have disappeared. Only the top of the Texaco gasoline sign is seen in the middle of photograph, and to the right the restaurant's roof can barely be seen. Looking to the left beyond bridge and guardrails, the Rezzonico home is visible with the water depth halfway up the porch. (MRW.)

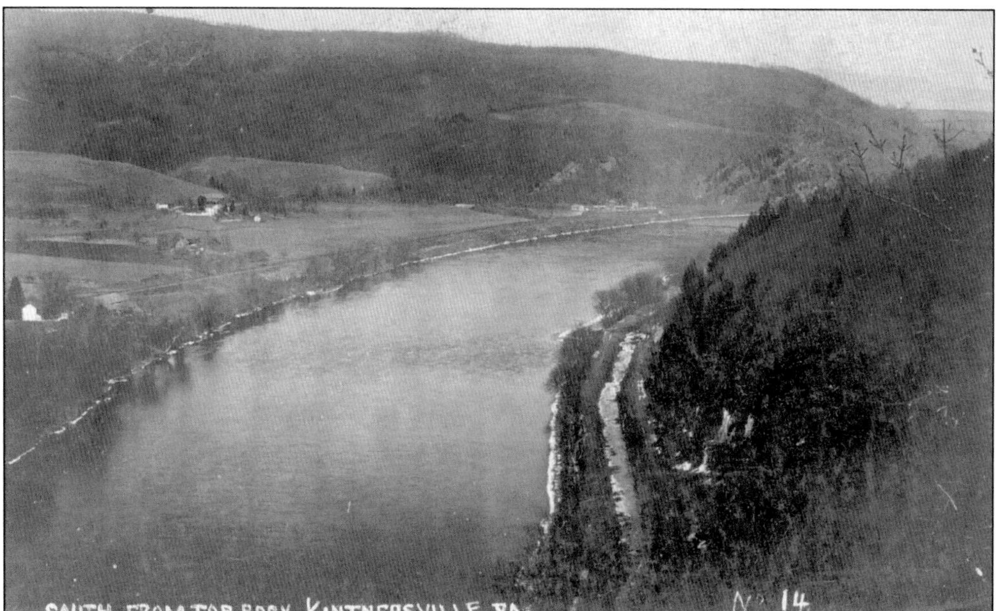

This view looking south on River Road from Top Rock provides a panoramic view of the surrounding countryside as well as the river and canal. Farmland, dwellings, and railroad tracks can be seen in the distance. Also known as Prospect or High Rock, this 500-foot-high rock of the Palisades family resembles a Native American profile. The colonial Shawnee village of Pechoqueolin, one of the largest Indian villages in Bucks County, was located nearby. (NHS.)

This waterfall is located along the Palisades of the Delaware on River Road. The majestic wall of Nockamixon cliffs rises some 400 feet from the brink of the river and sometimes harbors Peregrine falcons. The dark, cool environment also supports a rare alpine plant community. Each season during the year presents a changing scene. Winter is very picturesque, when snow and masses of ice form over the rock ledges and sparkle in the sunlight. (NHS.)

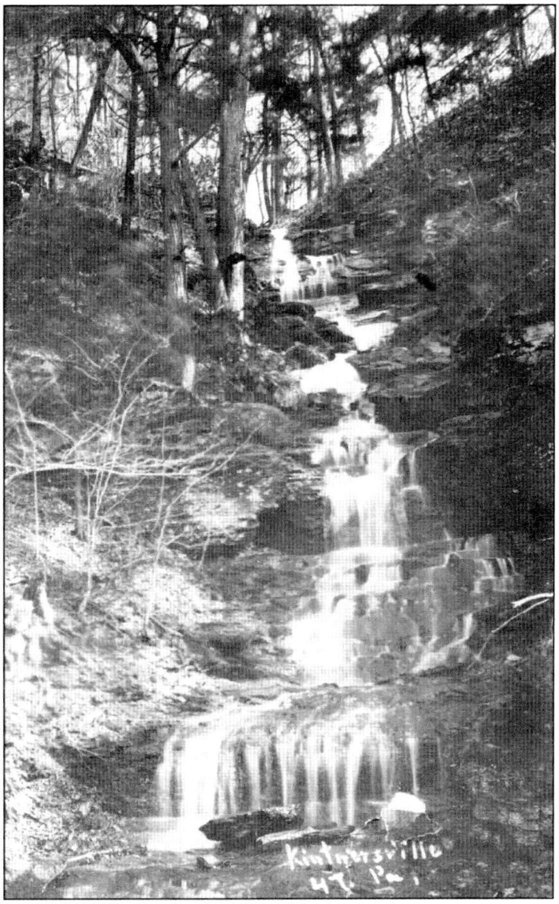

This early-1900s photograph shows Narrowsville, a small hamlet rear of the river hills, on River Road south of Kintnersville. The community of 14 houses included the lock tender's house and Mahala (Herstine) Fulmer's home on the right. Canal traffic workers used a covered bridge over the canal to reach the sawmill located between the canal and river. A sawmill used to cut logs floated down river years ago. Mills once stood along the canal and the lower end of narrows on the Delaware River. (MRW.)

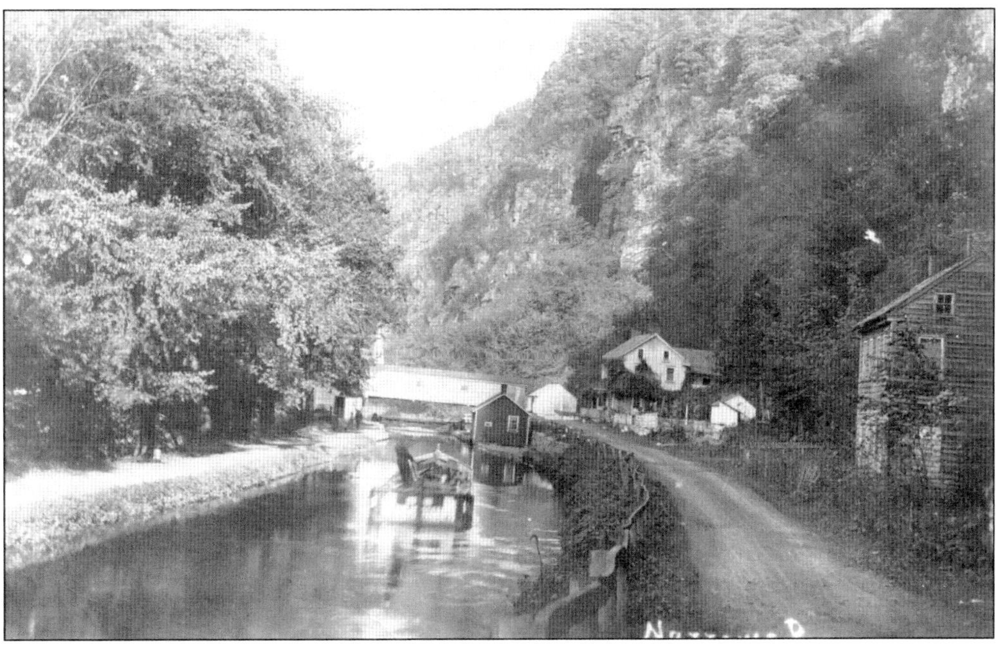

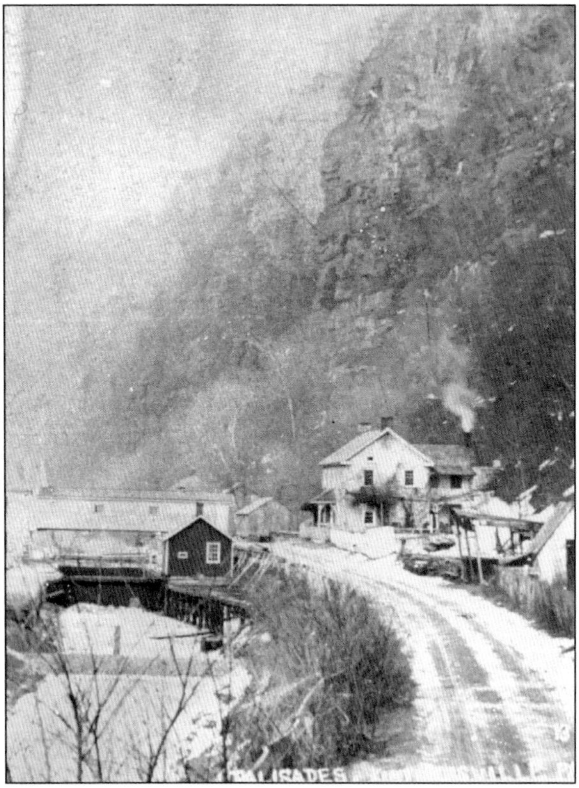

Here is a winter scene along the Narrows between Kintnersville and Upper Black Eddy, with snow and ice covering Narrowsville. The postcard was mailed—with 1¢ postage—on March 20, 1906, at 8:00 a.m. from Milford, New Jersey. The message reads, "Arrived yesterday in 8 inch snowstorm on 3:50 train. Took supper with us. I took her suitcase up. Chas." The postcard arrived in Brooklyn, New York, that same day at 3:00 p.m. (CLK.)

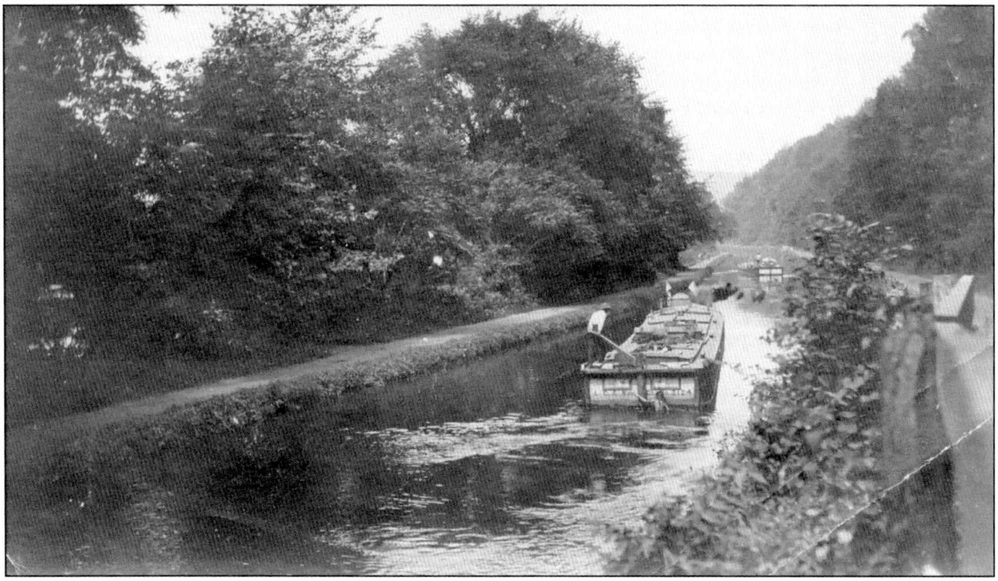

Two canal boat pilots maneuver down the Narrows. A boy in the water assists the front boat with its rudder. The boatman would blow a conch shell approaching Kintnersville, calling the Narrowsville lock tender to prepare to put the boat through the lock. Children raced down River Road to watch. Canal construction began in 1827 and finished in 1832. This major route in the mid-1800s carried 3,000 boats a year until the Pennsylvania Railroad was completed. The last barge passed through Kintnersville at the end of 1931. (RBK.)

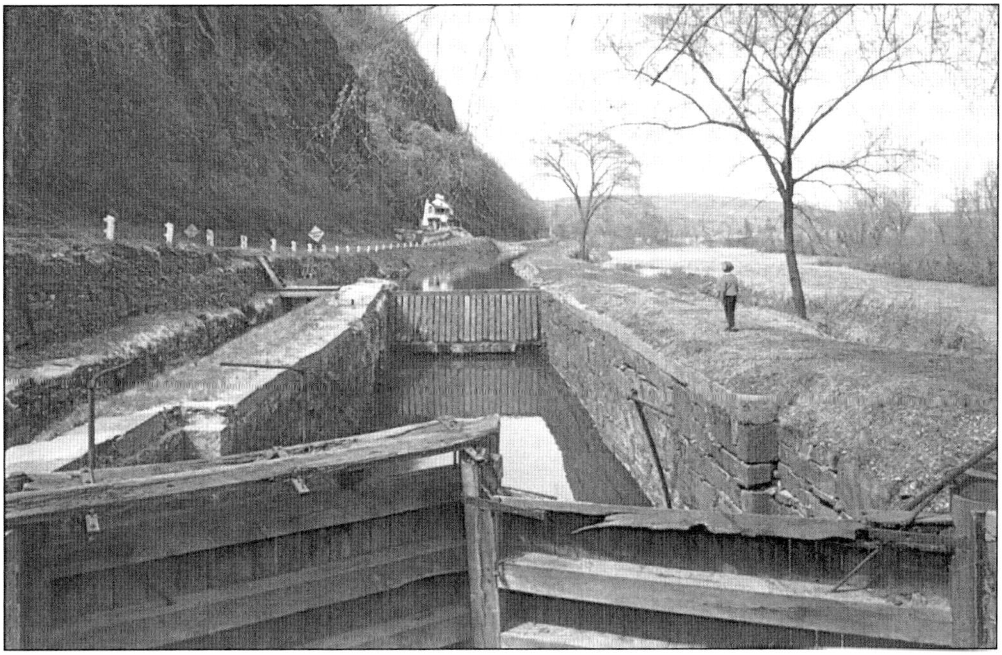

This picturesque scene is along the Delaware River between Kintnersville and Upper Black Eddy. The Narrowsville Hotel is in the distance on the left. The 1976 postcard features the Delaware Canal Lock No. 20 at Narrows. Canal locks were used to raise or lower the canal boats from one water level to another on the canal, which ran from Bristol to Easton. Walking the towpath is a popular pastime of residents and visitors. (MRW.)

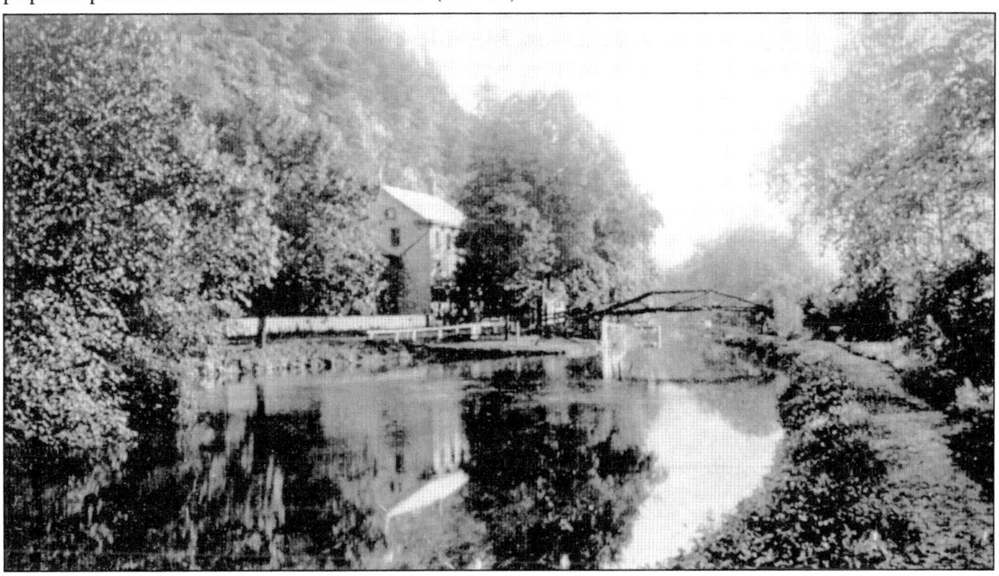

Indian Rock Inn at the base of Palisades cliffs along Delaware River, built by Jacob Krouse in 1820, has a long history. John Derr, owner from 1837 to 1854, expanded the Rising Sun Hotel for lodging. Mathias Lehman renamed it the Narrowsville Hotel in 1854. A well-known resort in the late 1890s and early 1900s, vacationers from Philadelphia came by train to Jersey Central Power's Gilbert Station. Crossing the river by boat, they continued across the canal bridge to the hotel. (NHS.)

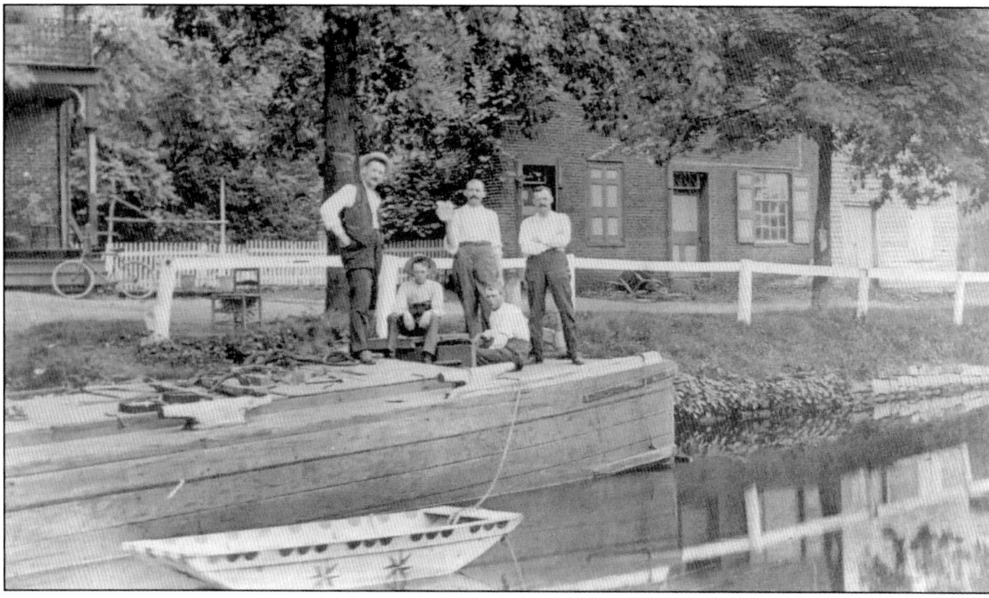

Villagers relax in front of the Narrows Hotel in this turn-of-the-century canal scene. Taking a boatman's holiday, the gentlemen stand on a canal boat watching youngsters play with a small decorated boat in the Delaware Canal. It looks like the men are taking a break from repairs since tools are on the boat deck. Canal barges often stopped at the hotel. The blacksmith shop and stables are behind the group on the right. (NHS.)

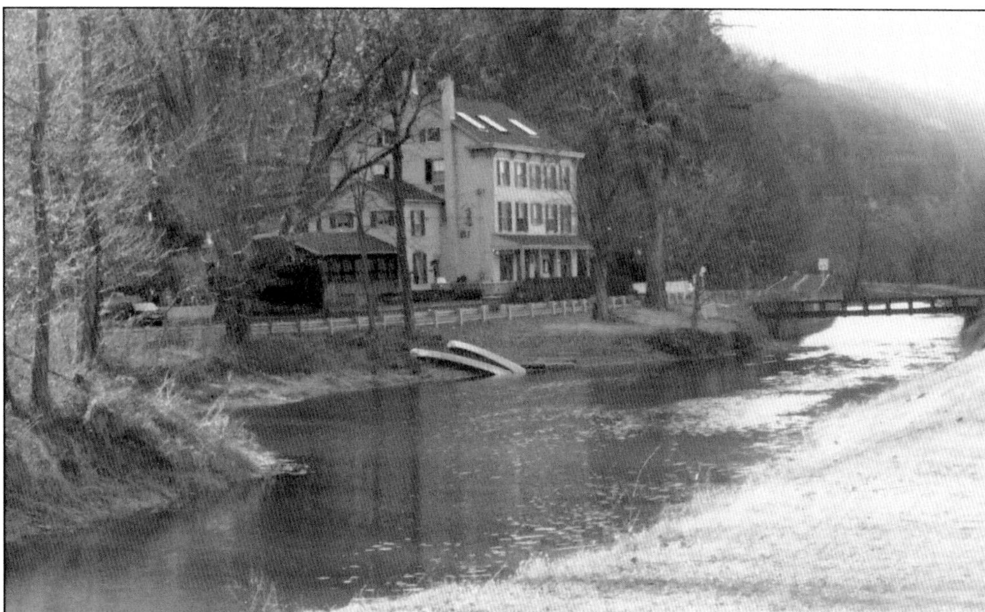

Indian Rock Inn, formerly Narrowsville Hotel, was located on River Road and served as a stagecoach stop on the Easton Morrisville line. Patrons passing through would take overnight lodging and an evening meal, enjoying a reprieve from the bumpy stagecoach trip. Canal barges also stopped in the mid- to late 1800s. Food was available for the crew, stables for mules, and a blacksmith shop for repairs. The Indian Rock Inn continues to offer hospitality with lodging, food, and entertainment. (NHS.)

Two

Early Families and Homes

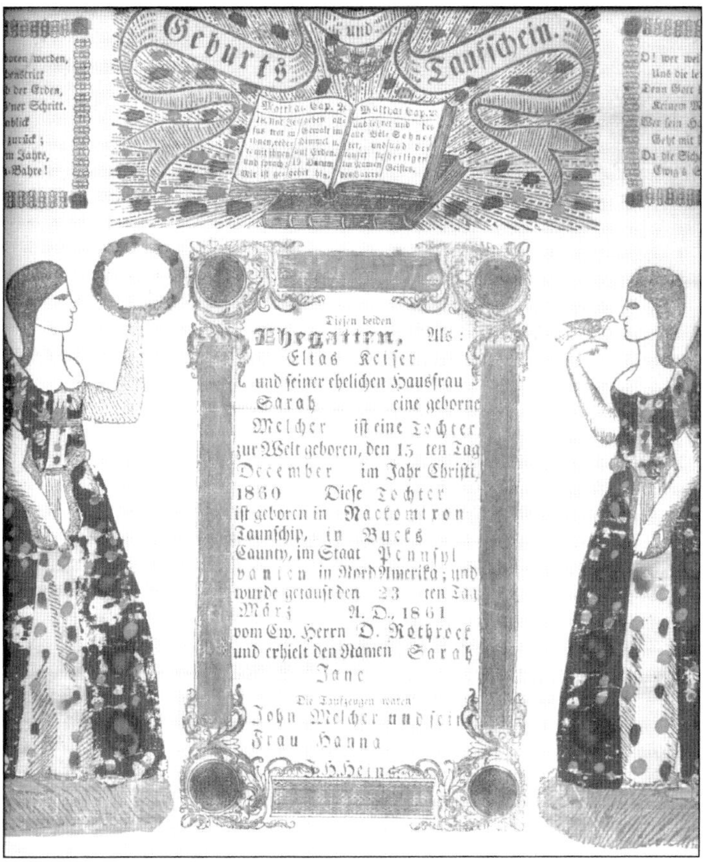

Elias Keifer and his wife, Sarah Melcher, had a daughter, born on December 15, 1860, in Nockamixon Township. She was baptized on March 23, 1861, by Pastor David Rothrock and named Sarah Jane. The godparents were John Melcher and his wife, Hanna. Pastor Rothrock served St. Luke's Reformed Church in Nockamixon from 1859 to 1892. The scrivener of the birth certificate fraktur was John Henry Heins. (NHS.)

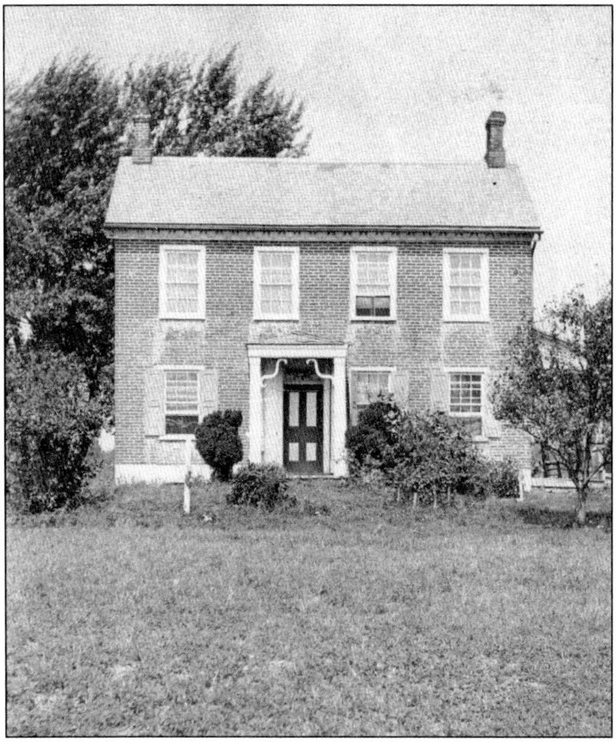

George and Mary (Randall) Butterfoss resided in a stately brick home on West Quarry Road in Harrow for a short time in the late 1890s. Named for the previous owner, the villagers knew the homestead as the Fox farm. The Butterfoss family, who emigrated from Holland, were boat builders by trade and enjoyed visiting the boats on the Delaware Canal. George built many homes in New Jersey—from the town of Stockton to Frenchtown. (RBK.)

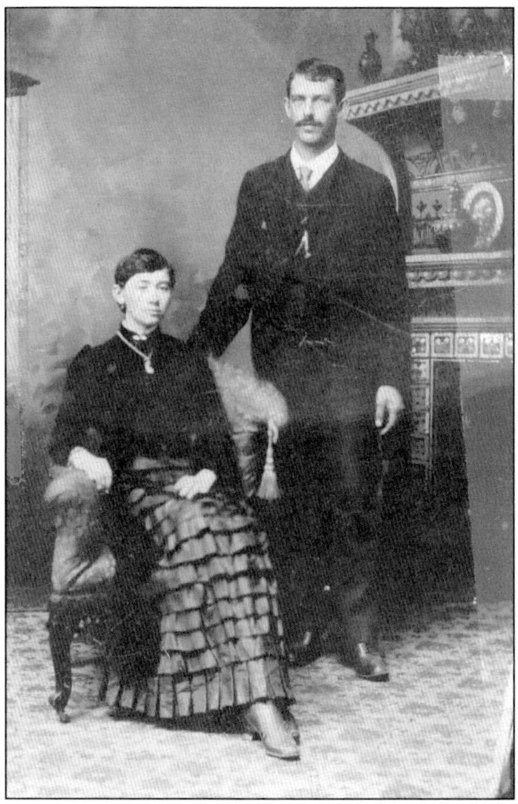

This tintype photograph shows George and Mary (Randall) Butterfoss, grandparents of Robert Butterfoss of Revere, sitting in their parlor. George, a skilled craftsman, made many improvements on the home. The ornate mantel in the photograph was one of the pieces of woodwork he built. Mary, a schoolteacher in New Jersey, taught Pitman shorthand, typing, and secretarial skills. They were the parents of four children: Joseph, Nell, Vivian, and Howard. (RBK.)

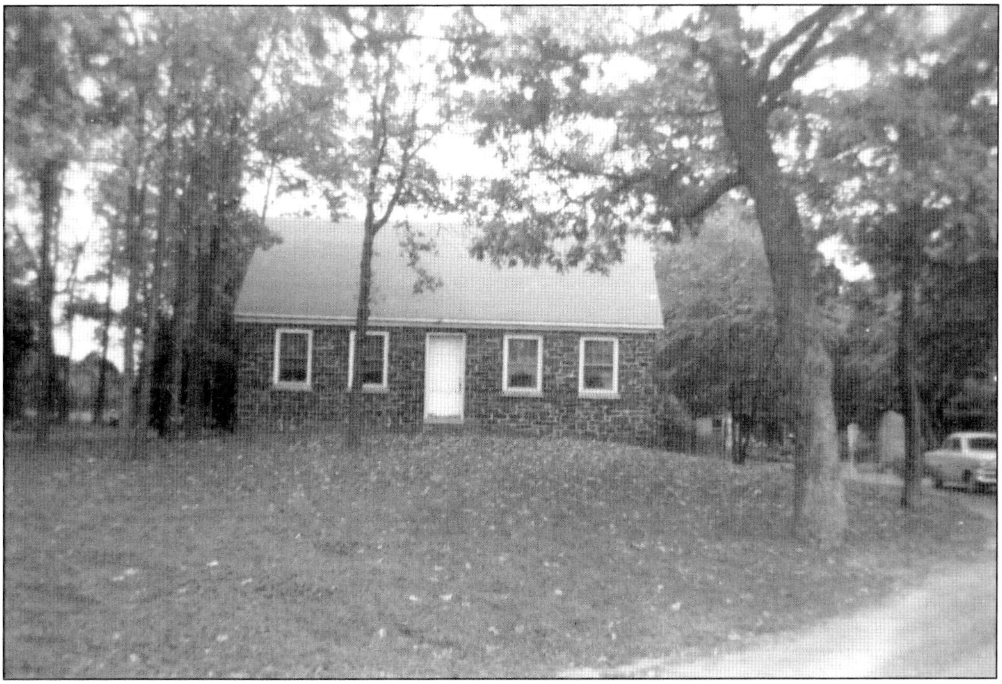

Alex "Babe" Zheltonoga started building the Zheltonoga home in 1947. Doing most of the labor, he subcontracted only the electric, plastering, and outside stonework. Alex and wife Salome (Trouts) moved into their Easton Road home in the village of Harrow in 1949 and continued to add features to make it cozy. Alex was originally employed by Bethlehem Steel. An excellent automobile-body technician, he later worked for Good Brothers and Neely Ford in Ottsville. (STZ.)

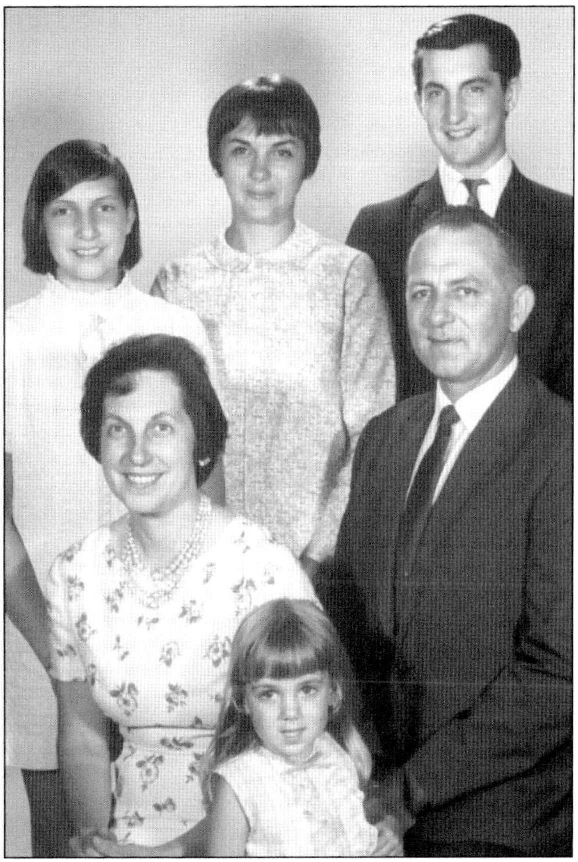

Salome Trouts of Harrow and Alex (Babe) Zheltonoga of Pleasant Valley, Springfield, met at Kellers Church social club, where young people came to dance and listen to country music. Alex, a great vocalist, often entertained with his buddies. Married in 1946, they celebrated their 65th anniversary in 2011. In this 1970s photograph, the Zheltonoga family members are, from left to right, (front) Salome, granddaughter Paige, and Alex; (back) daughters Sally and Judy and son James. (STZ.)

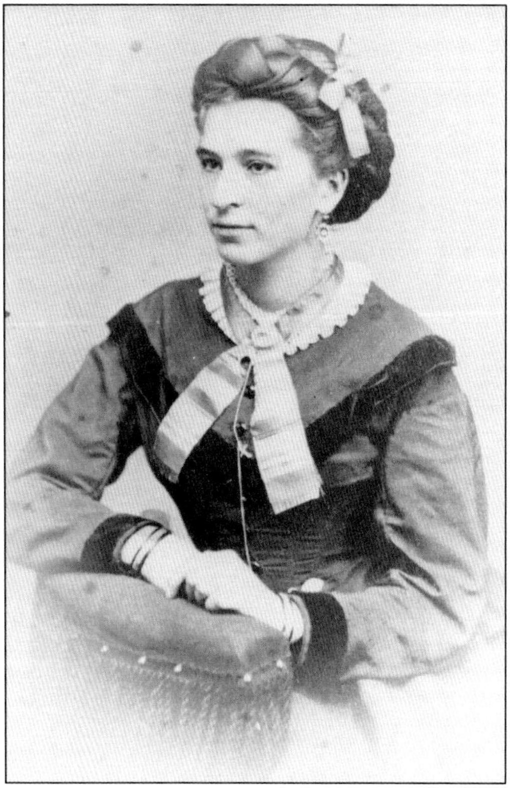

Isabella (McCarty) McCarty, daughter of Sarah (Beam) McCarty and Abner D. McCarty, was born in 1855 and passed away in 1923. This 1870 photograph was prior to her marriage in 1877 to Thomas Y. McCarty. Mother of Leo, Angelo, Roscoe, Alacoque, Florence, Ethel, and Charles, Isabella was a strong woman in body and spirit. Family albums show her helping in farm fields as well as cleaning clothes in the washtub outside. (RMC.)

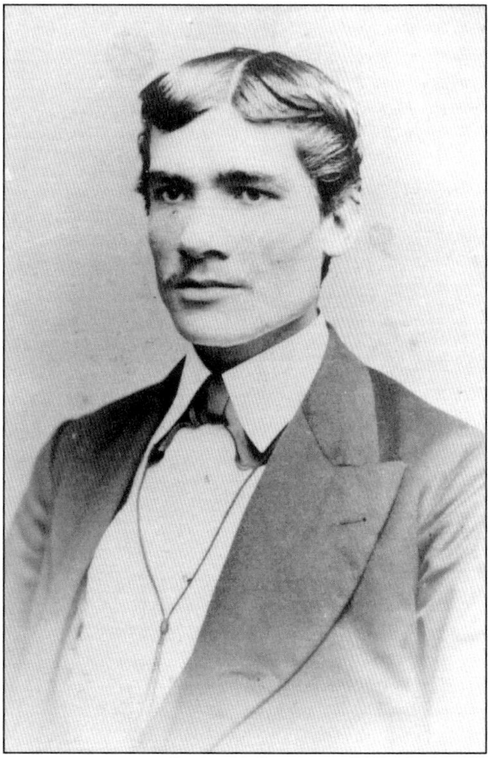

Thomas Y. McCarty, the sixth generation and youngest son of Paul Abner and Louisa (McIntyre) McCarty, was born in 1850 on the original McCarty farm in Bucksville and passed away in 1934. Husband of Isabella McCarty, and father of seven children, he is seen here in 1870. In addition to superintending the family farm, Thomas was also a stagecoach driver, schoolteacher, and auctioneer during his lifetime. (RMC.)

Thomas Y. McCarty, seen here around 1890, looks out from the second floor of the family barn, built in 1812. He was the Bucksville postmaster and carried on an extensive business dealing in general merchandise at his Durham Road store that opened in 1878. Thomas's presence was known in Bucks County as well as the state. He served as county jury commissioner and director of the poor, and he also worked at the Philadelphia Mint. (RMC.)

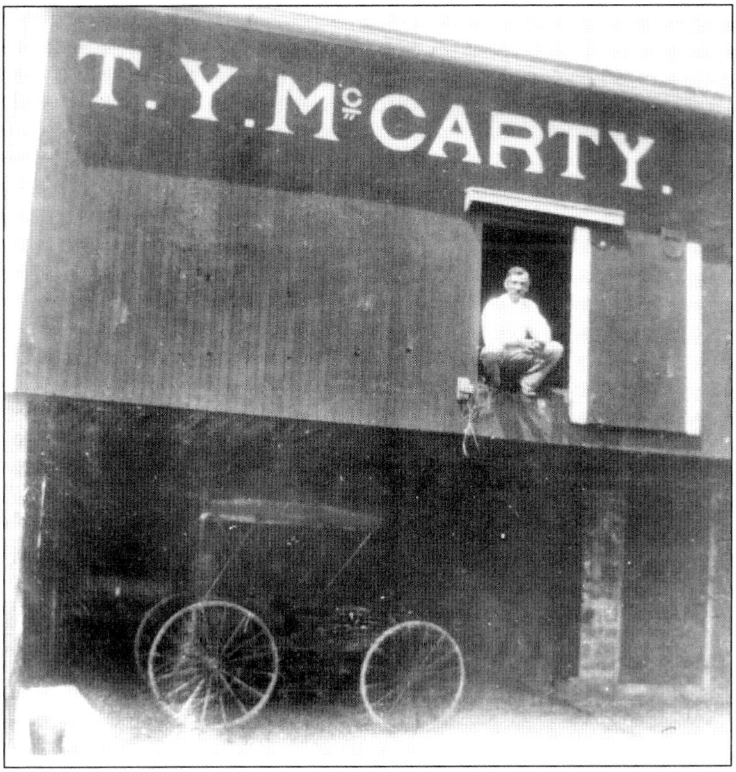

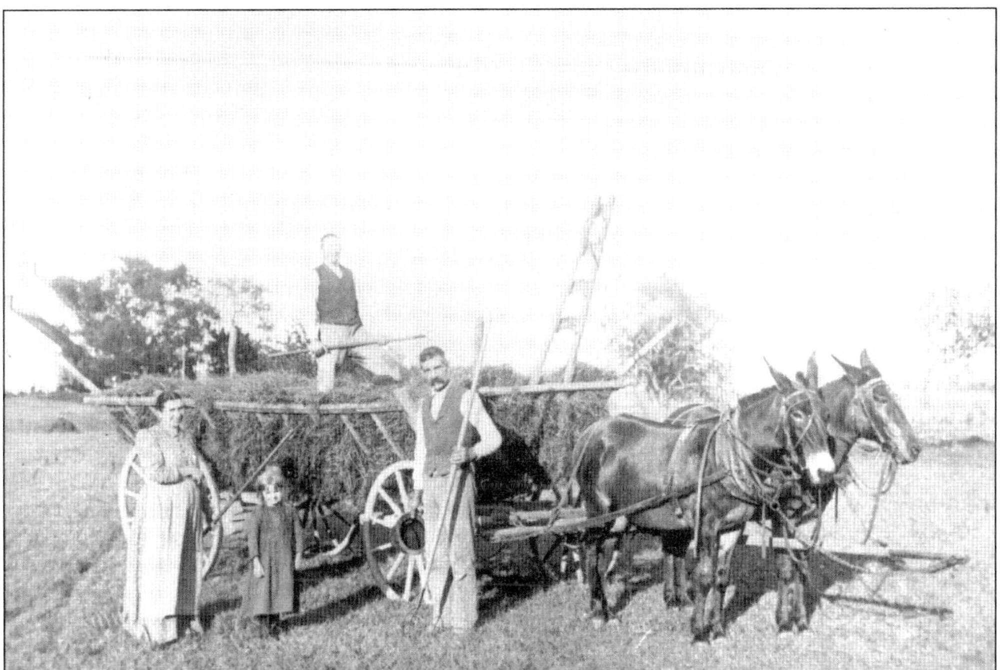

Isabella McCarty and daughter Florence come out and check on Thomas and a helper working out in the fields stacking hay sheaves in 1890. When the large hay wagon was full, two mules would pull it back to the barn where it would be stored. (RMC.)

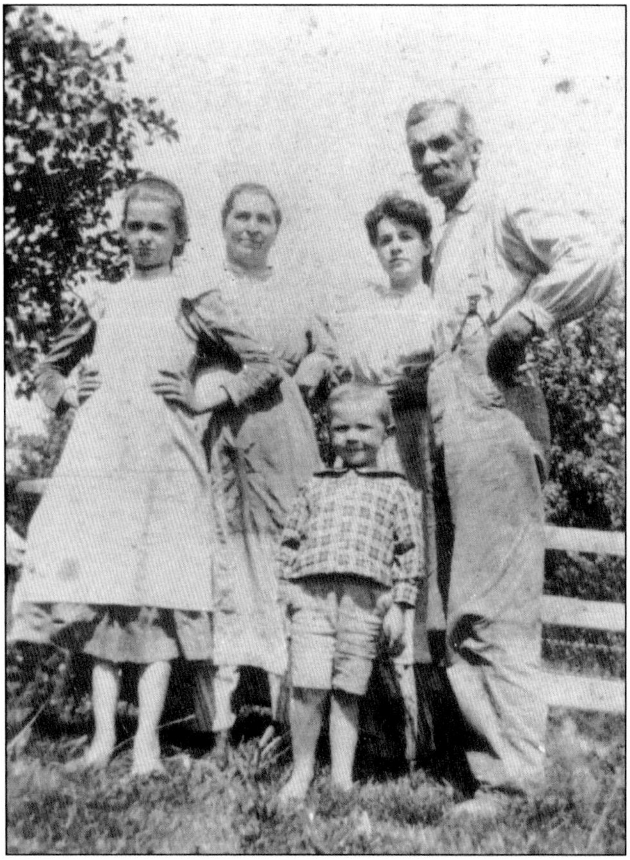

From left to right, daughter Florence, mother Isabella, son Charles, daughter Alacoque, and father Thomas Y. McCarty stop working in the garden to pose for this 1902 photograph. There was always plenty of work and daily maintenance to do around the family farm, and all members assisted with their share. (RMC.)

The family gathers at Thomas Y. and Isabella McCarty's home for the wedding of Thomas Roscoe McCarty to Mary Francis Fleck in September 1909. Young Thomas McCarty, Leo's son, is in front; on the porch, from left to right, are Florence McCarty, Martha (Beam) Kohl, Angelo McCarty, Isabella McCarty, Cecelia McCarty, Sarah (Beam) McCarty, Ethel (McCarty) Haney, Emma McCarty, Leo McCarty, Vincent Kohl, Roscoe McCarty, Thomas Y. McCarty, and Mary (Fleck) McCarty. (RMC.)

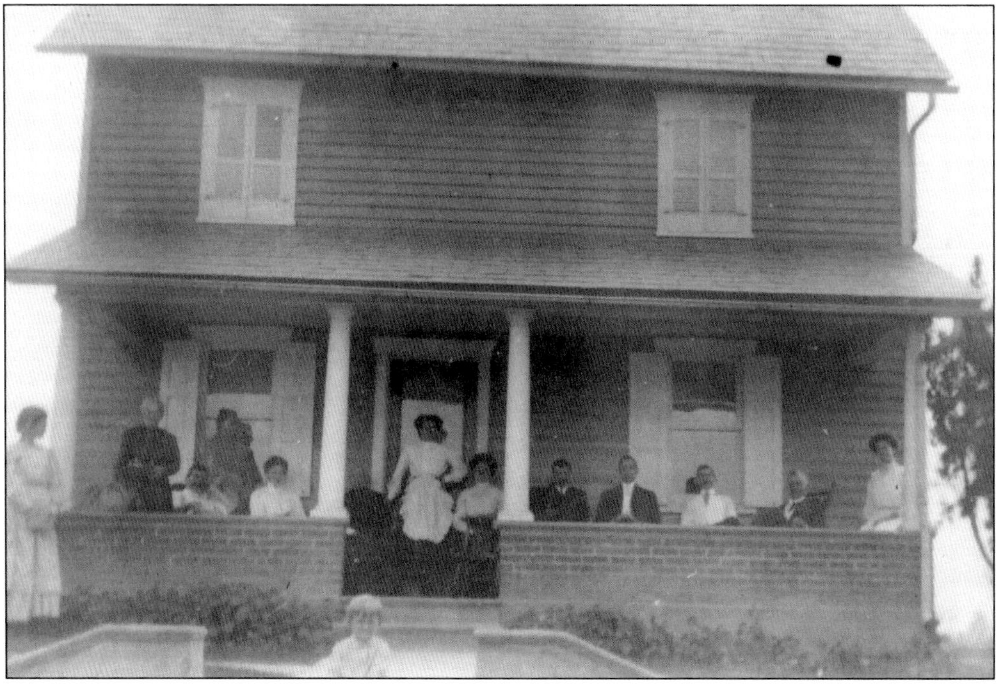

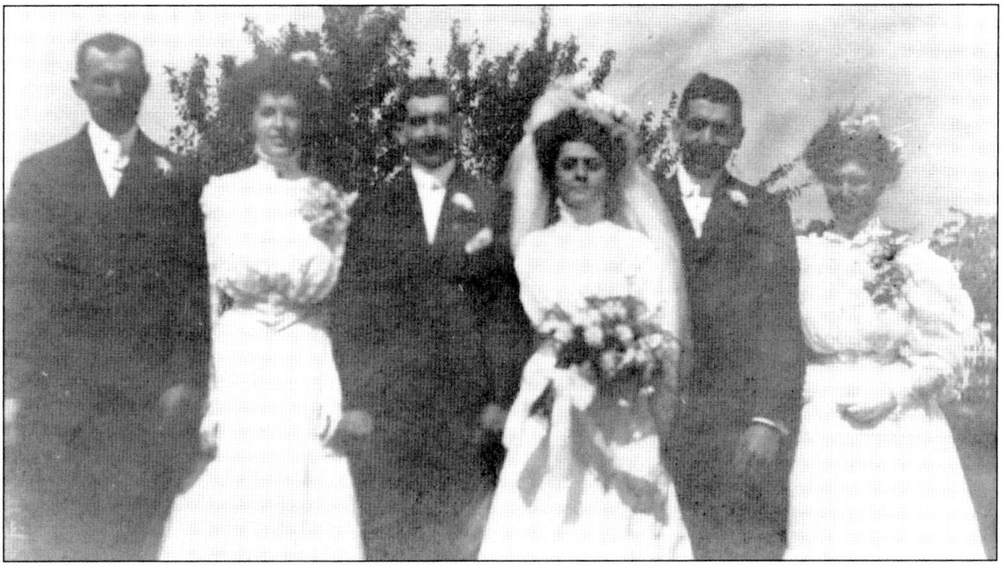

Thomas Roscoe McCarty and Mary Frances (Fleck) McCarty were married on September 30, 1909. Officiated by Rev. Joseph A. Schaefer, the wedding ceremony was held at St. John the Baptist Church in Haycock Run, Pennsylvania. Witnesses standing up for the couple were Joseph Fleck, Margaret Alacoque (McCarty) Kane, and Angelo and wife Cecelia (Kellaghran) McCarty. (RMC.)

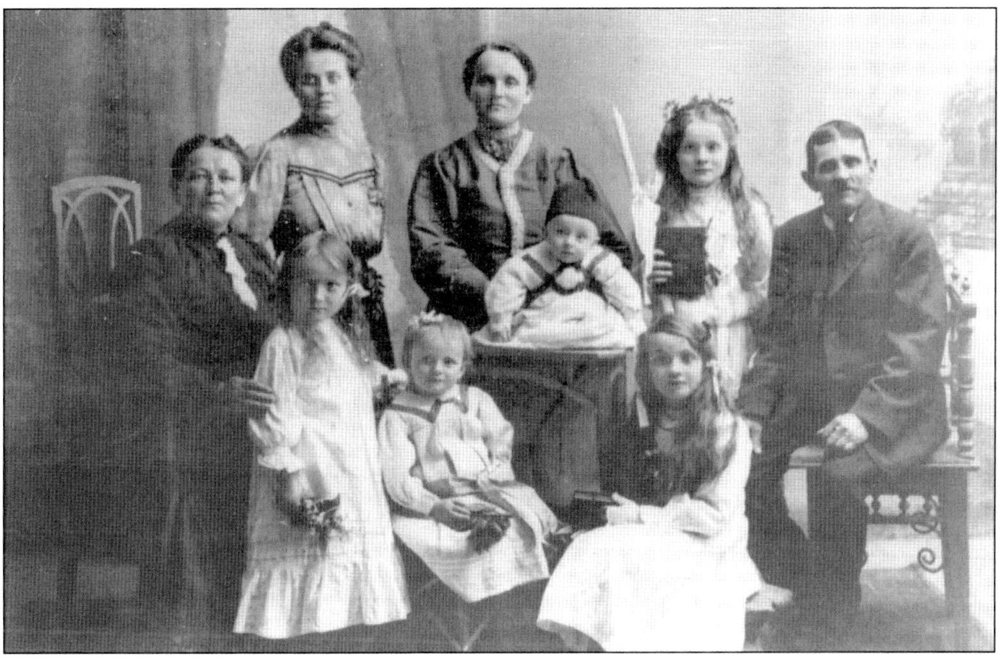

The Balbirer family is shown before sailing from Europe to the United States in 1913 to join father Andrew Balbirer, who came to Pennsylvania several years earlier. From left to right are (first row) daughters Victoria, Emma, and Regina; (second row) Eleanor Loeffelman (Ottilia Balbirer's mother), Kate Birl, Ottilia (Loeffelman) Balbirer holding son Robert Balbirer, daughter Rose Balbirer, and Peter Balbirer (Andrew Balbirer's father). The ship's crew assisted Ottilia with the children. (RMC.)

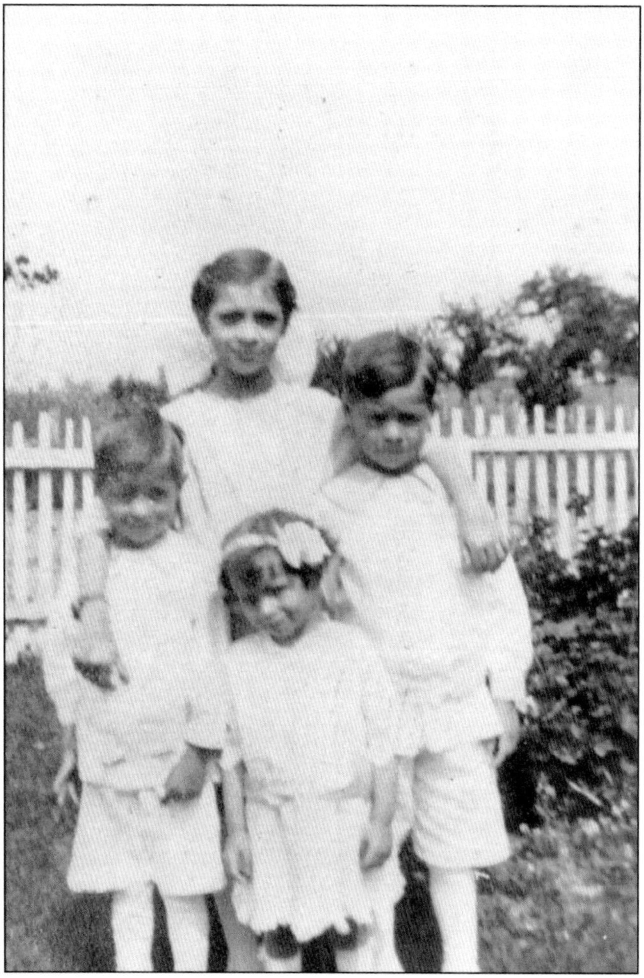

From left to right, Vincent, Helen (Thaler), Ethel (Sister Mary), and Charles P. McCarty—young children of Roscoe and Mary McCarty—pose for a family portrait in 1920. The girls are wearing stylish frocks. Ethel is wearing a headband with an attached flower, while Helen has her hair pulled back with a large bow. The boys are wearing choirboy-type shirts and knickers with high socks. (RMC.)

Friends and family celebrate Andrew and Ottilia Balbirer's silver wedding anniversary on October 16, 1923, at their Bucksville home. From left to right are (first row) John Holziger and a young boy; (second row) Emily Polley, Julia Balbirer, Anna Balbirer, Jacob Birl, and Robert Polley; (third row) Emma Balbirer, Anna Burkey holding Mupsie, Frank Urban, Ottilia Balbirer, Mrs. Miller, Katie Birl, and Andrew Balbirer; (fourth row) Regina Balbirer and Andrew Snyder. (RMC.)

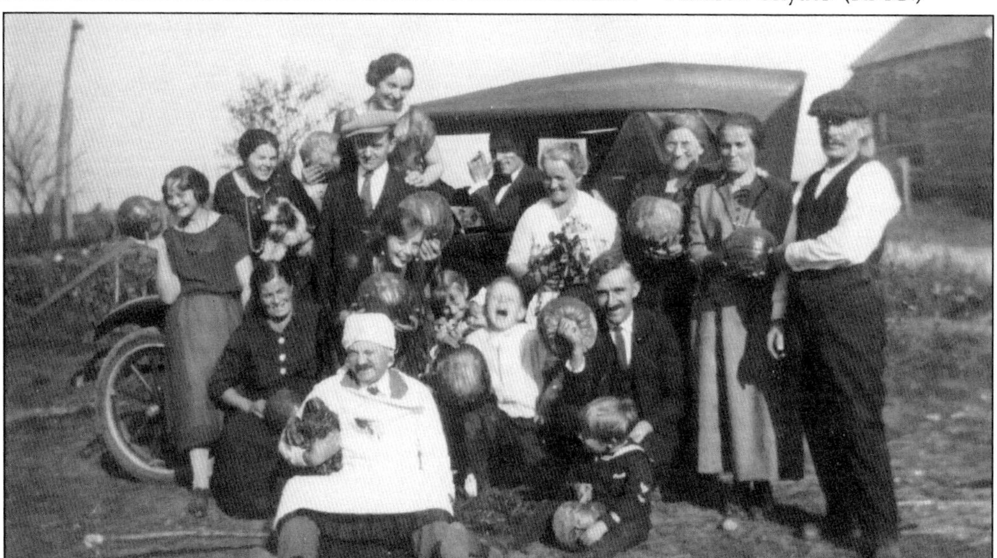

It looks like the day turned out to be cold and blustery when this 1925 photograph was taken on the farm. Both Barbara Damjanits (left), mother of Joseph Damjanits, and Ottilia Balbirer, mother of Victoria (Balbirer) Damjanits, are bundled up and holding onto the reins, bringing the horse to the barn. Victoria, Joseph's wife, is petting her dog. (RMC.)

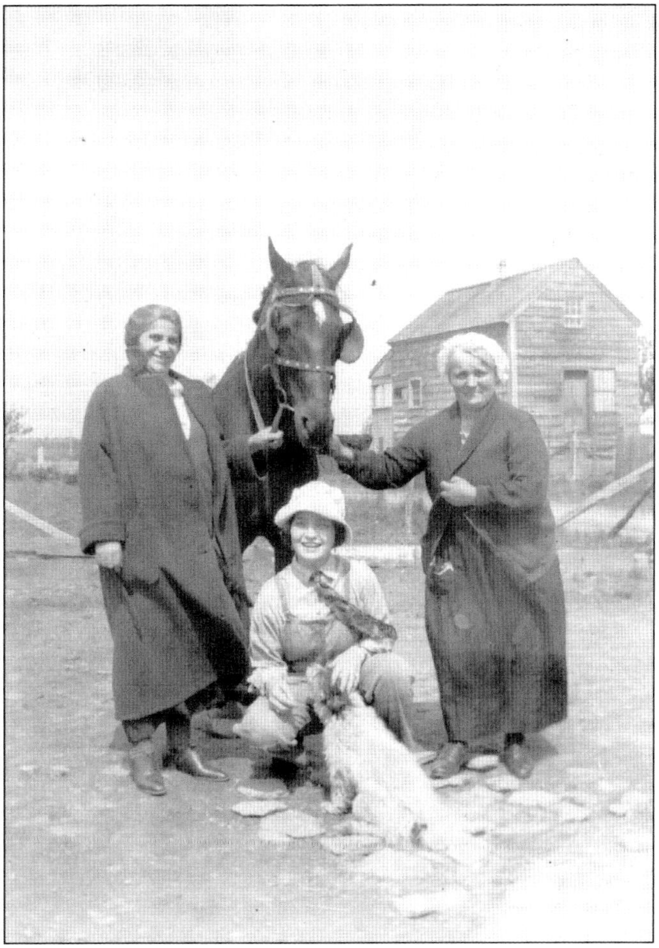

Women and children pose outside a family gathering in 1927. Somehow three young men snuck in the photograph. Posing from left to right are (front row) Matilda Rausch, Victoria (Balbirer) Damjanits, Fred Reichelt Jr., Ottilia Balbirer, and Regina Snyder; (second row) Mrs. John Rausch, Emma (Balbirer) Foltz, Jacob Foltz, Irma Rausch, Arthur Bahnck, Eleanor Omensetter, Lena Focht, Julia Reichelt, and Anna Balbirer holding Andrew Snyder Jr. (RMC.)

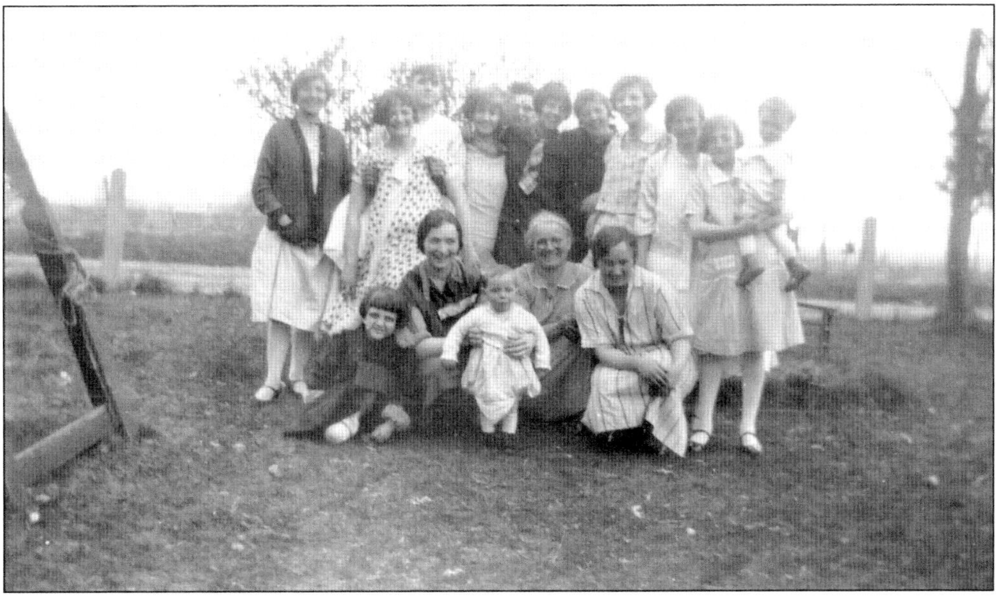

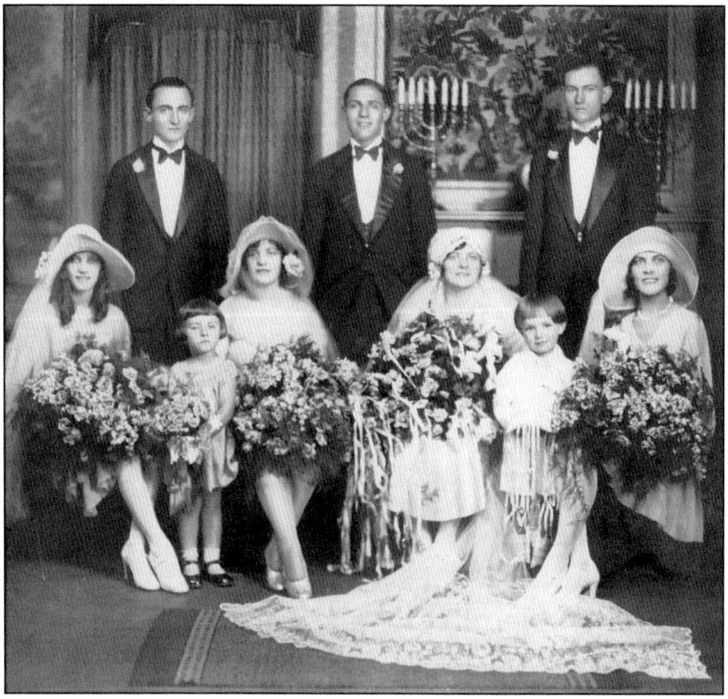

Jacob and Emilia "Emma" (Balbirer) Foltz celebrated their wedding on June 6, 1929. The happy couple poses with their attendants, from left to right, (first row) Marie Foltz, Helen Trechauska, Stephanie (Loeffelman) Denning, Emilia "Emma" (Balbirer) Foltz, Andrew Snyder Jr., and Eleanore Omensetter; (second row) Robert Balbirer, Jacob Foltz, and Anthony Mattern. Sadly, Jacob Foltz passed away in 1933. (RMC.)

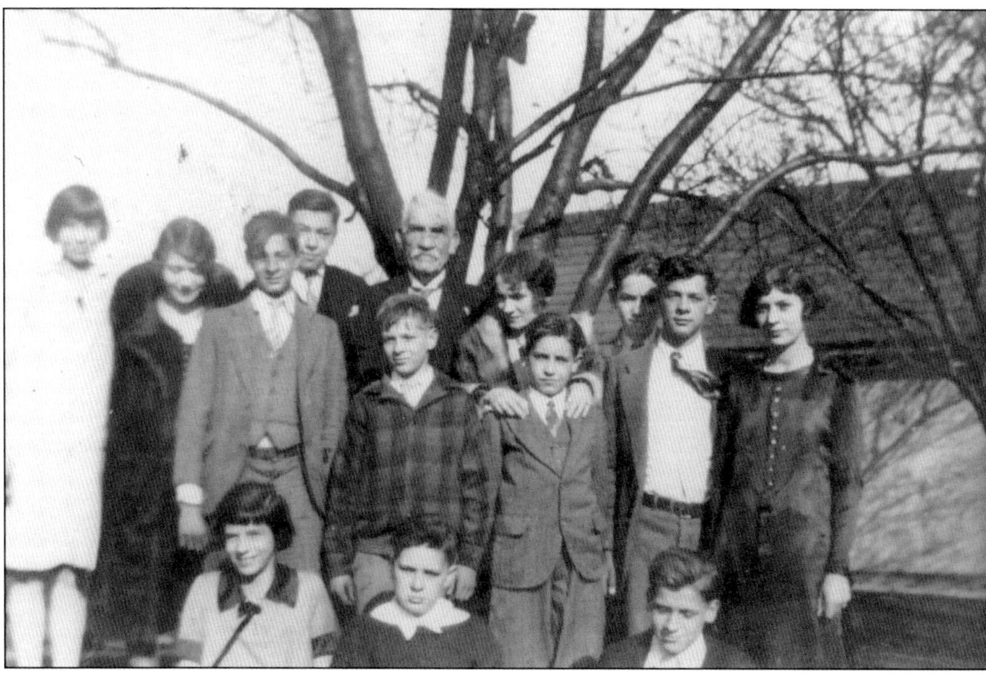

The McCarty grandchildren celebrate grandfather Thomas Y. McCarty's 80th birthday at the family homestead in 1930. Assembled from left to right are (first row) Ethel McCarty (Sister Mary) (Roscoe), Anthony Kane (Alacoque), and Raymond Haney (Ethel); (second row) Vincent and Herman McCarty (Roscoe), Gerald McCarty (Leo), Charles McCarty, and Helen (McCarty) Thaler (Roscoe); (third row) Isabella (McCarty) Ebner (Angelo), Catherine (Leo), Joseph Kane (Alacoque), Thomas Y. McCarty, Edna McCarty, and Leo McCarty Jr. (Leo). (RMC.)

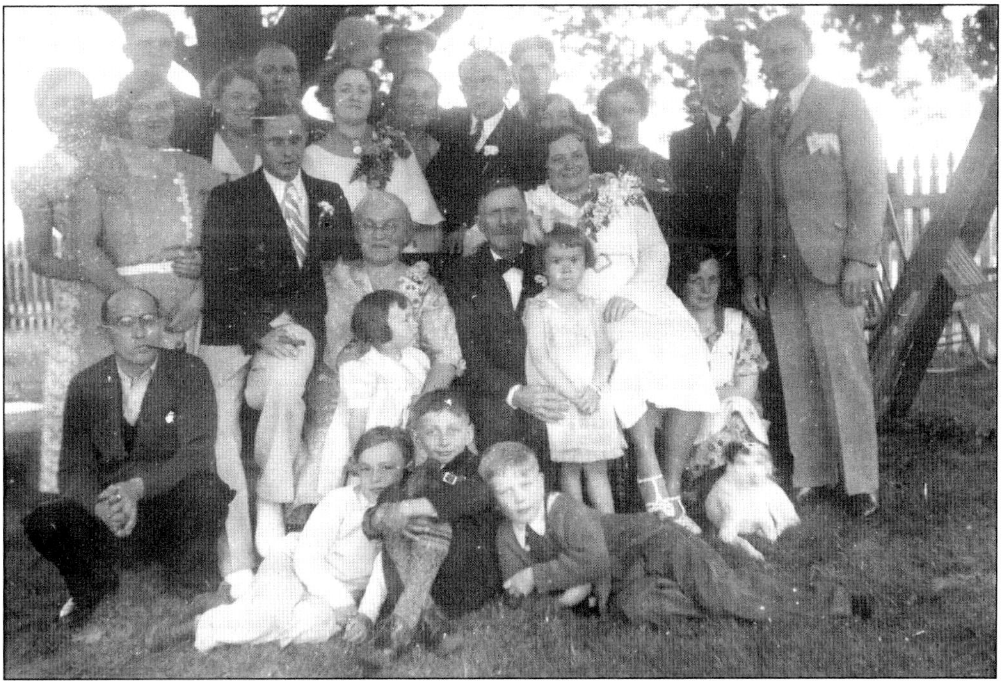

Seen here is the Arthur Bahnck and Emma (Balbirer) Foltz wedding in May 1934. From left to right are (first row) Andrew Snyder Jr., Fred Reichelt Jr., and Ernest Reichelt Jr.; (second row) Andrew Snyder Sr., Eleanor Snyder, Helen Damjanits, Arthur Bahnck, Ottilia Balbirer, Andrew Balbirer, Emma Bahnck, Julia Reichelt, and Carl Schunke; (third row) Emma Reichelt, Frieda Kluge, Anna Balbirer, Fred Reichelt Sr., Josephine Schunke, Emma Votens, Walter Reichelt, Reinhold Kluge, Joseph Damjanits, Ernest Reichelt, Edward Reichelt, and Walter Votens. (RMC.)

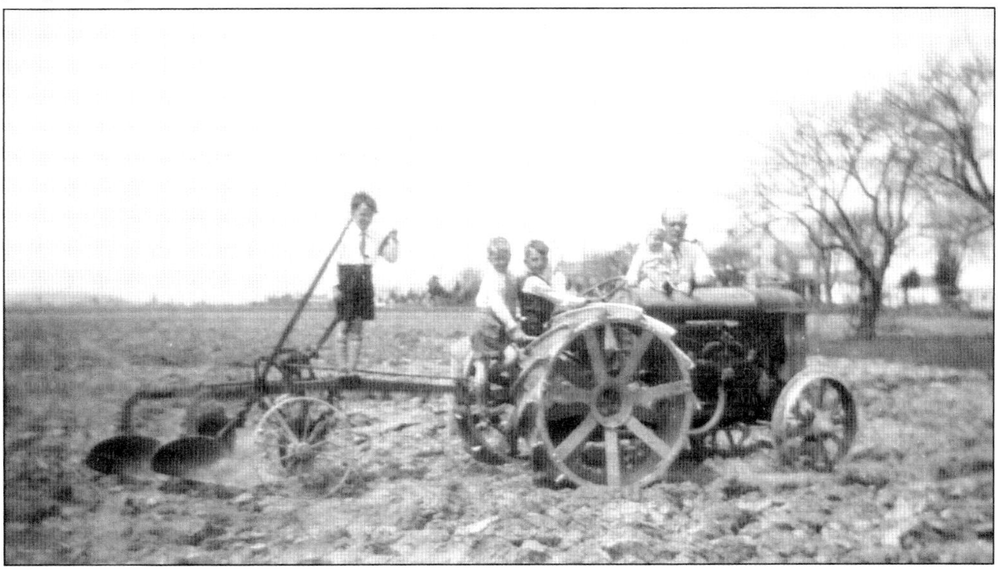

From left to right, young Balbirer family cousins Andrew Snyder Jr., Ernest Reichelt Jr., Fred Reichelt Jr., and Eddie Reichelt are enjoying their day. The four boys are learning the rudiments of farming. They are busy assisting Ernest Reichelt Sr. in harrowing the fields on the Reichelt family farm in 1934. (RMC.)

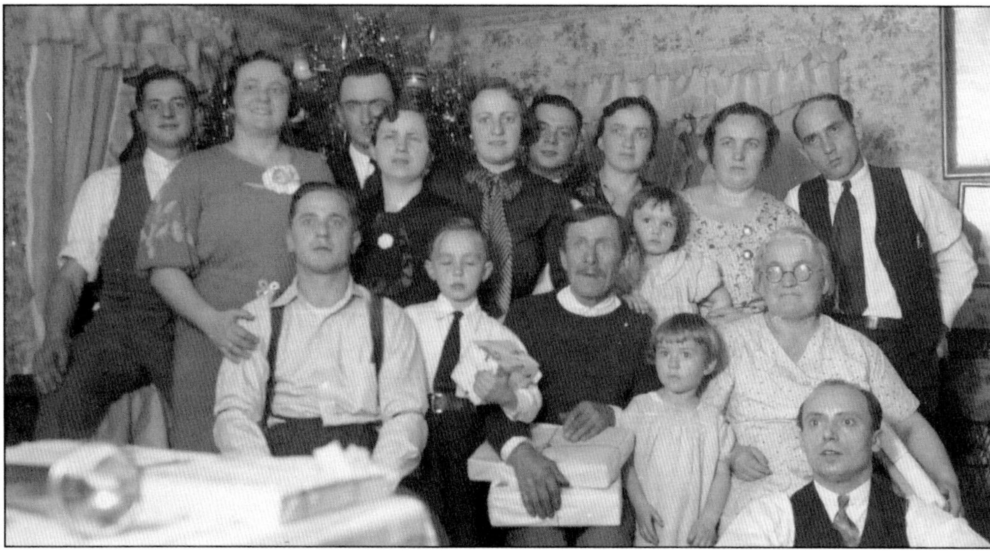

A large group of extended family members and friends have gathered here to celebrate Christmas in 1934. Sitting in front is Joseph Damjanits and from left to right are (first row) Arthur Bahnck, Andrew Snyder Jr., Andrew Balbirer, Helen Damjanits, and Ottilia Balbirer; (second row) Vincent McCarty, Emma Bahnck, Robert Balbirer, Anne Olinick, Anna Balbirer, Charles McCarty, Victoria Damjanits, Regina Snyder holding Eleanor Snyder, and Andrew Snyder Sr. (RMC.)

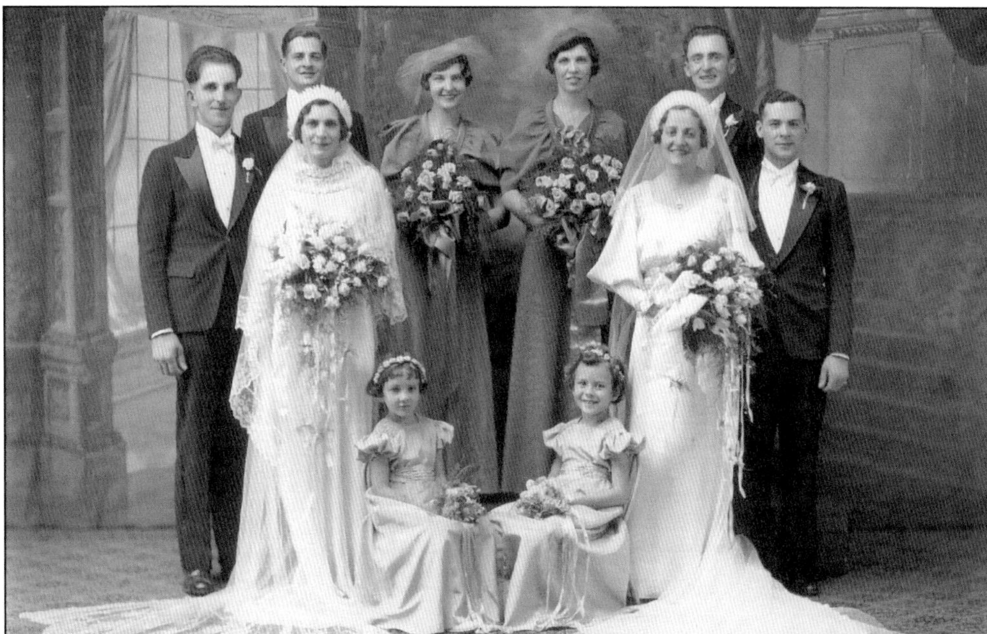

The double wedding of Charles P. and Anna (Balbirer) McCarty and John and Helen (McCarty) Thaler was celebrated on September 26, 1936, with a St. John the Baptist Church ceremony in Haycock Run. The newlyweds pose for a formal photograph. From left to right they are Mr. and Mrs. John Thaler and Mr. and Mrs. Charles P. McCarty; flower girls Eleanor Snyder and Helen Damjanits; and attendants, Vincent McCarty, Mary Thaler, Isabella McCarty, and Robert Balbirer. (RMC.)

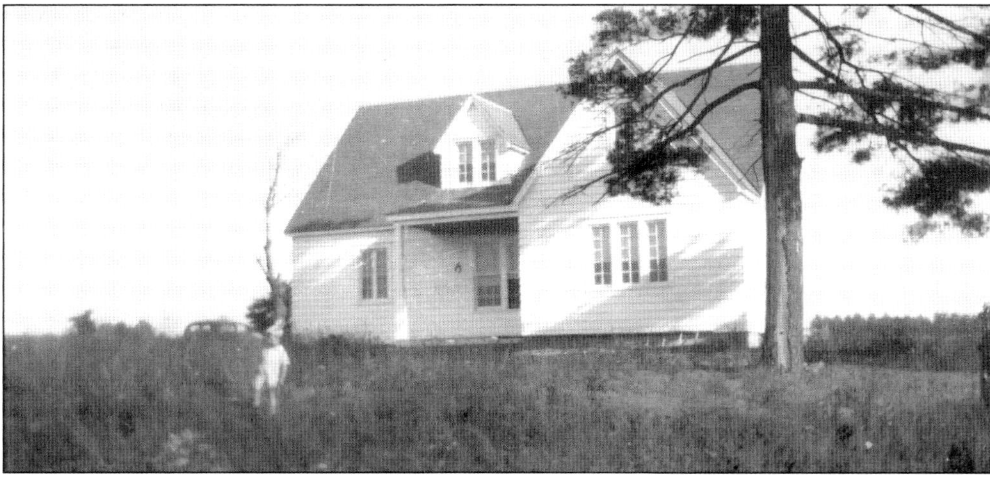

The home of Charles P. and Anna (Balbirer) McCarty was built in 1940. They joined the many members of the McCarty family living on Church Lane in Bucksville. Several years later, the family grew with two daughters and one son: Rosanne, Charles G., and Paulette. This photograph is unusual since its original form is in color, and black and white images were prevalent at the time. (RMC.)

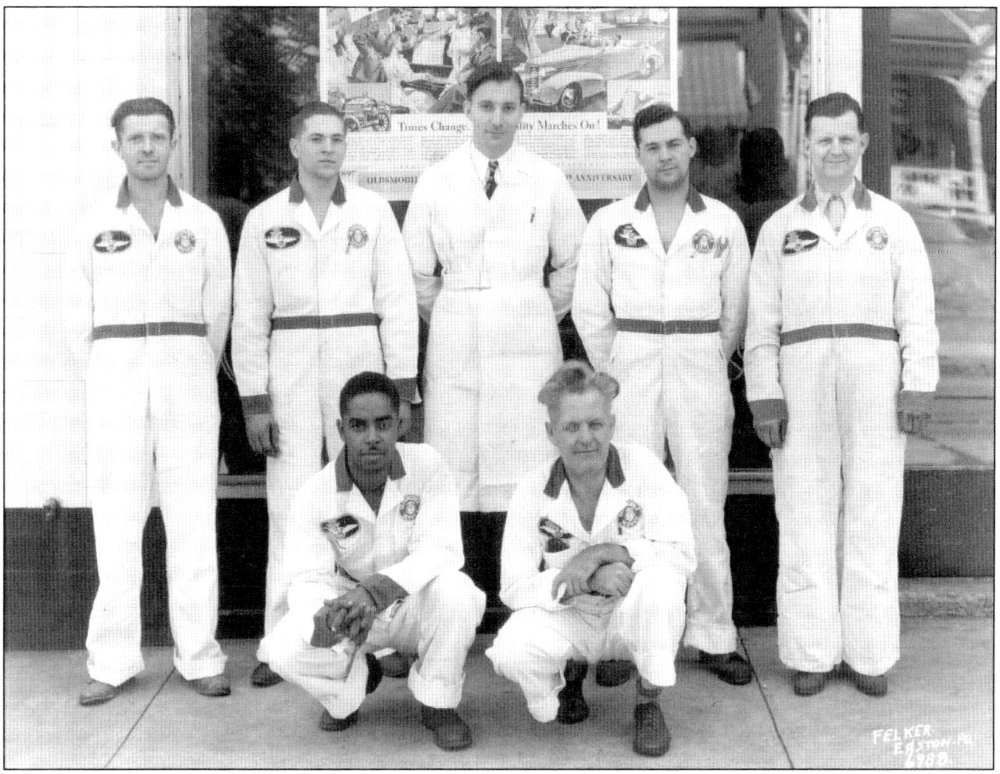

Several Nockamixon residents were employed by Swartz Motor Company of Easton in 1940. The automobile dealership sold various manufacturers: Chrysler, Plymouth, DeSoto, and Oldsmobile. An era advertisement in the window shows the popular slogan, "In My Merry Oldsmobile," extolling the Oldsmobile automobile. From left to right are (kneeling) unidentified and Pappy Gardner; (standing) Russell Flick, Herman McCarty, Dutch ? , Charles P. McCarty, and Maynard Stone. (RMC.)

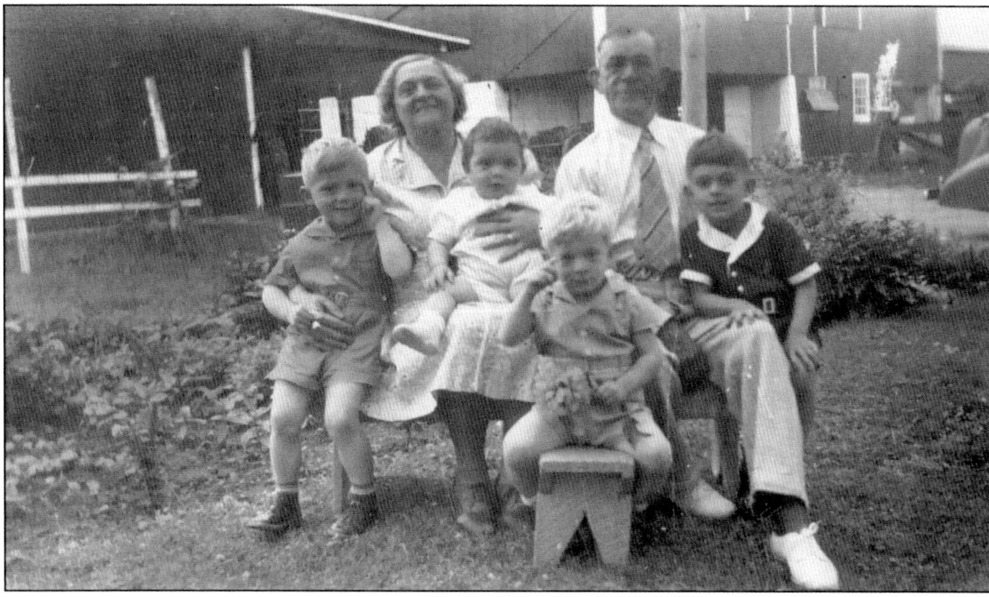

Another early color photograph in the McCarty family album, this was taken in front of the Roscoe McCarty homestead in 1941. Grandparents Mary (Fleck) McCarty and Roscoe McCarty pose with their young grandsons. Robert Thaler is seated on the bench in front, with (from left to right) Edward Thaler, baby James Thaler, and John V. Thaler behind him. Helen (McCarty) Thaler, Roscoe and Mary McCarty's daughter and the boys' mother celebrated her 100th birthday in 2011. (RMC.)

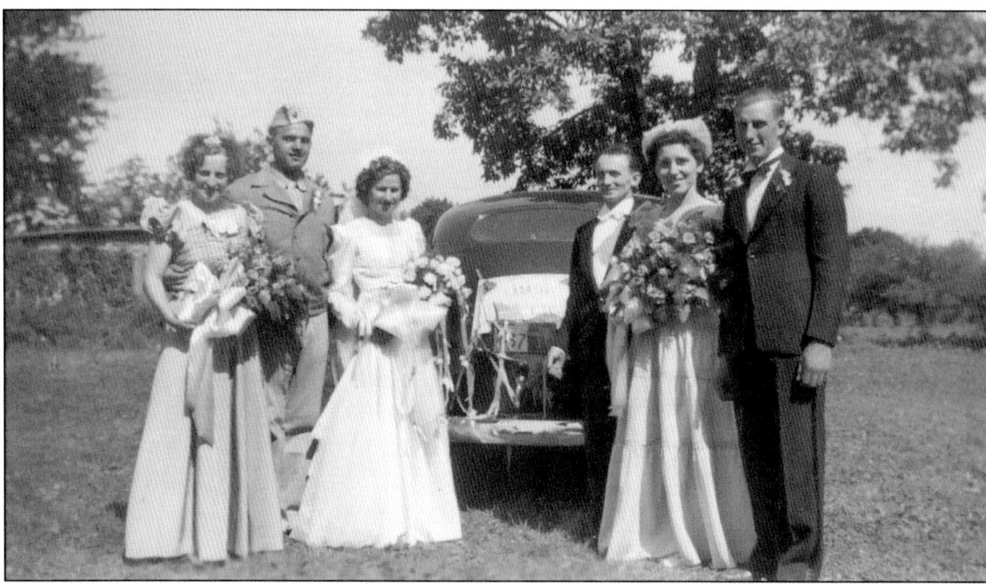

The wedding of Robert Jacob Balbirer and Mary Miketta took place on October 3, 1942. The happy couple poses outside with their attendants after the ceremony. From left to right are Anna (Balbirer) McCarty, Robert Miketta, bride Mary (Miketta) Balbirer, groom Robert Balbirer, Emily (Wagner) Schmidt, and Joseph Miketta. The Balbirer car is decorated with a "Just Married" banner and ribbons. (RMC.)

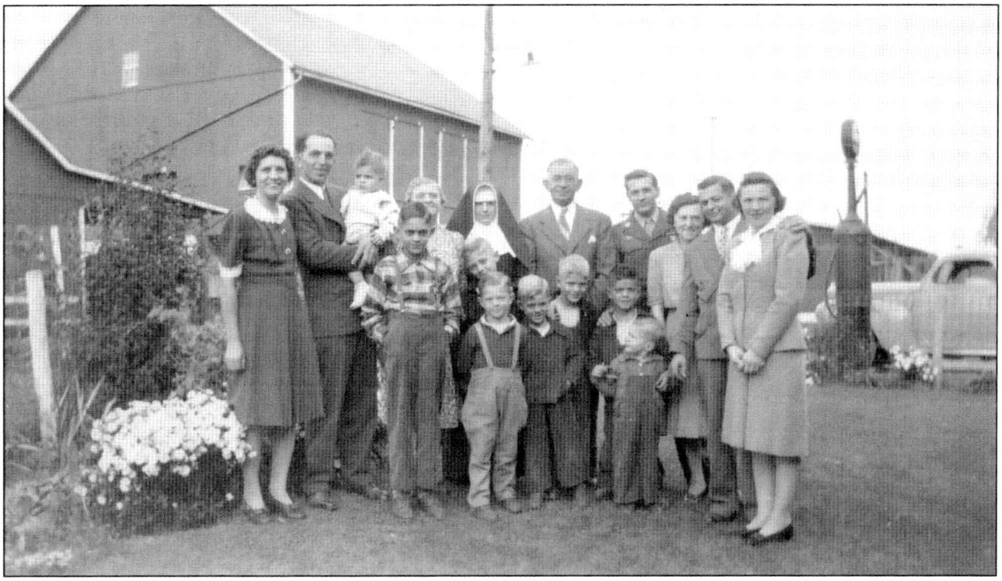

A family get-together at the Roscoe McCarty farm on September 30, 1945, was photographed for the family album. From left to right are (first row) Jack Thaler, Edward Thaler, V. Dennis McCarty, Gerry Thaler, Robert Thaler, James Thaler, and Philip McCarty; (second row) Helen (McCarty) Thaler, John Thaler holding Joseph Thaler, Mary McCarty, Sr. Mary McCarty, Roscoe McCarty, Herman McCarty, Catherine Schaeffer, Vincent McCarty, and Catherine (Reitter) McCarty. (RMC.)

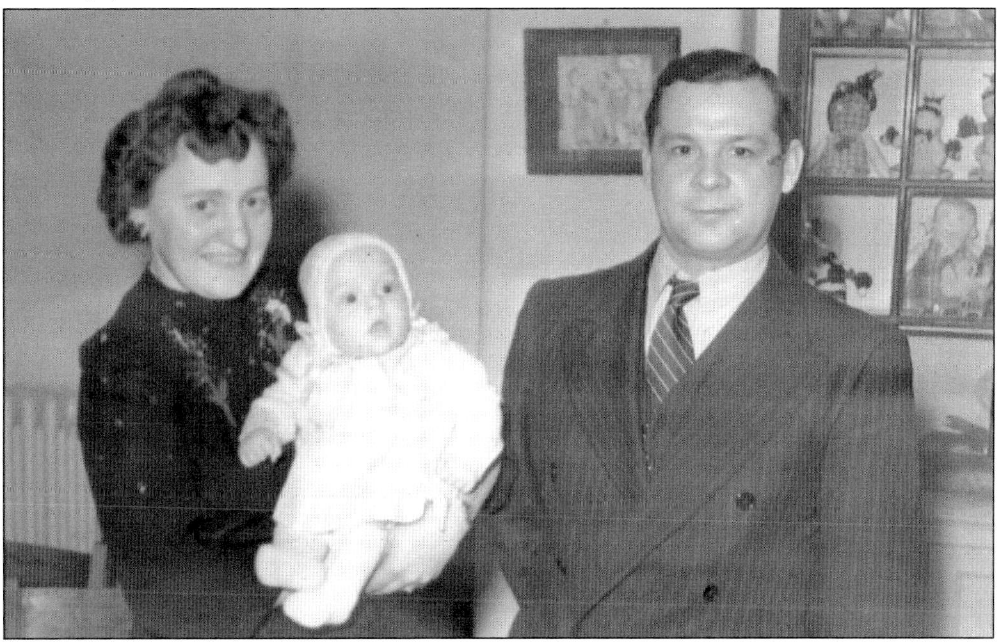

Anna (Balbirer) McCarty, holding Rosanne M. McCarty, and Charles P. McCarty pose for their first family photograph at Sacred Heart Hospital in March 1945. Through Sr. Mary's (Ethel McCarty) influences, the proud parents had just adopted five-month-old Rosanne. The McCartys adopted two more children, Charles G. McCarty and Paulette E. McCarty, through the Philadelphia Catholic Diocese. They also assisted other family members and friends with adoption. (RMC.)

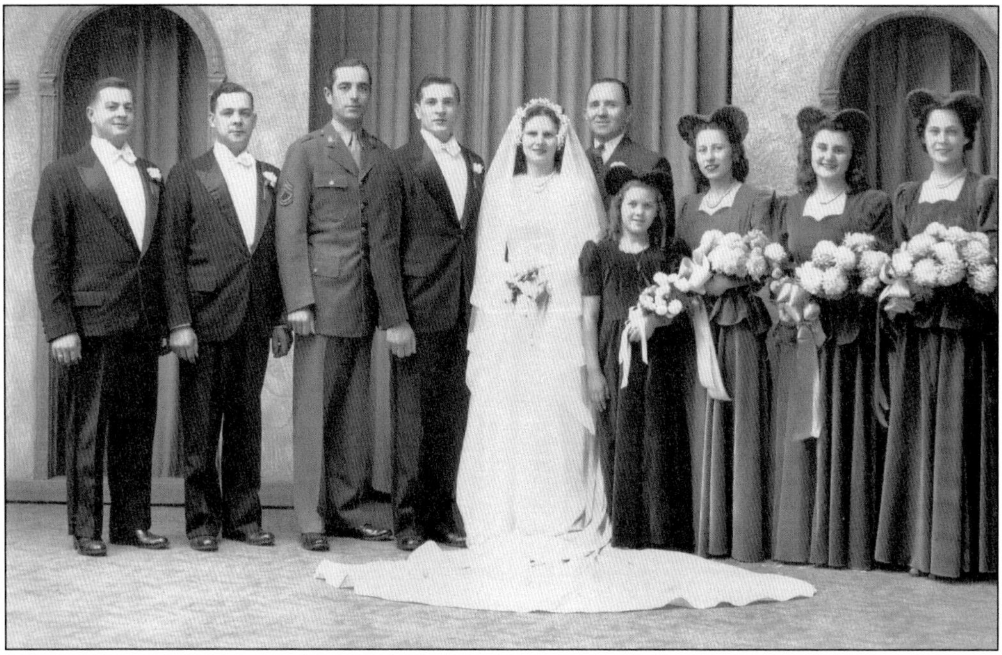

The wedding of Herman and Helen (Somp) McCarty was celebrated in November 1945. Posing for a formal photograph around the happy couple are their attendants, from left to right, Vincent McCarty, Charles McCarty, Walter Beam, Rudolph Somp, Claire Somp, Marie Weinbel, Ruth Somp, and Anna Kimenhour. (RMC.)

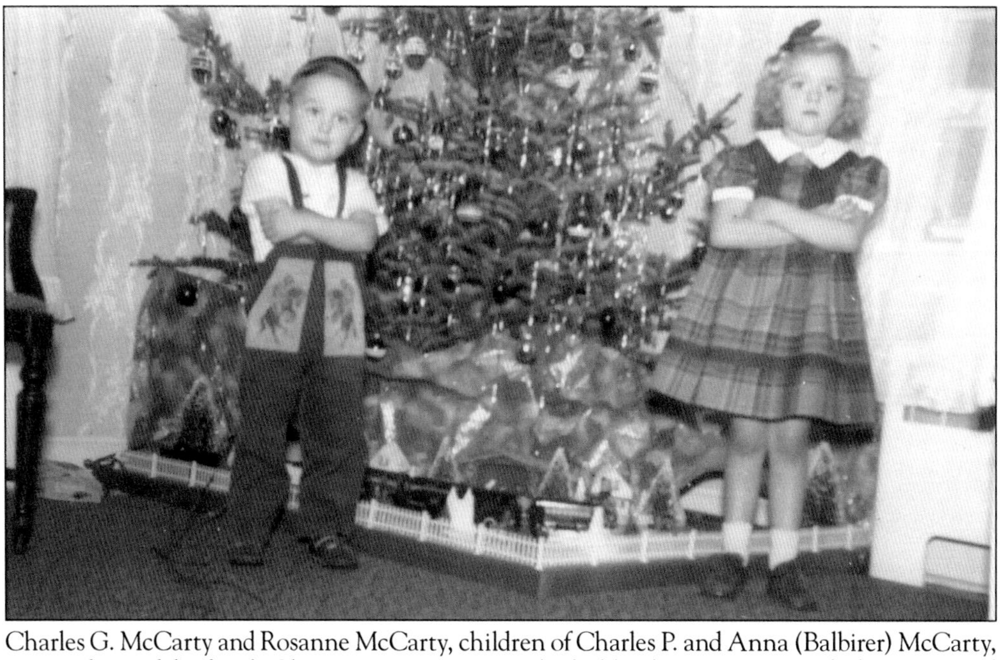

Charles G. McCarty and Rosanne McCarty, children of Charles P. and Anna (Balbirer) McCarty, pose in front of the family Christmas tree in 1949. It looks like they are wearing clothing received as presents: Charles's trousers have cowboys and horses, and Rosanne is wearing a pretty dress. The children look anxious, however, and are probably ready to play with the train set under the tree. (RMC.)

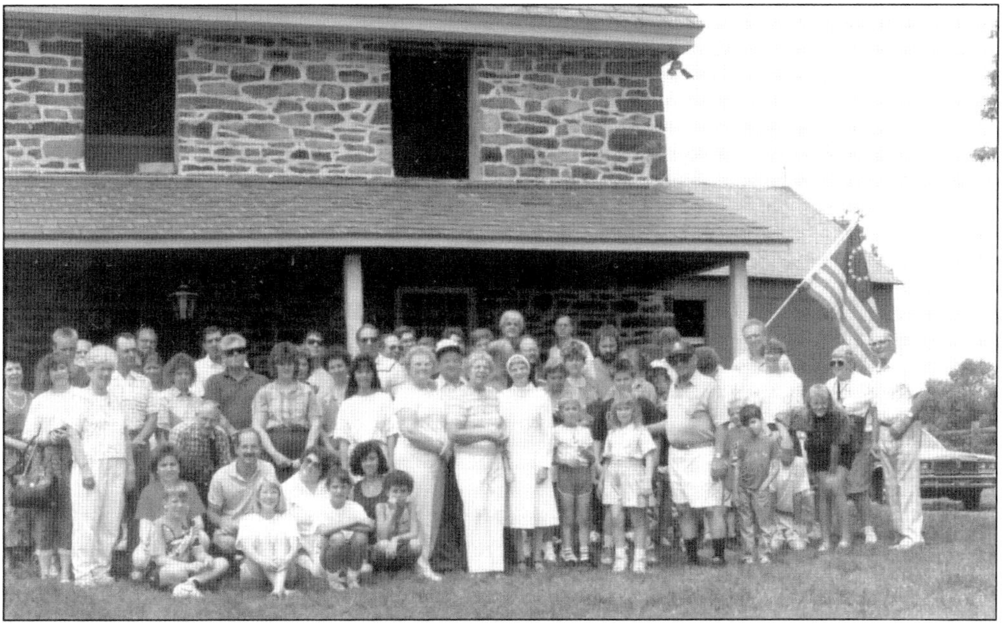

This McCarty reunion photograph was taken at the family homestead on Church Lane in Bucksville in July 1991. Built by Nicholas (third generation) and Albertina (Kohl) McCarty in 1776, it was used as a Mass house by Catholics in the area. The home on the former Roscoe McCarty (seventh generation) farm has been completely renovated. The owner graciously allowed the McCarty family to congregate for this photograph. (RMC.)

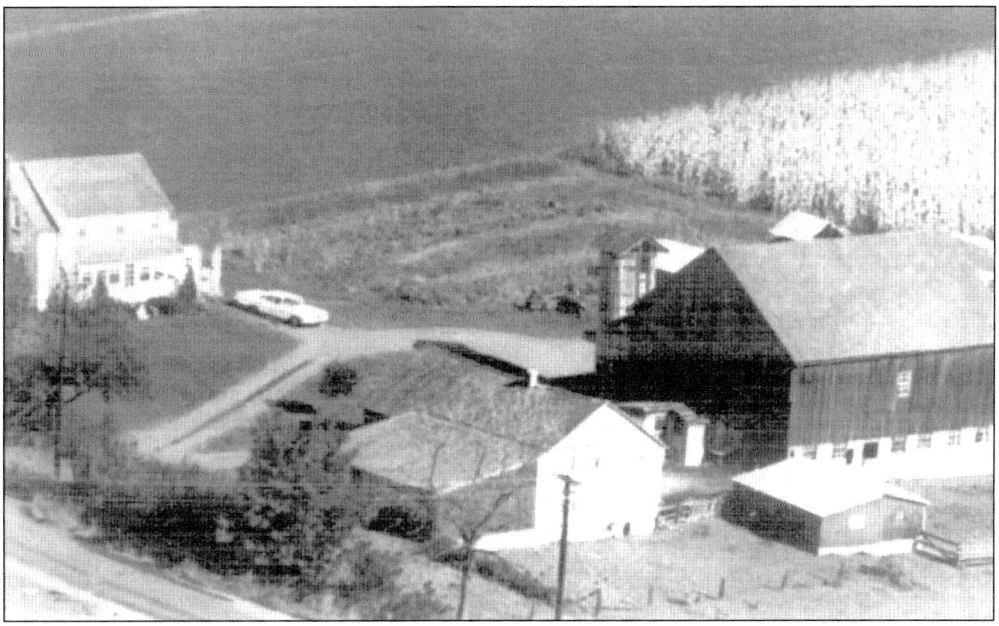

T. Earl Michener and wife, Ruth Gretchen, moved their family to Revere, purchasing the Marienstein farm in 1939 but not the farmhouse. There were six boys and two girls: Robert, Norma, Charles, twins James and Joan, Alfred, Lester, and Louis. Daughter Norma (Michener) Fox remembers living over the farm shed above the barn for five years while her father and carpenter built farmhouse. They had no running water, so it had to be carried inside. (NMF.)

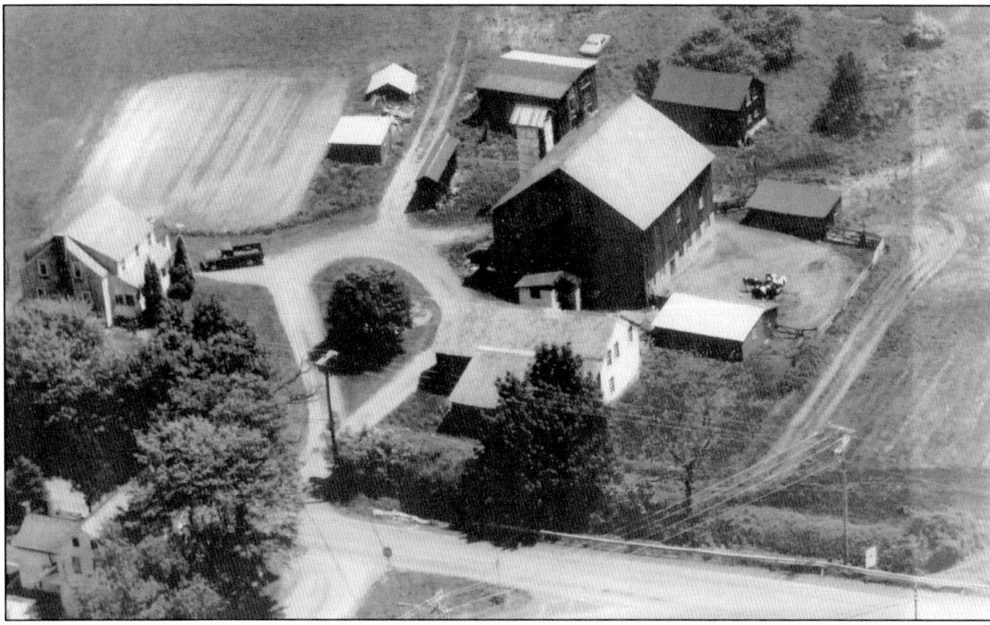

Farming most of the fields and renting some to Penn Rare Metals, T. Earl Michener grew many different crops and raised two breeds of cows, Jersey and Holstein. The family always had plenty of food grown on the farm. Mother Ruth planted a garden each year and canned for winter, and the children pitched many a hay bale. Norma remembers celebrating her 16th birthday in the family's new home with a master bedroom and conveniences. (NMF.)

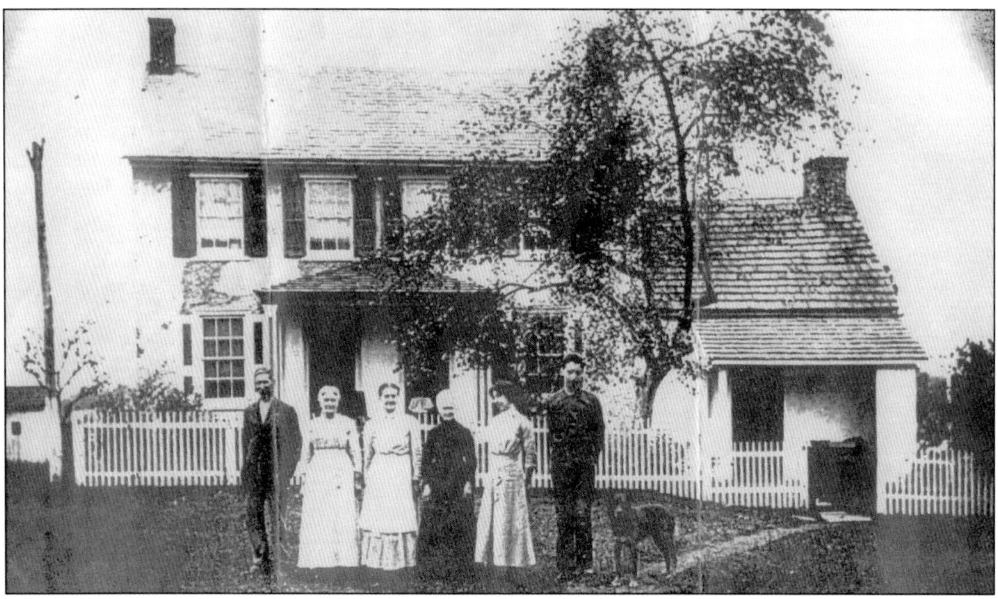

The stone farmhouse, on Marienstein Road in Revere on the 1798 tax map, saw many inhabitants. Stone wall boundaries show larger acreage. Peter Neamand's pot shop in the early 1800s made earthenware pottery. Wilmer Trauger, born and raised in his grandparents' Kohl home, graduated from Nockamixon High School in 1914, taught at Revere School, and graduated from Harvard University. Trauger family members visit in this 1911 photograph. In the 1920s, the family residence became Sylvester Moninghoff's, a Revere store owner. (RCD.)

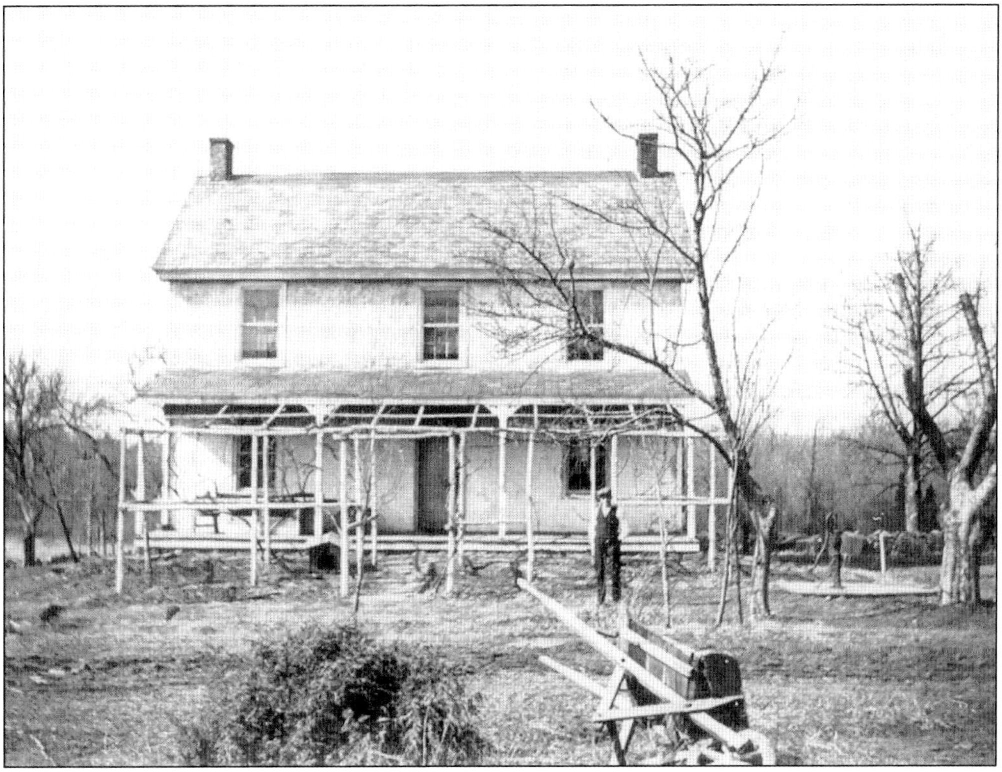

The Sebastian Schwar family homestead on Rock Ridge Road, near Marienstein Road in Revere, is seen here. Sebastian, the gentleman standing in front of the house, arrived in the United States in 1853. He came directly to the Nockamixon area, since his family members were already living here. A stonemason, he built houses primarily along Easton Road in Nockamixon Township. (MGS.)

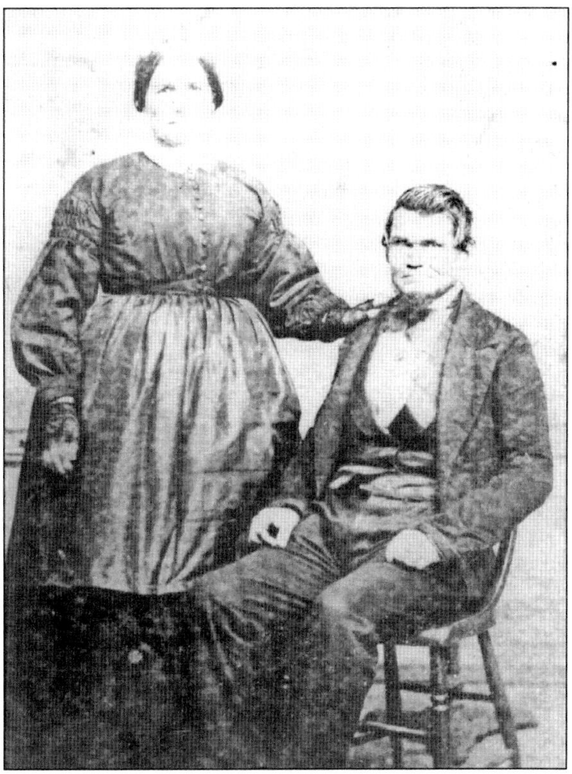

Sebastian and wife Theresa (Philipp) Schwar are shown in this mid-1800s photograph. The Schwar family did the masonry work in the building of St. Joseph's Marienstein, St. John's Catholic mission church, located in Revere. The local Schwar brothers, employed as stonecutters, may have been relatives of Sebastian. They opened a quarry in the 1860s in Harrow, the site of the current quarry. (MGS.)

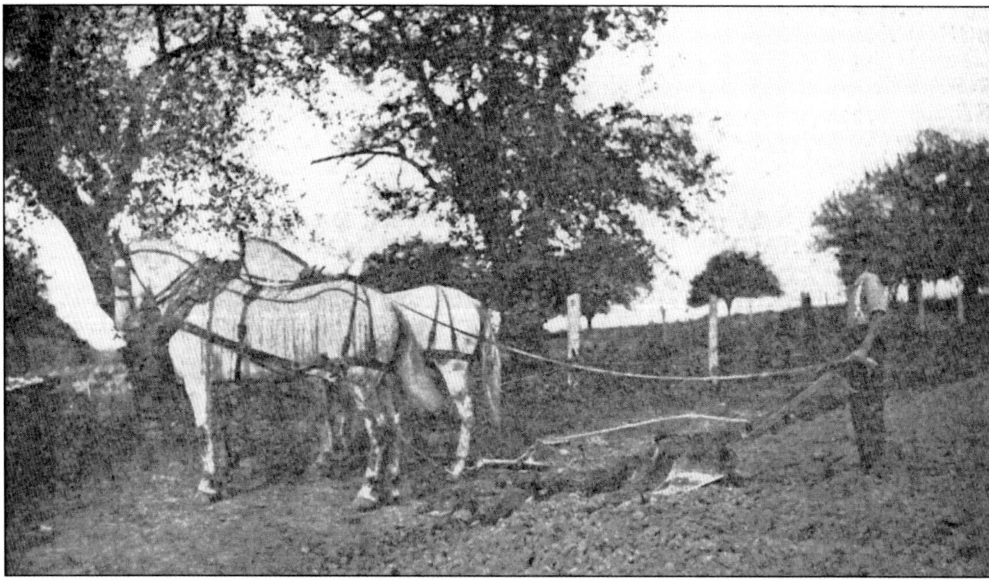

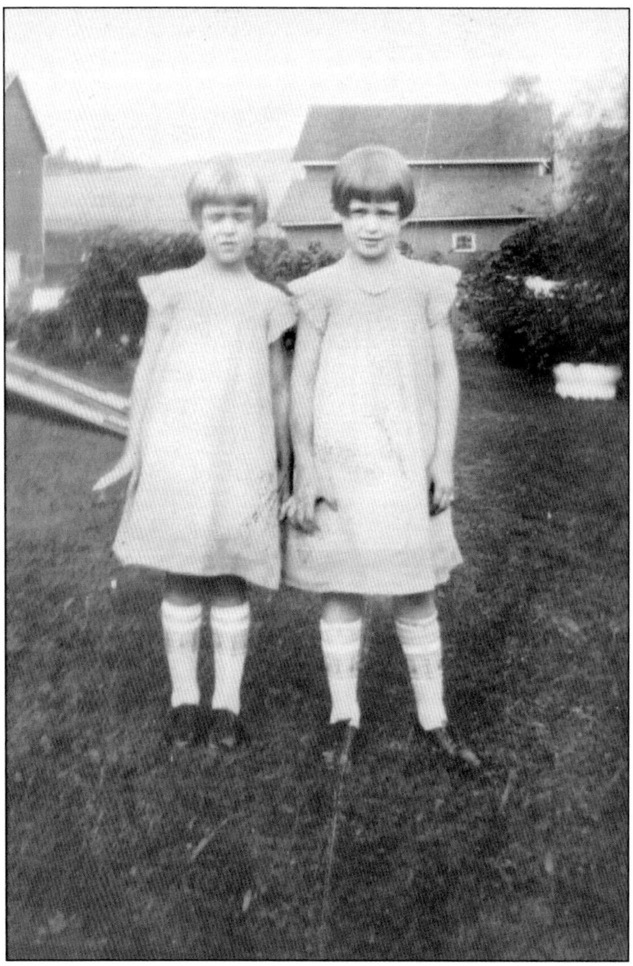

Elmer Stone plows the field at his Easton Road farm in Ferndale. Elmer, wife Estella (Shick), and daughter Verna resided on the homestead. Verna married Peter Henry Bartman, and they had three daughters: Doris, Blanche, and Rowena. Blanche (Bartman) Wehrung was born in her grandparents' stone farmhouse. When Elmer had a stroke and could no longer farm, the family rented the house and built a new home nearby. (BBW.)

Peter Henry and Verna (Stone) Bartman's farm was on a hill across from the Ferndale post office. Peter, with brother Ervin, worked at the Ford, Lincoln, Mercury dealership in Riegelsville that was started by their father. Daughters Doris, Blanche, and Rowena enjoyed living there. Blanche remembers their dog going to school with them and returning to take them home. Blanche (left) and Doris pose in 1927, with a barn on left and an outbuilding on the right. (BBW.)

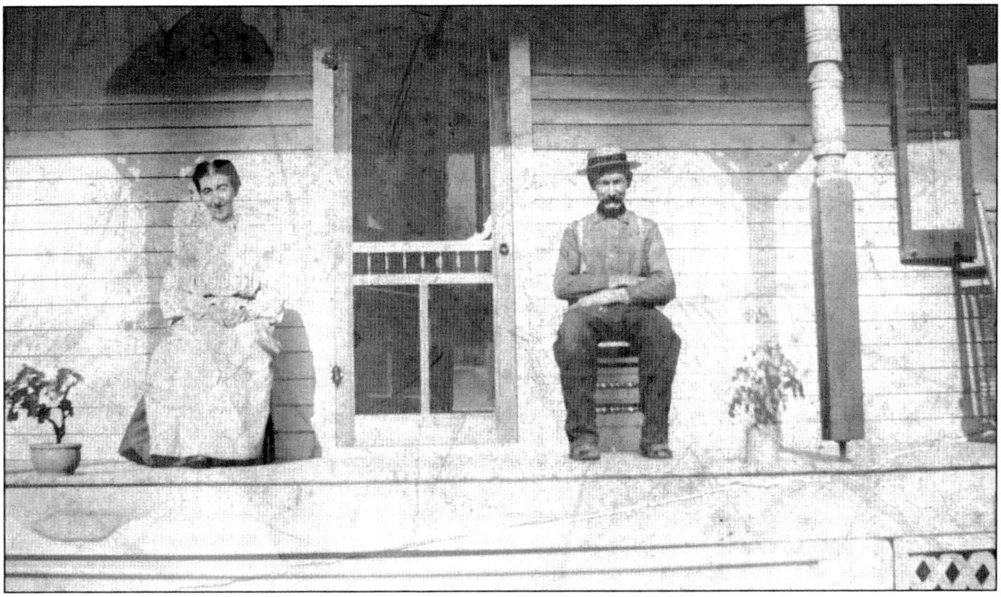

William Shick is seen with daughter Ella, who kept residence at their Ferndale home in the 1920s. William's wife, Emma Jane (Kohl) Shick, died at the age of 26, leaving three children. Estella and Minnie married brothers Elmer and Harvey Stone, who worked at William Shick's boot and shoe factory, located near the corner of Center Hill and Easton Roads. It was later torn down. William, Blanche Wehrung's great-grandfather, died in 1926 when he was struck by a bus on Easton Road. (BBW.)

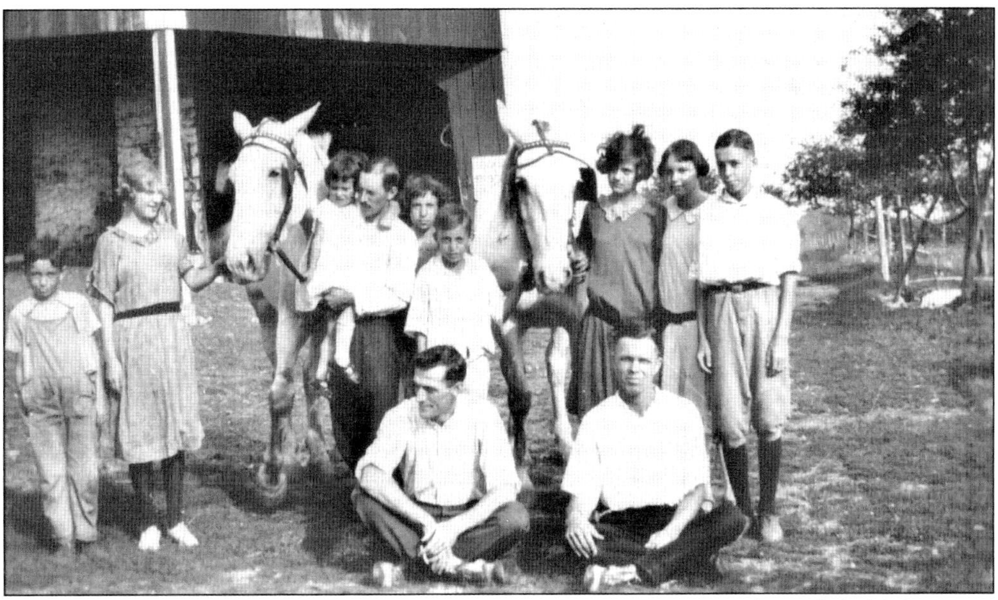

Philip and Bessie Strott settled on their Ferndale farm in 1920. Visitors from Philadelphia came via trolley to Doylestown. Philip picked everyone up in his automobile traveling backcountry roads. Photographed in 1925 with work horses are, from left to right, (first row) unidentified and Herb Matter; (second row) Mervin Matter, Lorraine Schlimm, William Romberger holding Laverne Romberger, Helen Romberger, Norman Romberger, Roxie Schlimm, Thelma Matter, and Charles Matter. (CJF.)

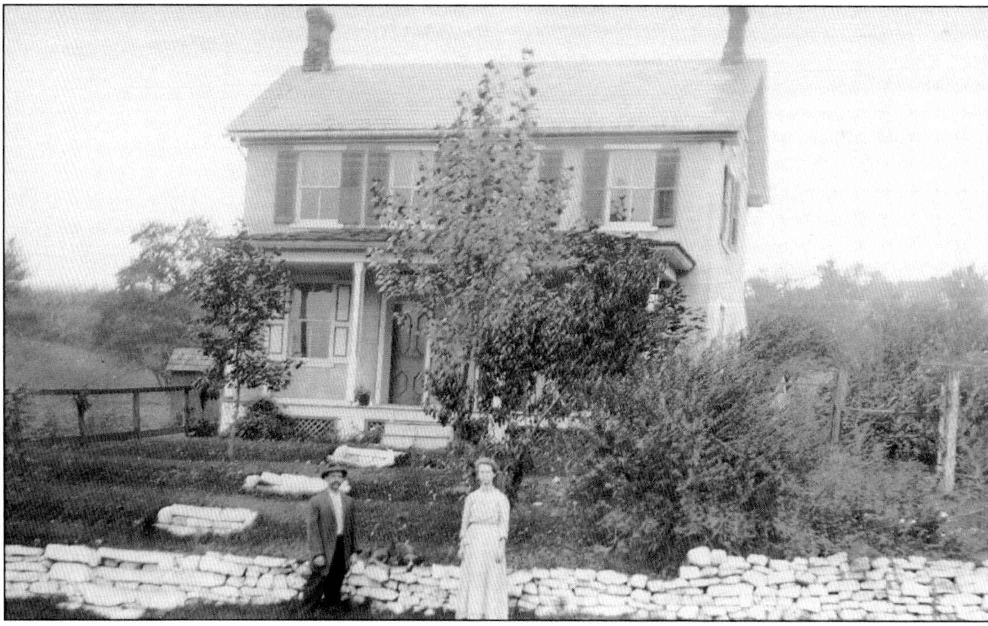

Harvey B. and Laura (Cressman) Keller stand in front of their home in Ferndale in 1927. They lived there with their only child, Lloyd. Harvey worked for the Ferndale Glove Factory in the village for many years, a branch of Keller Glove Manufacturing of Plumsteadville. Their son was named after the owner. (LHK.)

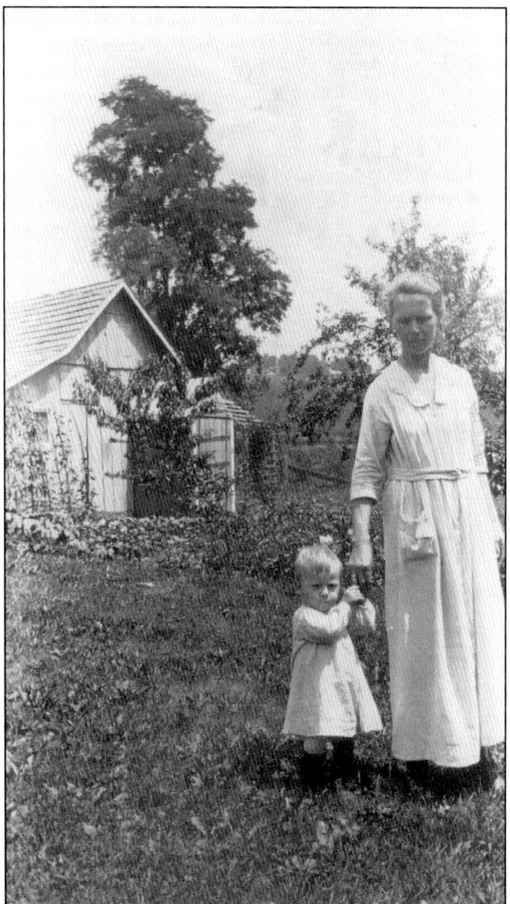

Laura holds the hand of her young son, Lloyd, in front of the well house on their farm. He was born on March 30, 1925, and was about two years old at the time this photograph was taken at the family homestead. Lloyd is wearing a long, shirt-type frock and high socks, typical apparel of young children during the era. (LHK.)

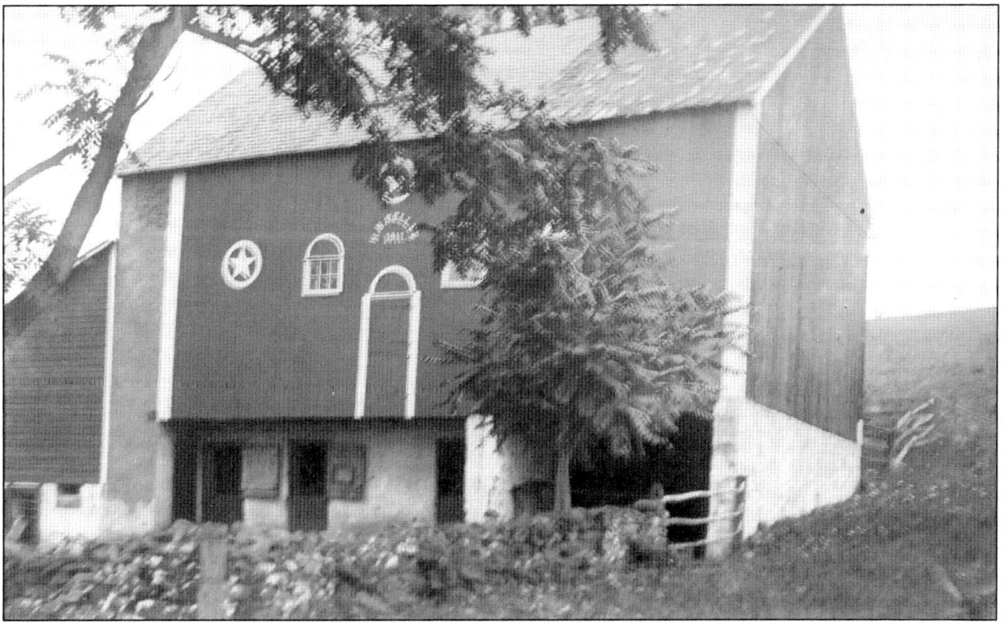

Harvey B. and Laura (Cressman) Keller purchased their farm from Steven Eccher. The barn, dated to 1911, was large—a good building to house animals and machinery. Judging by the slope of the land, it was possibly a four-bay bank barn. This was the first farm they owned. Several years later, they decided to move closer to the village of Ferndale. (LHK.)

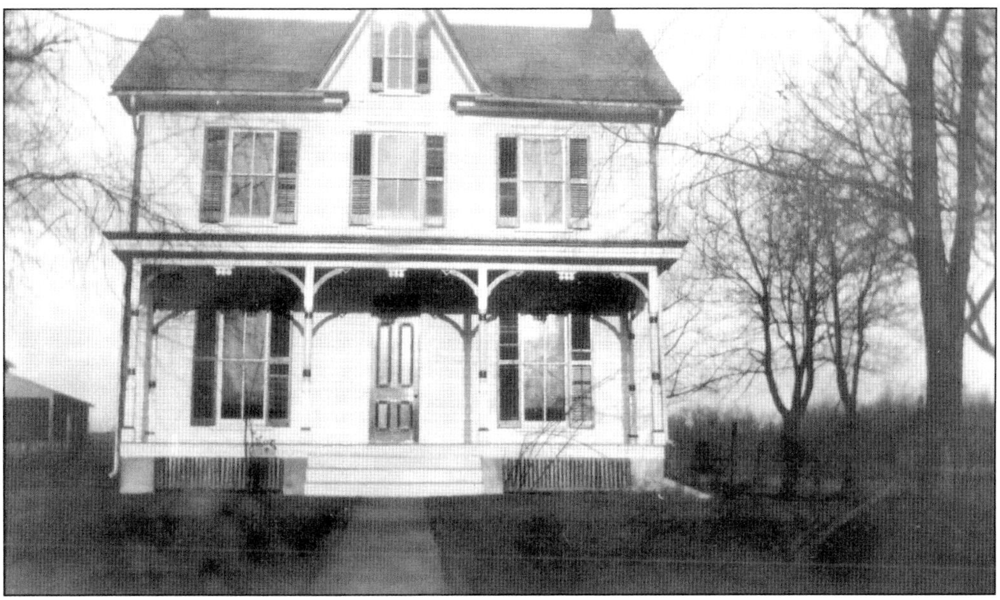

This photograph shows a Victorian home on Easton Road in Ferndale that was owned by Harvey and Laura Keller. It was centrally located in the village and the third home for the family. A perfect house for the family, it was two stories high, with a full front porch and a large addition on the rear with another small porch. The house still stands; however, it has seen many alterations over the years. (LHK.)

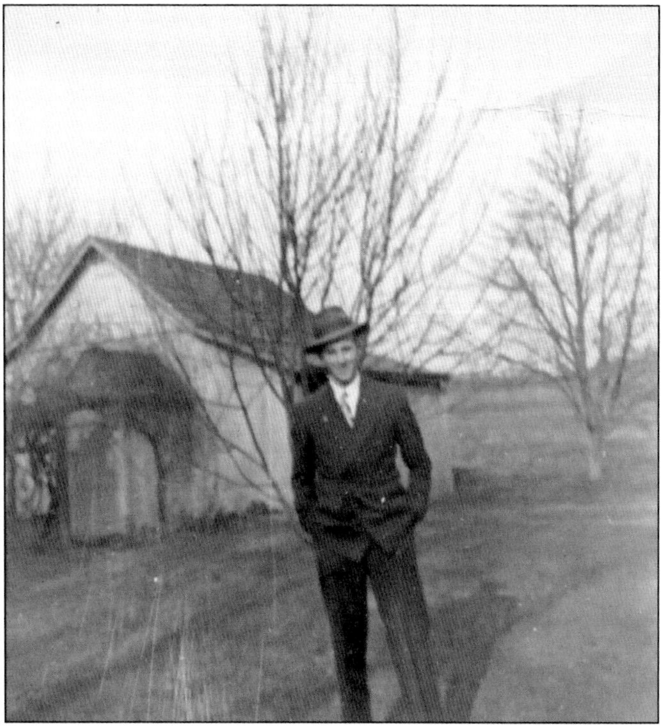

Lloyd Keller returned to Nockamixon in 1945 after serving in the military during World War II. Wearing the correct dress for gentlemen in the 1940s—a fedora hat, suit, white shirt, and tie—Keller returned to work at the Ferndale Glove Factory in the village. His father was also a longtime employee there. (LHK.)

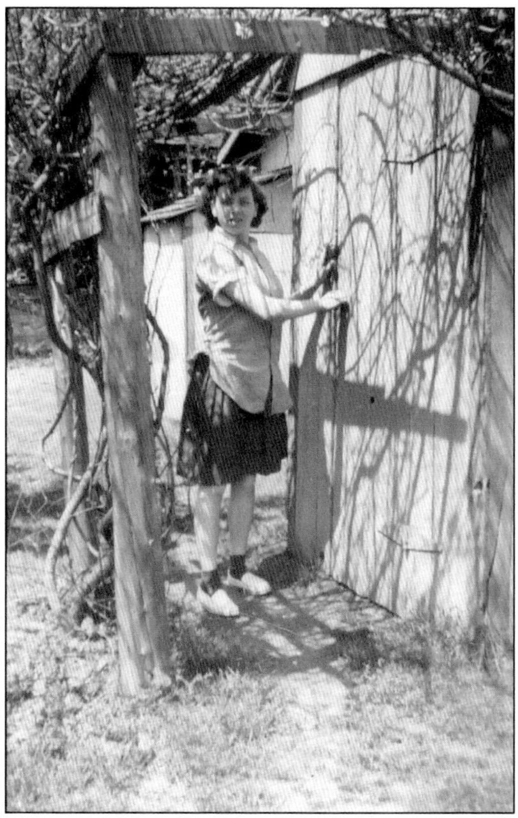

Newly married Hilda (Ketterer) Keller is caught here visiting the outhouse in a 1945 photograph. At the time, her husband, Lloyd, was in the process of remodeling their home in Ferndale and doing alterations on the bathroom. Hilda was born in Tohickon, the village that was flooded and is now under Lake Nockamixon. (LHK.)

The third generation of Kellers—Ronald, Thomas, John and Donald, sons of Lloyd and Hilda Keller—were born and raised in Ferndale and attended the local schools. Wearing their Sunday best and on good behavior, this photograph was taken before the family left to attend St. Luke's Lutheran Church on Christmas day in 1957. (LHK.)

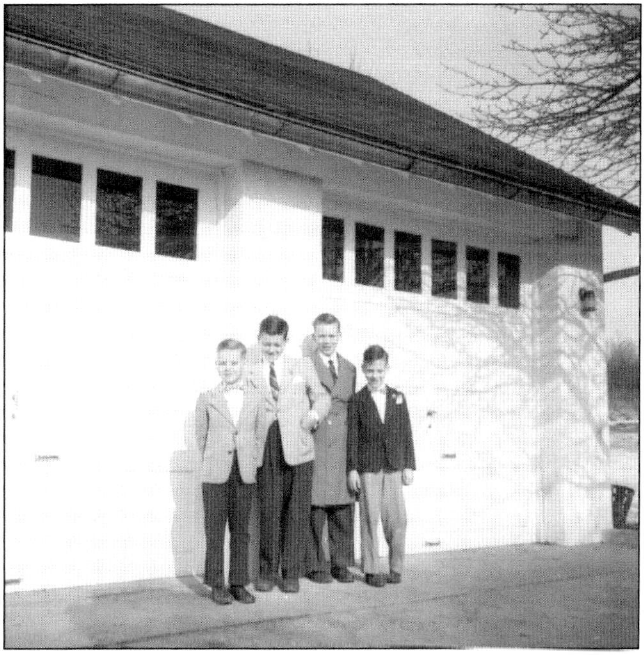

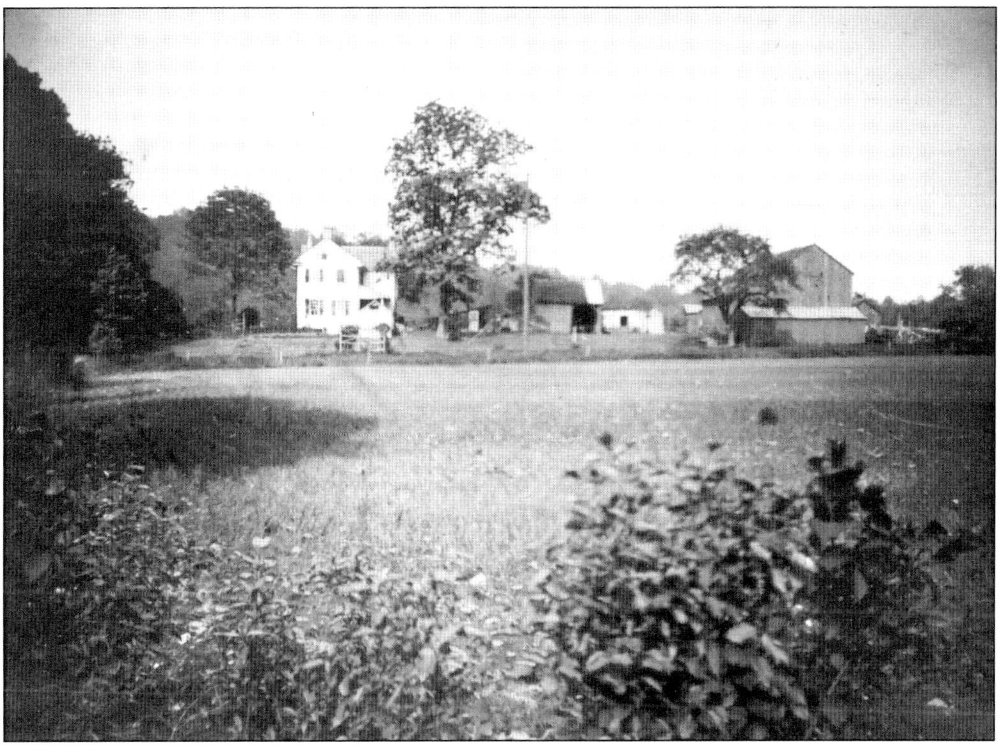

Nicholas and Anna Griffaton purchased a 42-acre orchard farm in Ferndale in the 1920s. It was the perfect place to raise their family, with a large farmhouse and several barns and outbuildings. Anna worked the farm and took care of the children, while Nicholas continued working as a tailor in Philadelphia. Elizabeth, born in 1909, was the oldest child and spoke only German until starting school. She later taught her parents English. (CGG.)

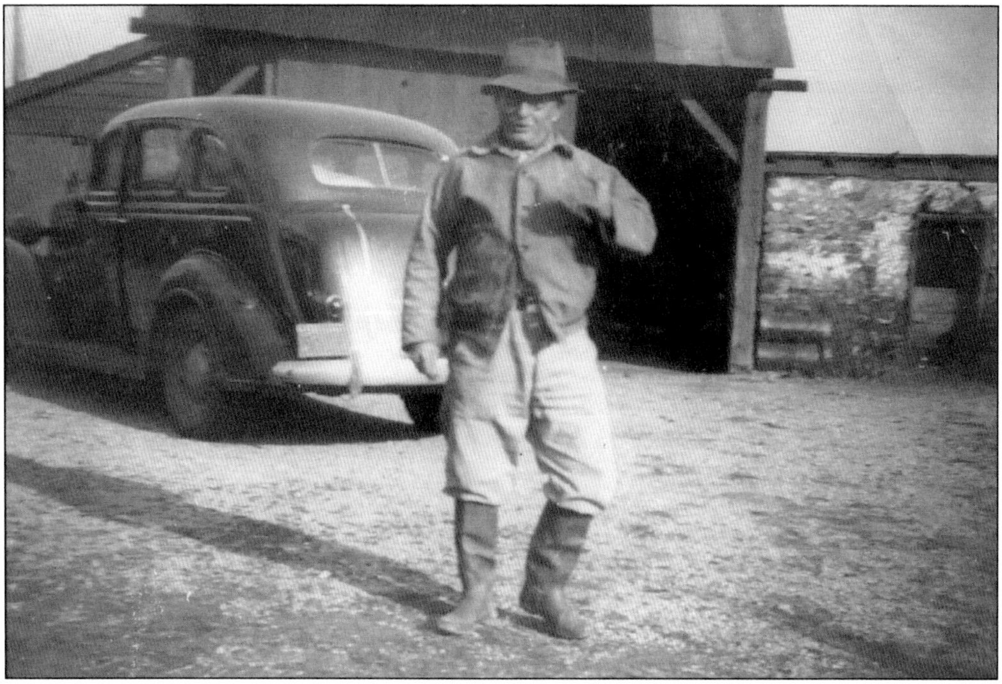

Nicholas Griffaton, a tailor by trade, might be considered a "dandy"—always dressed impeccably with white shirt, tie, vest, trousers, and jacket. Even though he continued as a tailor, later relocating to Doylestown, Nicholas thoroughly enjoyed working around the family's Ferndale farm when he came home on weekends via the trolley. (CGG.)

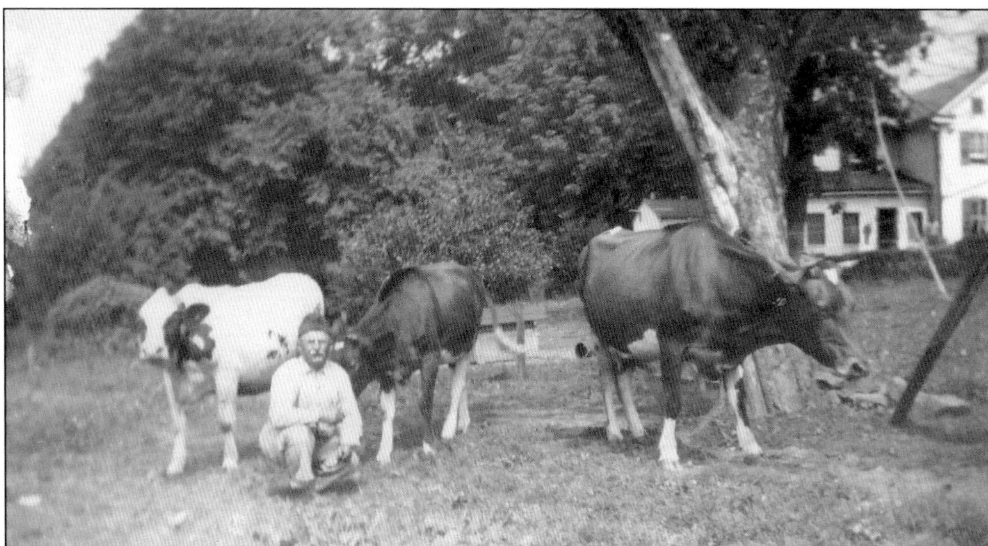

Nicholas Griffaton is seen in the fields taking care of the cows during the summer of 1946. Eventually he was able to leave his work as a tailor and enjoy country living on the homestead full-time with his family. Nicholas had a wonderful tenor voice and often could be heard singing the German songs he loved while working around the farm. (CGG.)

Elizabeth Griffaton is wearing a blouse with fashionable sailor pants, a popular outfit worn by young women during the 1920s. She helped her mother, Anna Griffaton, with the children when they moved to Ferndale and learned how to cook. Elizabeth enjoyed bringing home recipes from school friends to share with her mother. Anna would bake the special pies and cakes along with the eight loaves of bread she made each week. (CGG.)

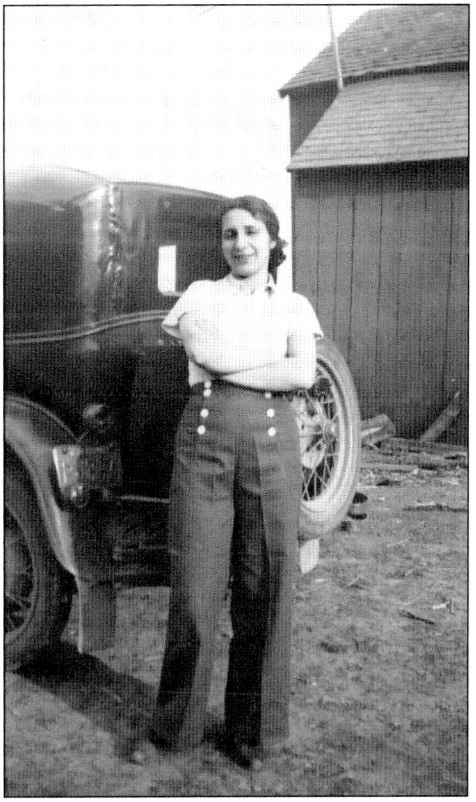

Helping out with chores on the farm in 1920s, Nicholas (Nick) Griffaton Jr. is bringing in two of the family's horses. As the oldest son, Nick was responsible for helping his mother around the farm handling the work his father would normally have done if he had been home. He was kept busy with the farm animals, feeding and taking care of them. (CGG.)

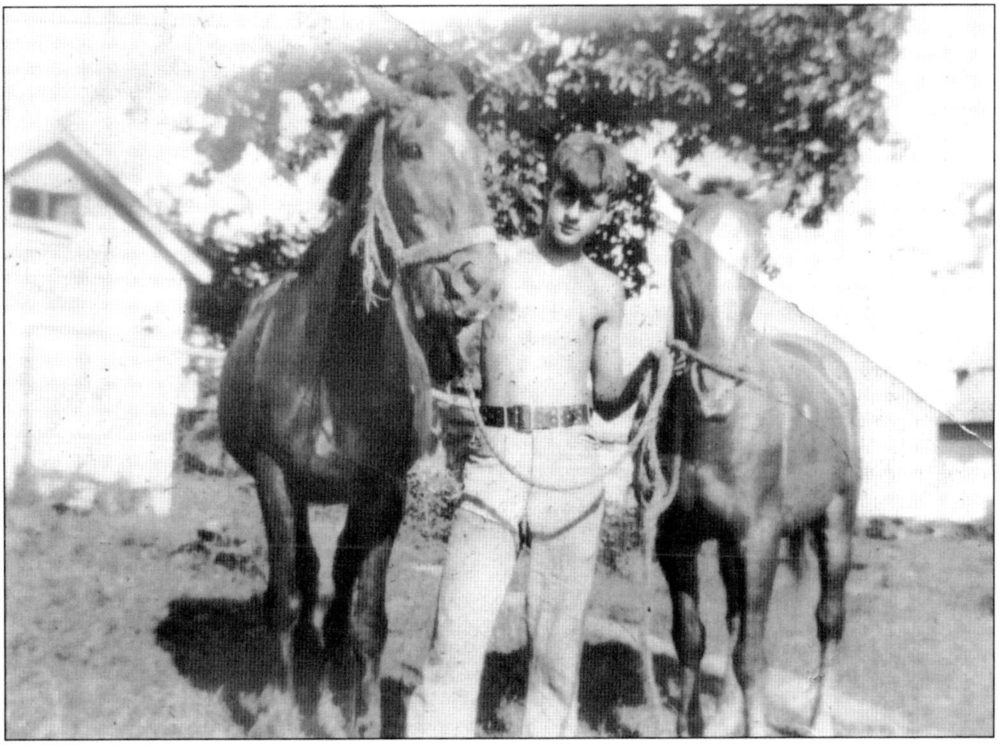

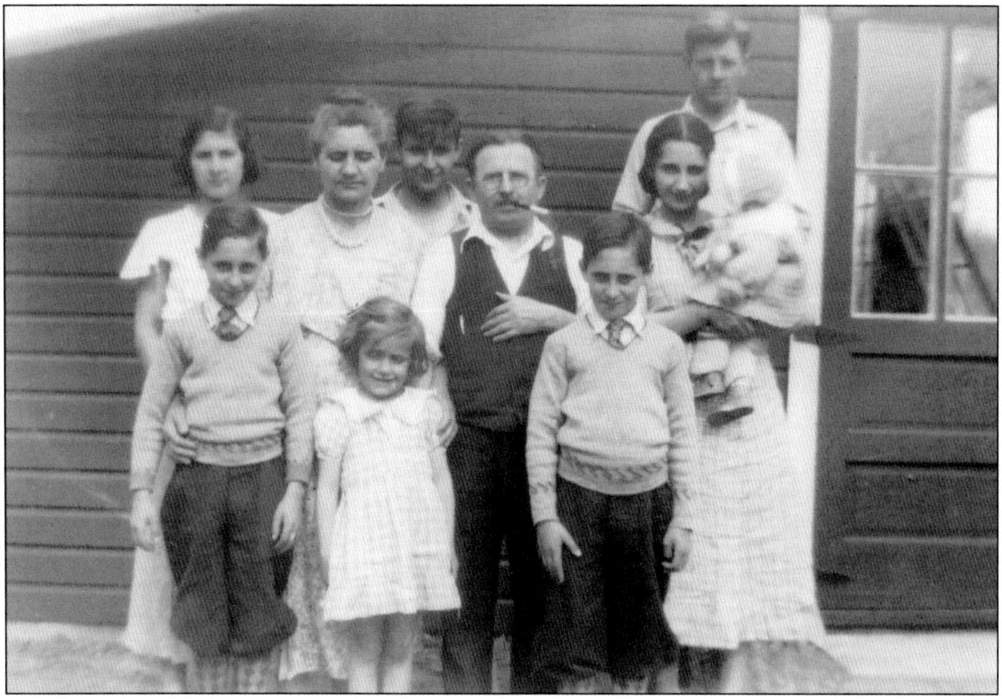

The Griffaton family poses outside their Ferndale home in this late-1920s photograph. Family members are, from left to right, (first row) daughter Ann and twin son Edward; (second row) twin son Leo, mother Anna, father Nicholas Sr., and daughter Elizabeth von Hohen holding her daughter Joan; (third row) daughter Joan, son Nicholas Jr., and Elizabeth's husband Erwin von Hohen. (CGG.)

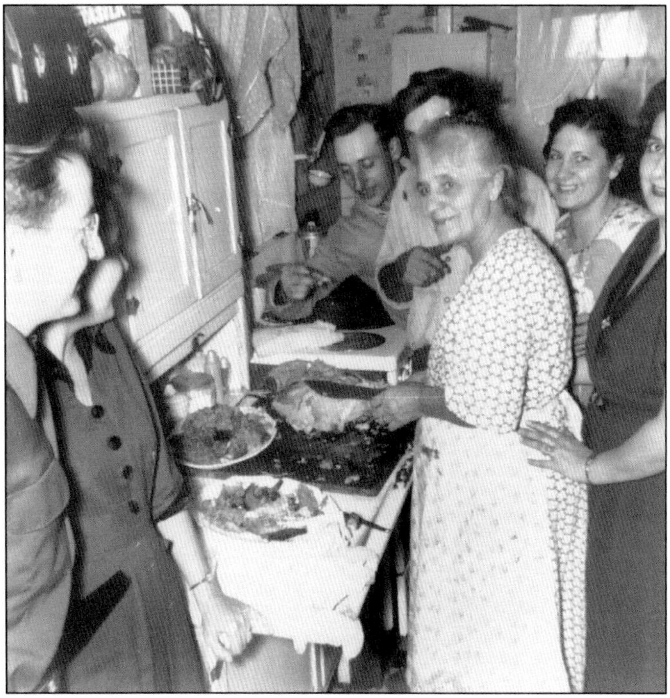

Anna Griffaton prepares a special Thanksgiving dinner in the 1950s at the Ferndale family home. Three generations gathered to celebrate the holiday and enjoy the wonderful food prepared by their mother and grandmother. Family members tasting samples are, from left to right, granddaughter Joan and husband Gerard, sons Charles and Andrew, along with daughters Ann and Elizabeth. Twins Leo and Edward were also there; one of them took the photograph. (CGG.)

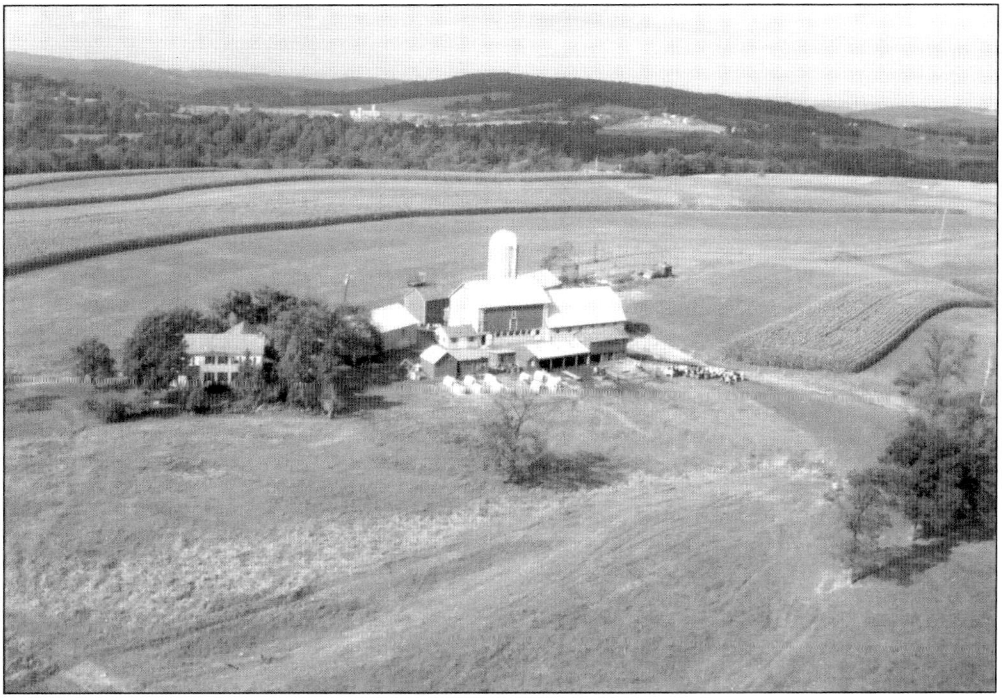

Clarence Berger's parents, Oscar O. and Katy (Nicholas) Berger, purchased their farm with 80 acres in Kintnersville from the Sigafoos family in 1907. The original 18th-century stone farmhouse had later additions on both ends. The home was large, having more rooms than most families needed. Clarence's family used two rooms in the beginning, while the rest remained empty. (CMB.)

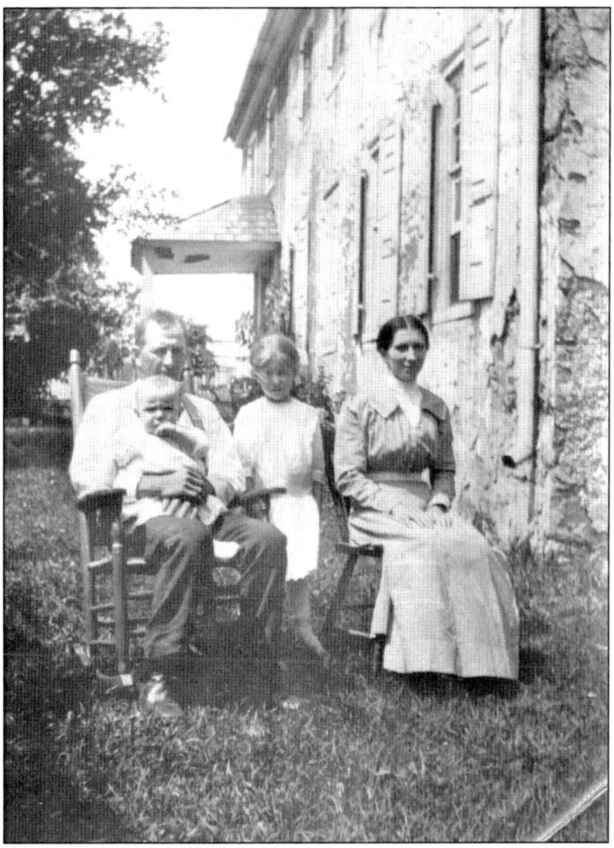

Oscar O. and Katy (Nicholas) Berger are pictured in 1913 with their children, daughter Evelyn, the oldest child, and son Paul. Clarence was born in 1923 and lived in the family home his entire life. He and wife Mabel (Sames) Berger continued to live there after they were married. Brother Paul and wife Rhea (Scholl) Berger lived in another home on the farm down the road. (CMB.)

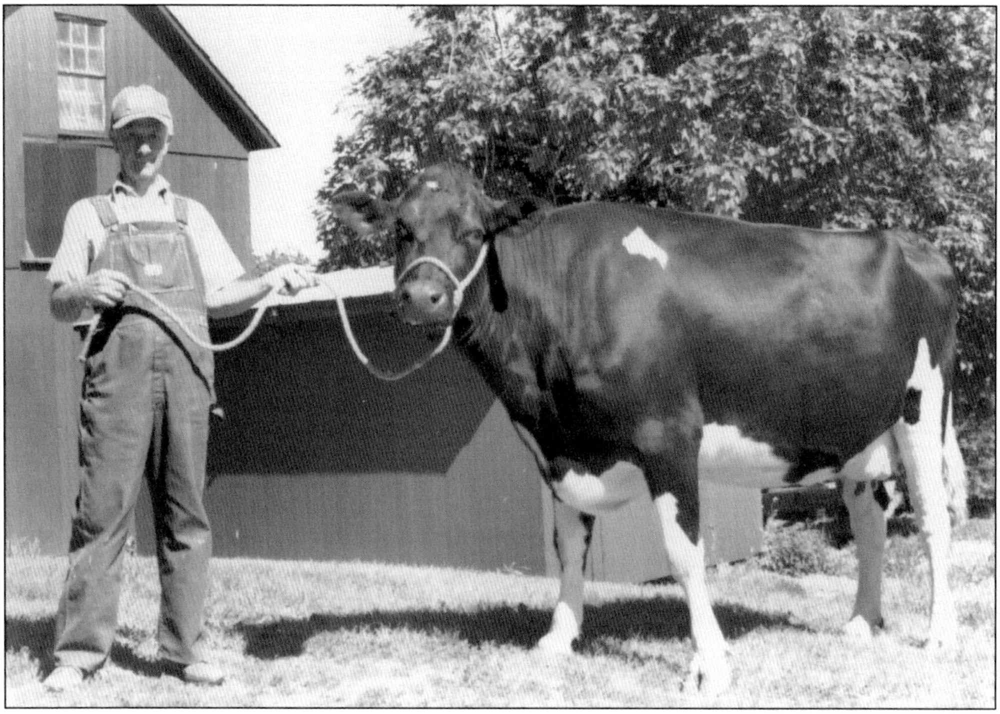

Clarence Berger is standing with Fanny, one of the family's cows, in 1979. The original Berger farm was primarily a dairy farm when his parents ran it. They also raised their own pork and beef and planted a garden. They made their own cornmeal, ground it themselves, and his mother used it for baking. The only items they needed to purchase were sugar and flour. (CMB.)

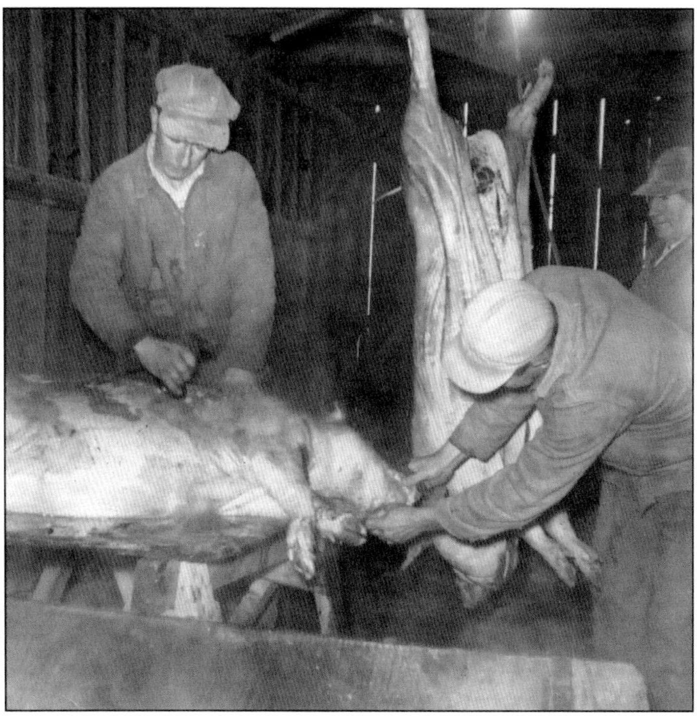

Clarence (left), his brother Paul, and father Oscar are seen at home butchering hogs, a yearly ritual. The process was done in the cooler months, usually November. Oscar was a farmer, and his two sons followed suit. Farming practices were carried out each day. They also tended to the dairy operation. As Clarence says, "It's been a good life." The Berger farmland is registered in the Bucks County Agricultural Preservation Program. (CMB.)

Clarence is plowing the field, getting it ready for planting corn in the 1950s. The Bergers still farmed with horse-drawn equipment until around 1956, when father Oscar passed away. The first tractor was purchased around 1939, but the family continued to use horses years later, depending on the need. They grew items for both family and livestock to eat. Living on a farm, there was always something to eat as well as work to be done. (CMB.)

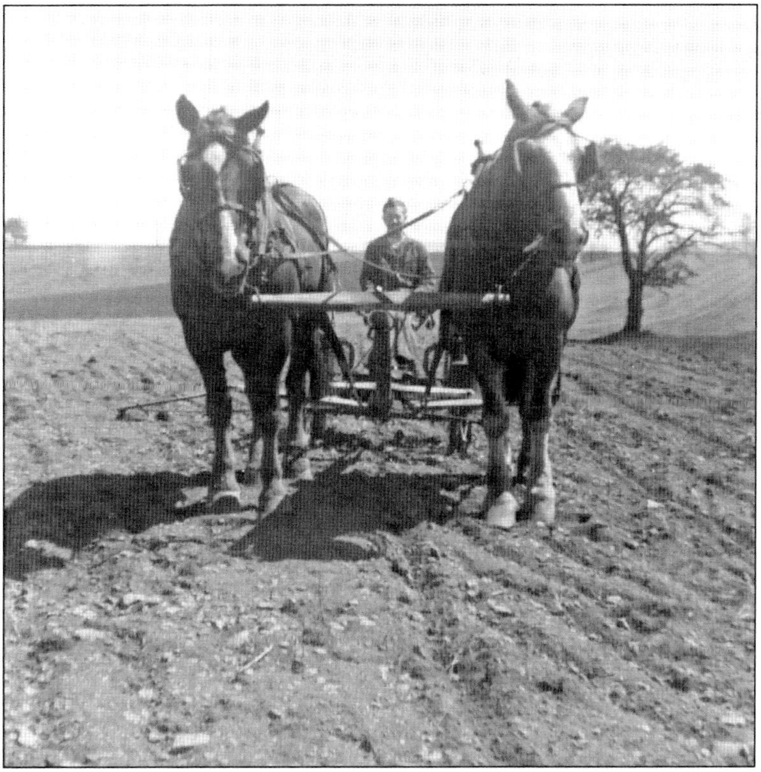

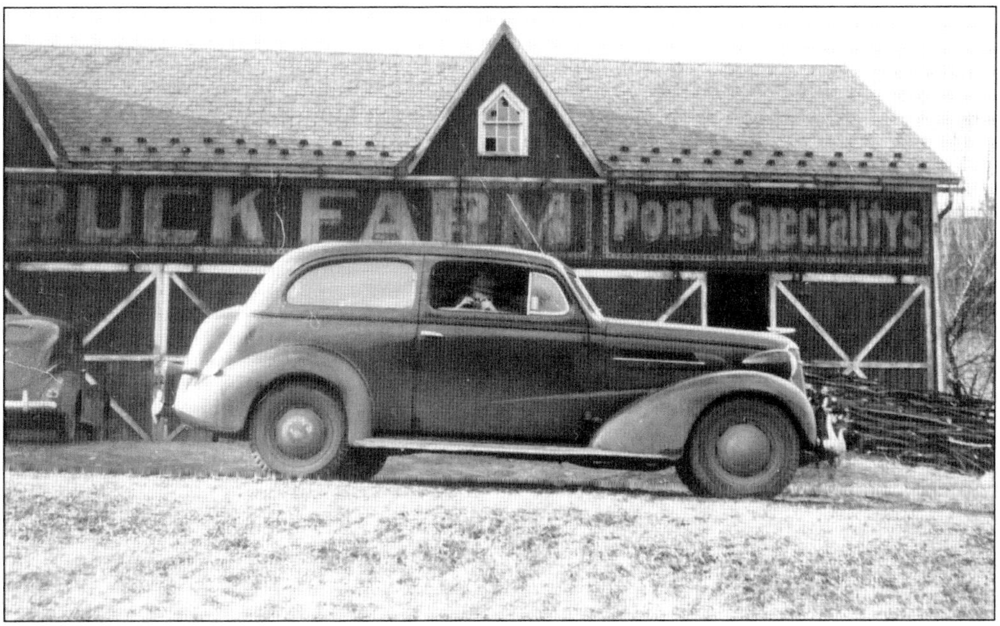

The Louis Jaffee building on Ealer Hill Road in Kintnersville is seen here in 1940. William Williams worked the truck farm that specialized in pork products. William and his wife, Miriam, lived in the farmhouse until they moved in the summer of 1942. The 1937 Chevrolet sedan was owned by their son Richard Williams. The large barn was later destroyed by fire, and new houses have been built on the Ealer Hill site. (MRW.)

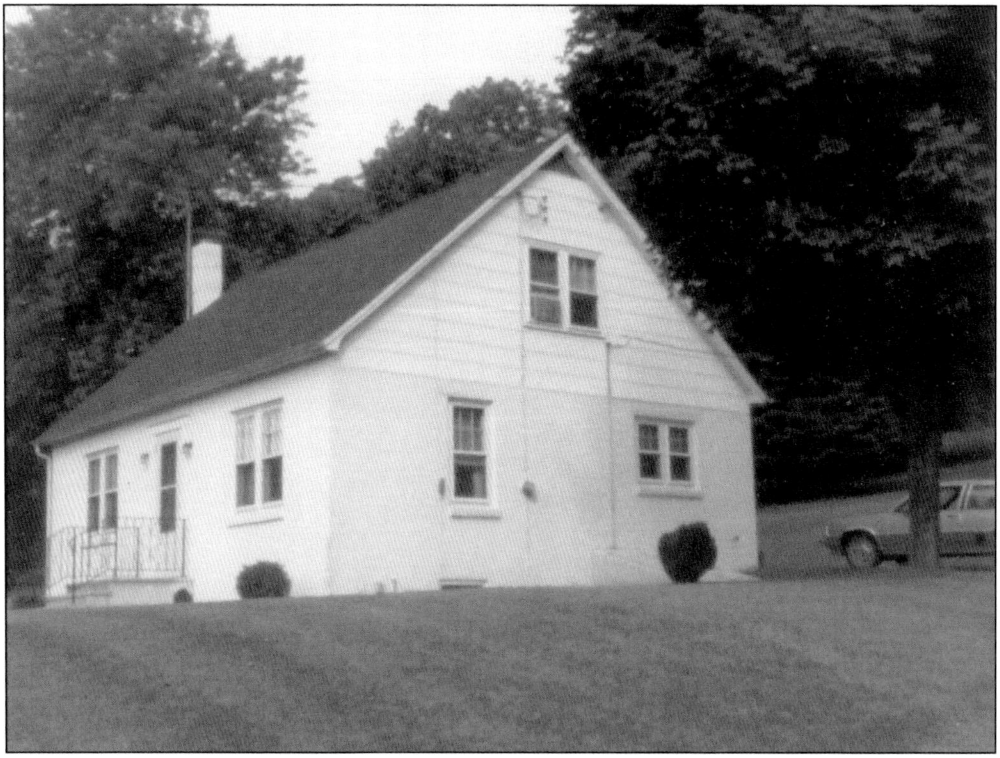

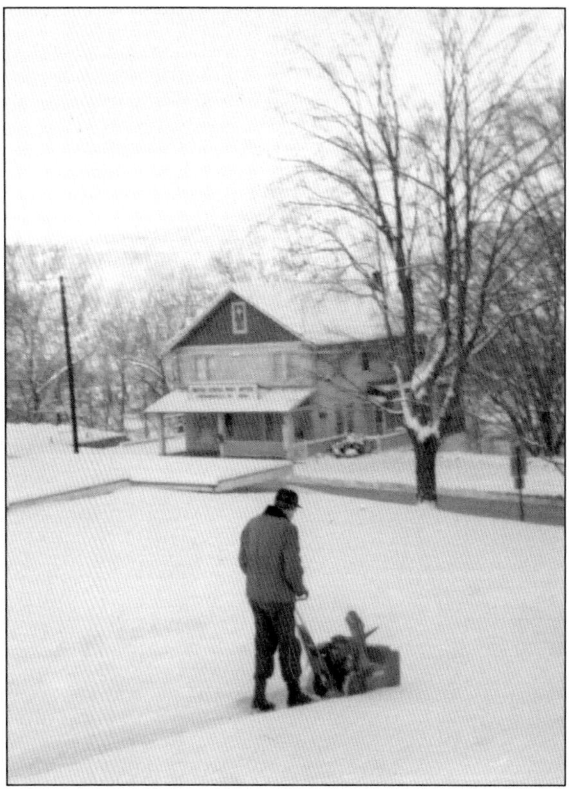

Mildred (Sigafoos) Williams met her husband, Richard, in the late 1930s, and they were married in October 1940. They built their Cape Cod–style home in 1951–1952 on a hill overlooking Easton Road. It was one of the last two houses built in the village of Kintnersville. The Williams raised their two sons, Leslie and Gary, there, and they attended township schools. (MRW.)

Richard Williams is seen clearing snow from his Kintnersville property after a sleet and snowstorm came through area in January 1968. Both Richard and wife Mildred were born and raised in Upper Bucks County. Richard was a superintendent at Riegel Paper, and Mildred worked as postal clerk in the Kintnersville Post Office. Mildred has always lived along the canal and Delaware River. Her father and grandfather worked on the canal as boat builders and carpenters. (MRW.)

Three

Education and Religious Life

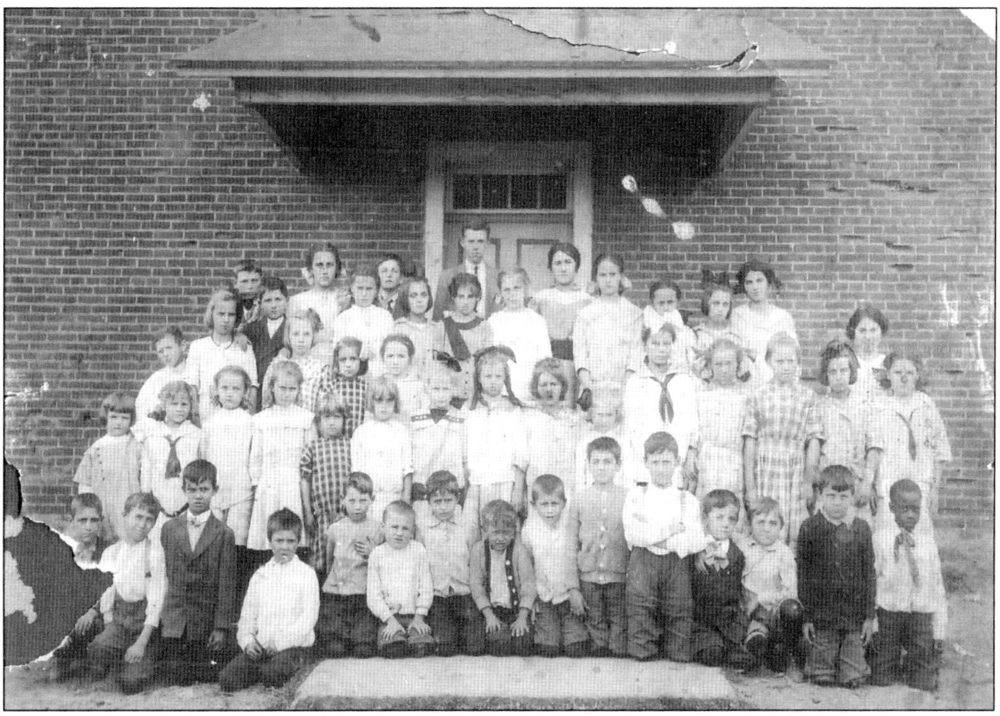

Revere School students, grades one through eight, are pictured with teacher Mary (Fox) Hindenach around 1915. Located on Schoolhouse Way off Marienstein Road, the two-story brick building replaced the original schoolhouse on the Conrad Custer farm. Ethel (Fabian) Lines, Ethel (Kohl) Kulp, Verna (Stone) Bartman, and Wilmer Trauger, all Nockamixon graduates, were teachers at Revere School. (NHS.)

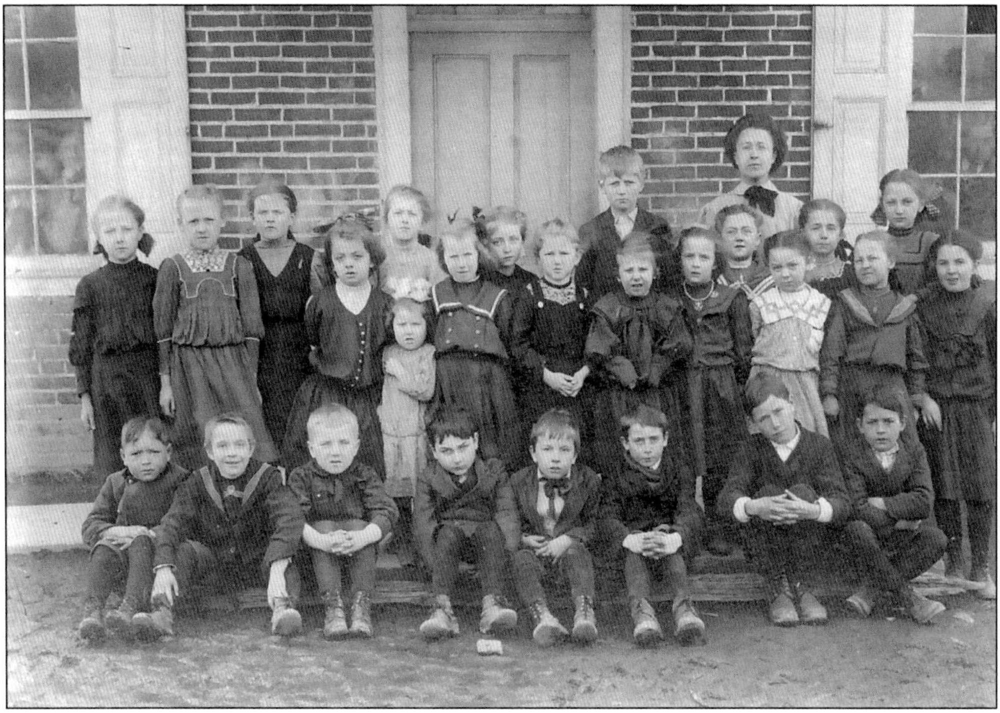

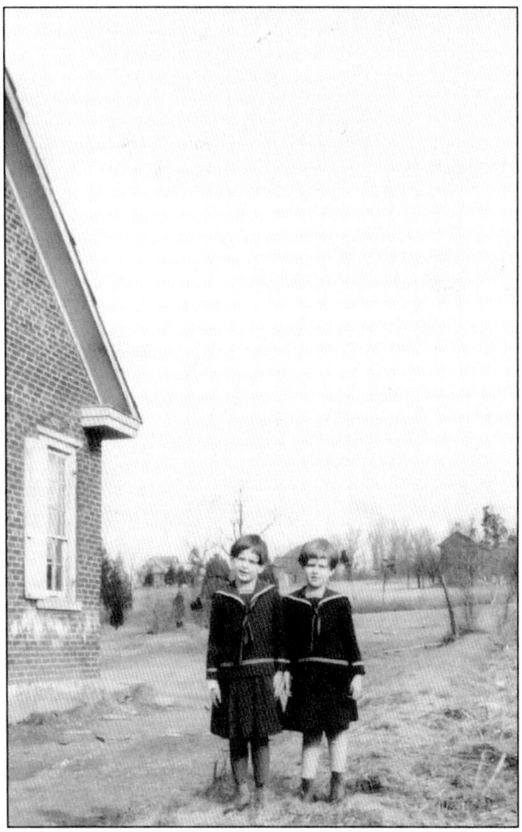

Teacher Anna Frankenfield is seen with Center Hill School primary-grade students around 1910. Nockamixon Lutheran Church built a two-room, log schoolhouse around 1771 on Center Hill Road in Ferndale. The Reformed Church also built a school there around 1773. The two congregations joined in 1812, building Nockamixon Union Church on the log schoolhouse site. In 1828, Union Church trustees were elected to care for the schoolhouse where English and German were taught. The school was leased to the township in 1838 and today is a private home. (NHS.)

Sisters Doris (left) and Blanche Bartman stand outside of Center Hill School in 1928. When six-year-old Doris began to attend school, Blanche cried that she wanted to go too. At only four years of age, her mother said okay. The girls walked up Center Hill Road from their home across from the Ferndale Post Office. Teacher Flora Litzenberger gave Blanche first-grade work. Each year she attended school, completed lessons, and went on to the next grade. (BBW.)

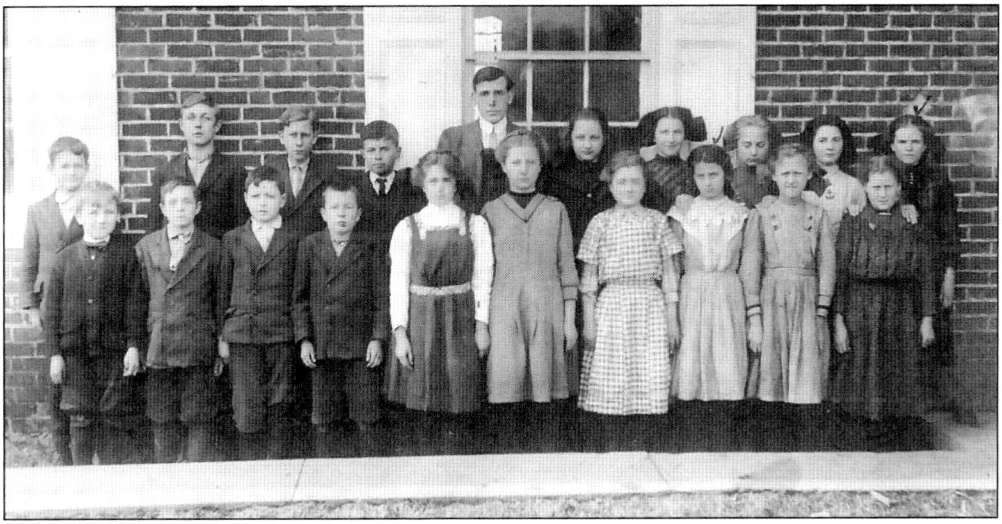

Grammar school students, grades five through eight at Center Hill School in Ferndale, are pictured with their teacher, Melvin Mann, in 1910. A graduate of Nockamixon High School, he attended Kutztown Normal School and then taught at Kintnersville, Lonely Cottage, and Center Hill Schools in Nockamixon. Mann later graduated from the University School of Veterinary Medicine in Philadelphia and opened a private practice as a veterinarian. (NHS.)

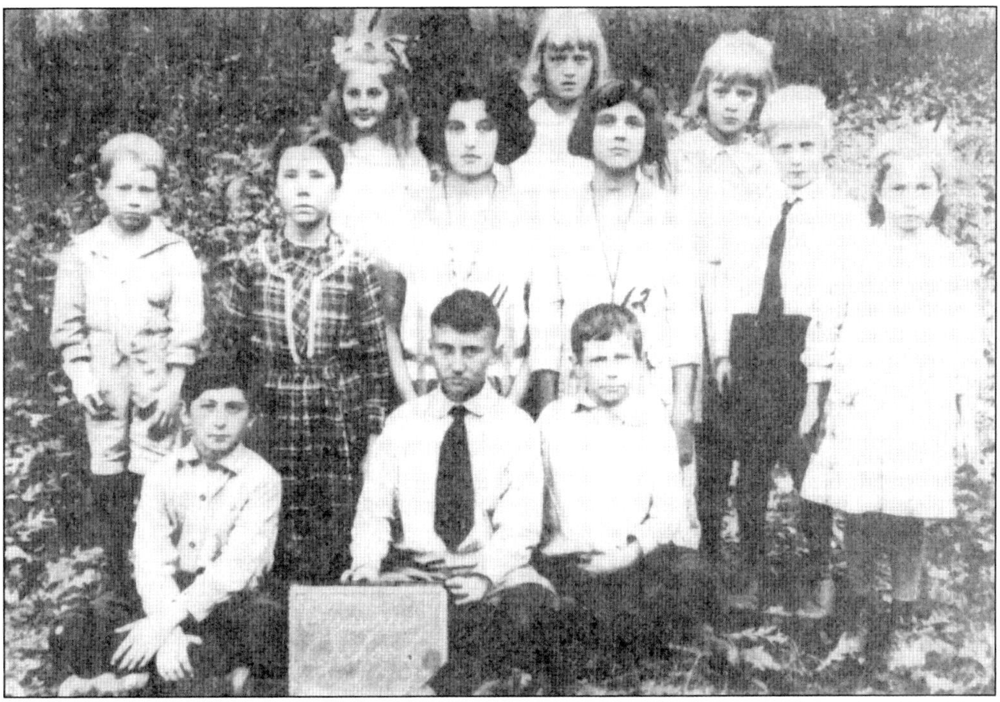

Primary grade students pose at Trauger's School in Kintnersville in 1922. This school building replaced an early one called Melchior's School, located on the road between the present Berger Farm and Camp Nockamixon, which was used until about 1900. Trauger's School was located in a wooded area belonging to Jacob H. Trauger. The brick school building was dismantled shortly after the construction of Nockamixon Consolidated School; however, the foundation remains. (NHS.)

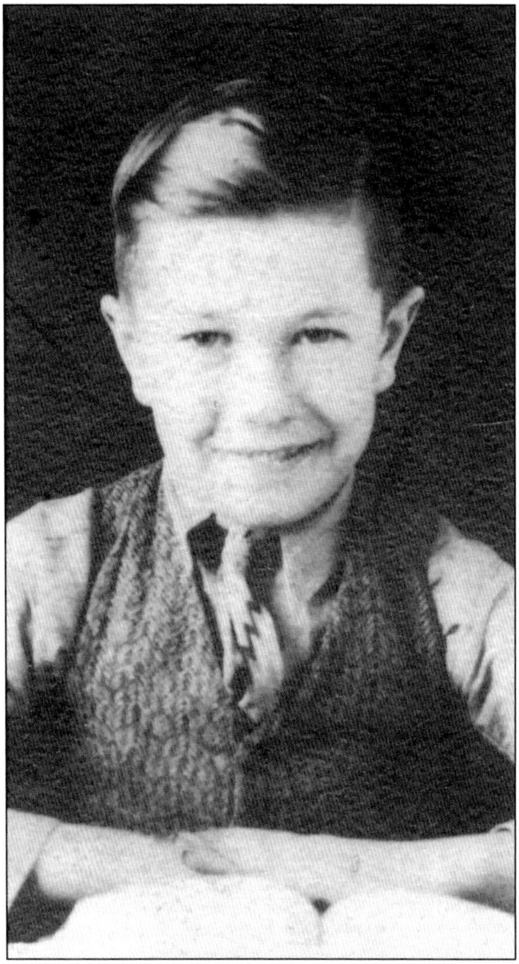

Clarence Berger of Nockamixon Consolidated School is seen in this 1933 photograph. Clarence originally attended Trauger's School, located down the road from his family farm near Camp Nockamixon, for one and a half years. When the building was demolished, he attended the new Nockamixon Consolidated School when it opened in 1930. Clarence continued his elementary school education and later graduated high school from the same building in 1941. Nockamixon Consolidated School is now an apartment building. (CMB.)

Young Revere School scholars are pictured in 1922. Teacher Ethel (Fabian) Lines, in the center of the back row, reminisced about a typical day. "Classes start 8:45 am. All eight grades and all subjects taught. Recess, twice a day with one hour lunch. School ended 4:00 pm. Discipline was in teacher's hands. Floor and blackboards were kept clean, and must keep large heater going with coal in winter. All this for $85.00 a month!" (NHS.)

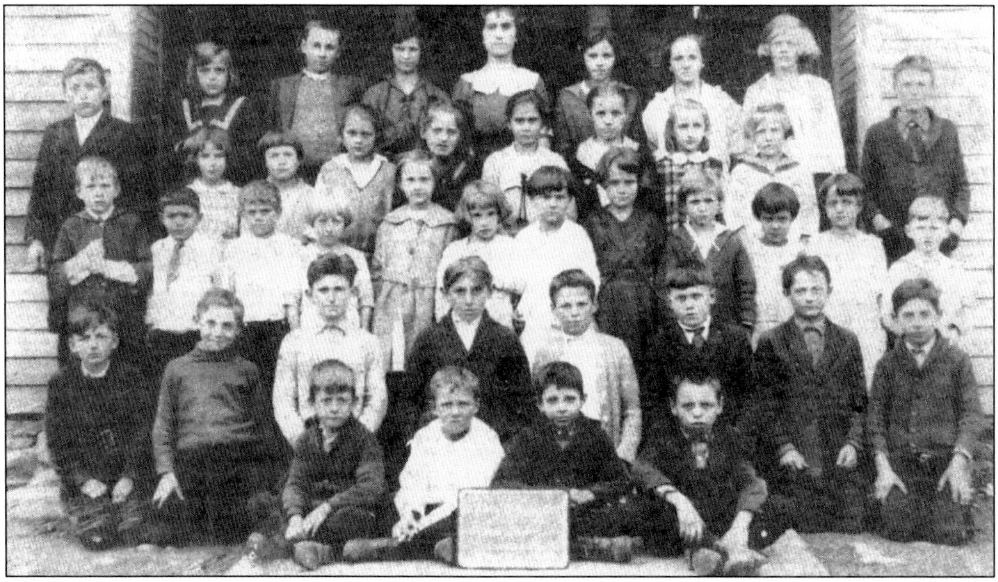

Here are school photographs of the Griffaton children, who were Center Hill School primary grade students. To the above left is Nicholas Griffaton Jr., the oldest son, and his young sister Anna is on the right. The twins, Leo and Edward, are pictured below. Their parents, Nicholas and Anna Griffaton, purchased a farm in Ferndale in the 1920s. One of children's teachers was their neighbor, Vema (Stone) Bartman, Blanche Wehrung's mother. (BBW.)

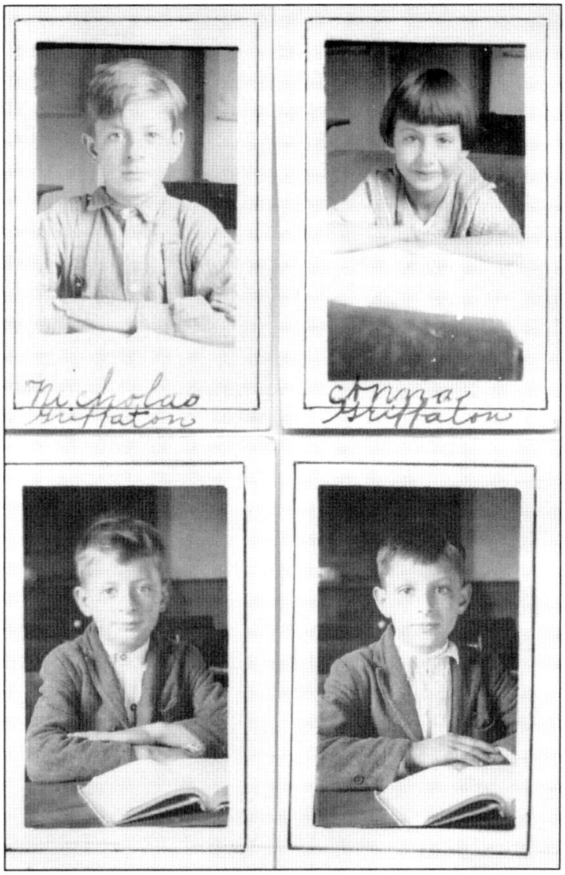

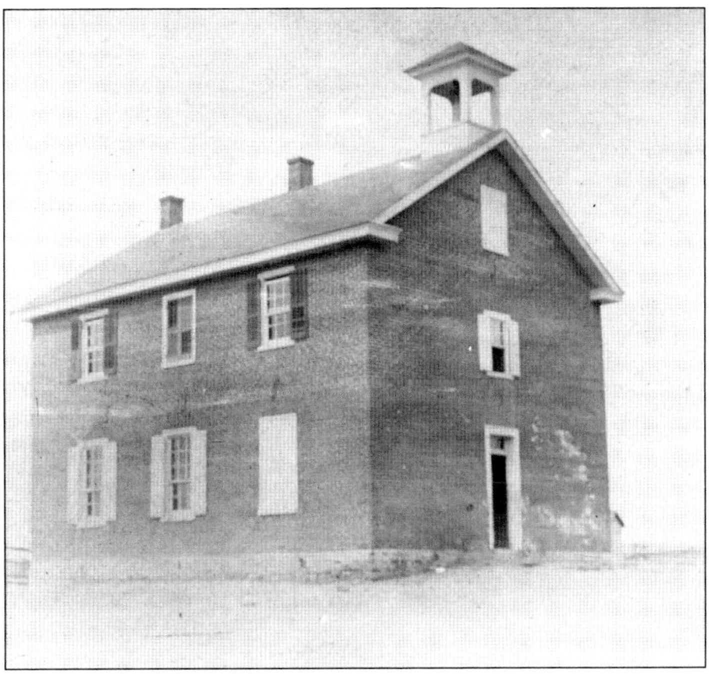

The Conrad Custer farm in Revere housed an early school around 1760. The land changed hands several times over the years. In 1838, John Rufe sold 20 perches to the Nockamixon School District, as well as an additional 40 perches in 1865. This two-story brick building was constructed in the late 1800s off of Marienstein Road on Schoolhouse Way. Grades one through four were on the first floor, with grades five through eight on the second; both were taught by two teachers. (NHS.)

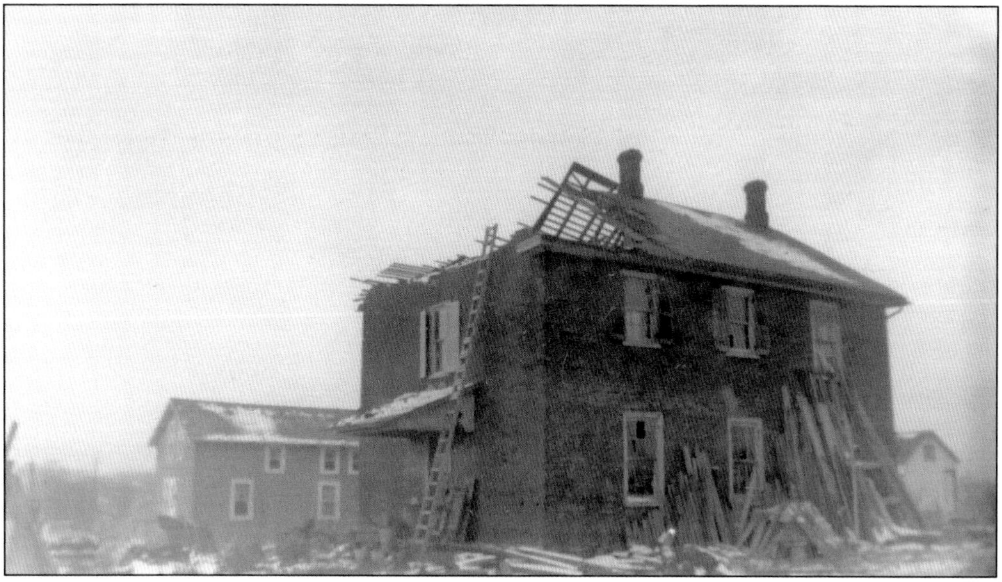

Elementary enrollments at Revere School increased. A temporary building constructed to accommodate additional students is seen to the left of the original school building. By 1904, enrollment dropped, and one teacher taught all grades. After Nockamixon Consolidated School opened in 1930, these two school buildings were sold in 1931 and used as residences. The original brick building was severely damaged in a 1955 storm and was demolished. (NHS.)

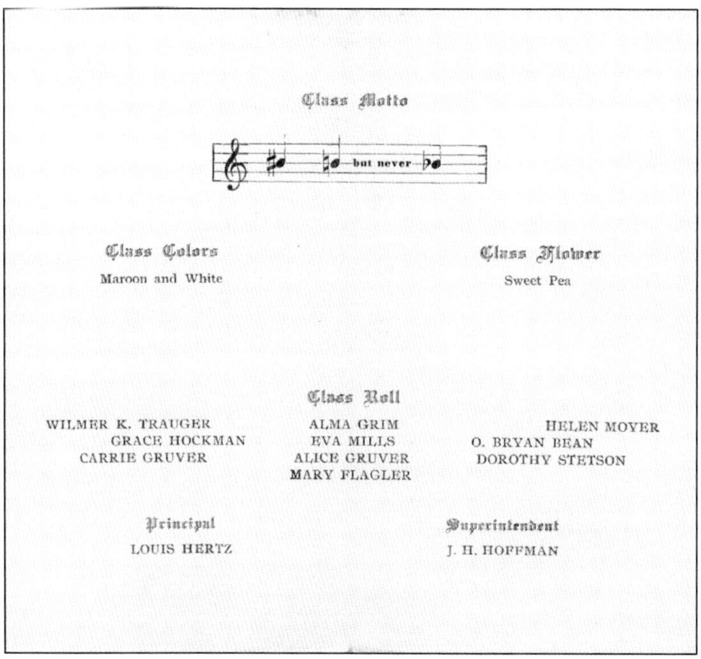

Class Motto

but never

Class Colors

Maroon and White

Class Flower

Sweet Pea

Class Roll

WILMER K. TRAUGER
GRACE HOCKMAN
CARRIE GRUVER

ALMA GRIM
EVA MILLS
ALICE GRUVER
MARY FLAGLER

HELEN MOYER
O. BRYAN BEAN
DOROTHY STETSON

Principal

LOUIS HERTZ

Superintendent

J. H. HOFFMAN

A formal graduation announcement states, "Senior Class of Nockamixon High School invites you to attend commencement exercises to be held in St. Luke's Church, Ferndale, Pennsylvania, Wednesday evening, April 13, 1913." Since only a two-year course was offered in 1913, four graduates—Wilmer Trauger, Eva Mills, Bryan Bean, and Pauline Caviezel—continued and completed a three-year course, graduating a second time on May 6, 1914. (NHS.)

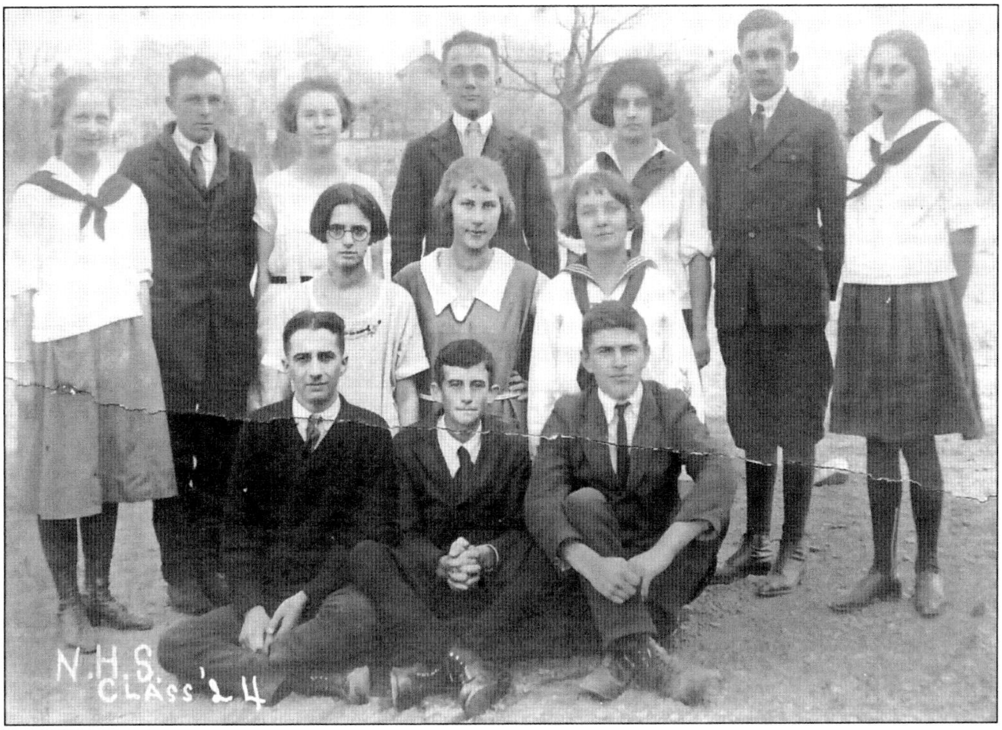

The 1924 Nockamixon High School graduating class is pictured at Center Hill School. Students attended classes there when they were no longer held at the Revere Store after a 1923 tornado tore the roof off the building. The graduates are, from left to right, (first row) Theodore Moyer, John Trauger, and Thomas Hale; (second row) Vergie Dunlap, Alma Seifert, and Margaret Trauger; (third row) Mabel Foellner, Samuel Litzenberger, Dorothy Fretz, teacher Raleigh Reinert, Stella Bean, Charles Kohl, and Esther Seifert. (NHS.)

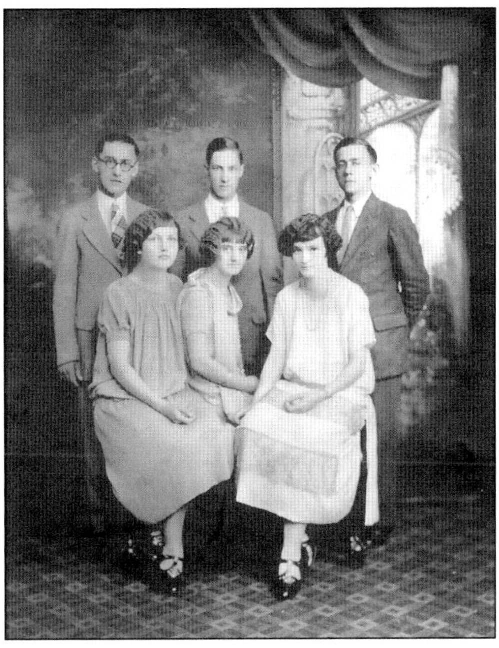

The 1925 Nockamixon High School graduation was held again at Center Hill School. Graduating class members are, from left to right, (first row) Evelyn (Morris) Trauch, Margaret (Hager) Kline, and Flora (Litzenberger) Shoemaker; (second row) Myron Bean, Robert Rufe, and principal John Shoemaker. Flora would later teach at Center Hill School in Ferndale. (NHS.)

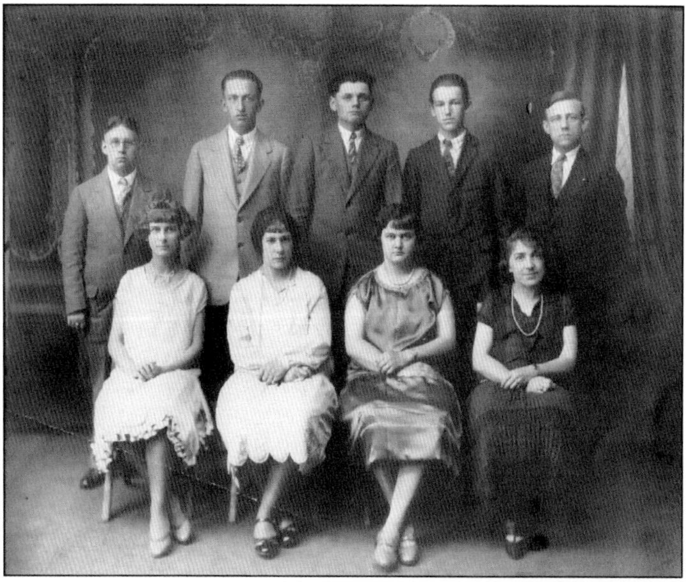

The 1926 Nockamixon High School graduates are, from left to right, (first row) Mildred (Foellner) Magee, Evelyn (Berger) Nicholas, Emma (Trauger) Roth, and assistant principal Elizabeth Grim; (second row) Ray Stover, Ray Foellner, Harry Zitlin, George Ottinger, and principal John Shoemaker. Grim taught at Center Hill School before assuming duties at the high school in 1921. She remained teaching there until her retirement in 1946. (NHS.)

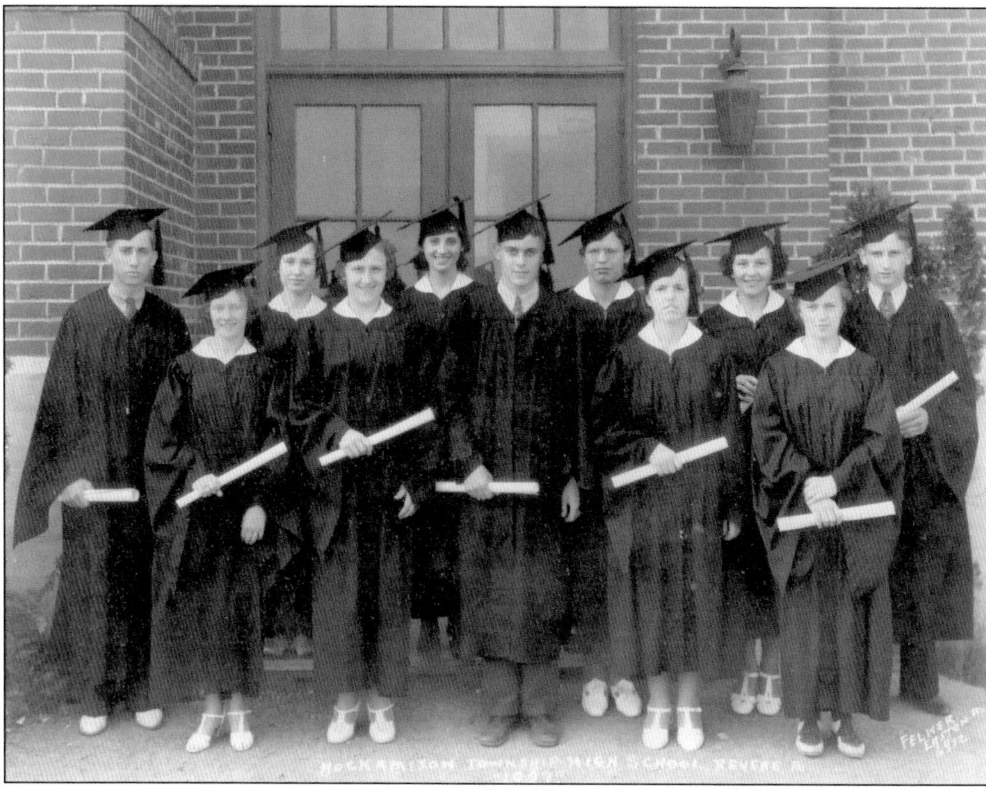

The 1937 graduating class stands outside Nockamixon Consolidated School. Built in 1930 on Easton Road in Revere, it housed grades 1 through 12. From left to right are (first row) Florence Shupe, Marie Schermann, Richard Williams, Ruth Mood, and Mildred Helman; (second row) Charles Sarber, Mary Rufe, Yetta Zeitlin, Norma Limbach, Betty Schaefer, and Oscar Frei. During their high school years, the eastern wing was added to building, with the WPA doing much of the work. (LLR.)

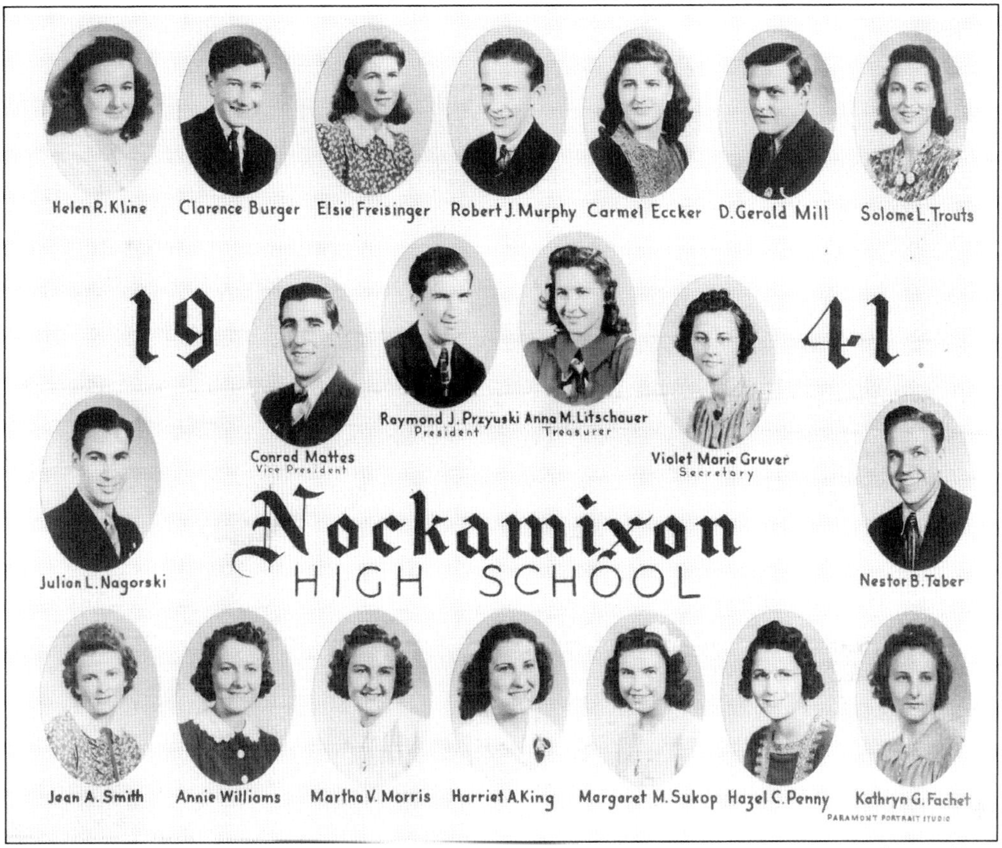

Twenty students graduated in 1941 from Nockamixon High School. From left to right are (first row) Jean Smith, Annie Williams, Martha Morris, Harriet King, Margaret Sukop, Hazel Penny, and Kathryn Fachet; (second row) Julian Nagorski, Conrad Mattes, Raymond Przyuski, Anna Litschauer, Violet Gruver, and Nestor Taber; (third row) Helen Kline, Clarence Burger, Elsie Freisinger, Robert Murphy, Carmel Eccker, D. Gerald Mill, and Salome Trouts. Music, home economics, and commercial subjects were added to the curriculum in the late 1930s. (NHS.)

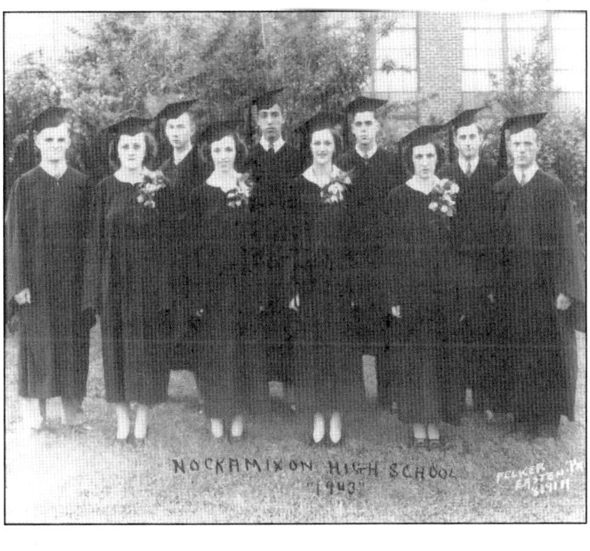

The 1943 Nockamixon High School class poses for a graduation photograph. From left to right are (first row) Herbert Krause, Eva Barron, Ruth (Unangst) Johnson, Rowena (Bartman) Krause, and Kathryn (Schmidt) Shive; (second row) William Murphy, Kenneth Piell, Robert Fink, Gustave Richtar, and Edward Litschauer. The first school cafeteria opened during the year and was welcomed by students. The following year, the class of 1944 issued the first yearbook, *N'tschutti*, meaning "beloved friend" in the language of the Delawares. (NHS.)

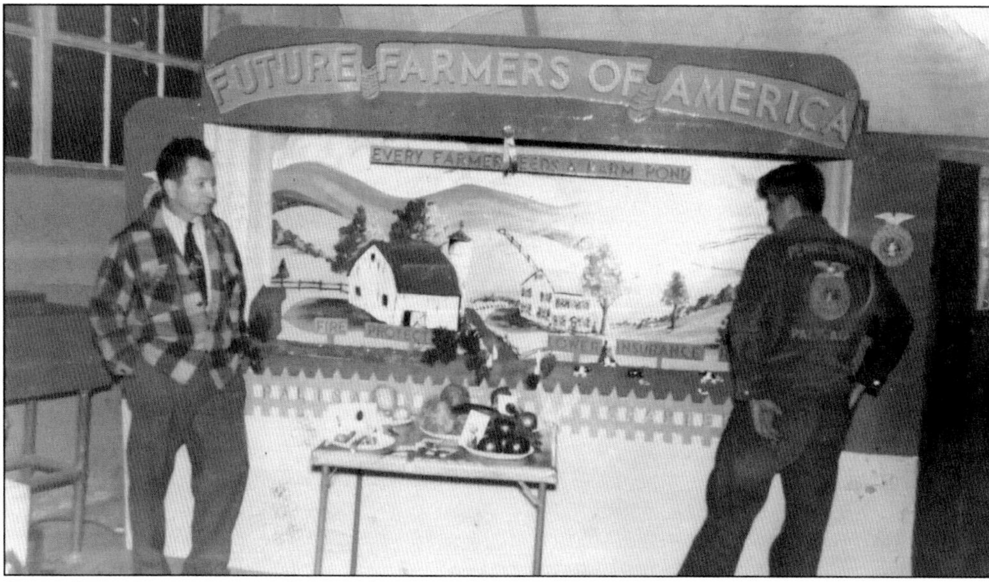

Started in 1942, vocational agriculture was an important field of study at Nockamixon High School. Students belonged to Future Farmers of America, an organization that augmented the instructional program. Frank Naska Sr. (left) and son Frank Jr. (a Palisades High student), attending the Nockamixon Fair in October 1953, check out a prize-winning display by Palisades students. The special events continued to be held at Nockamixon School after Palisades High School opened in 1953. (BNB.)

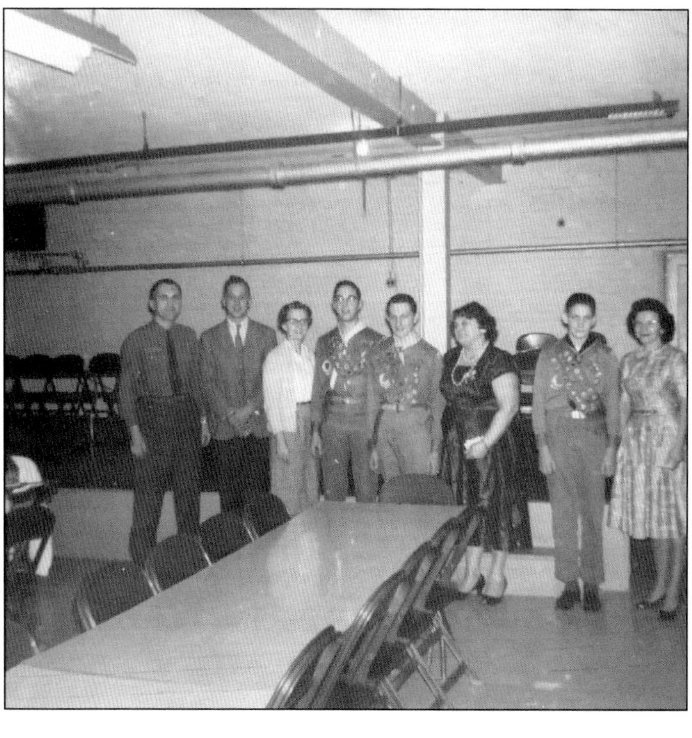

At a January 8, 1962, ceremony at Nockamixon School, three members of Nockamixon Boy Scout Troop 27 were awarded the rank of eagle scout. Christopher Hampton, Benjamin Naska, and Ronald Houseworth received this high honor from scoutmaster Fred Fischer for their leadership projects. Photographed after the ceremony with their parents are, from left to right, scoutmaster Fred Fischer, Mr. Hampton, Mrs. Hampton, Christopher Hampton, Benjamin Naska, Mrs. Julia Naska, Ronald Houseworth, and Mrs. Houseworth. (BNB.)

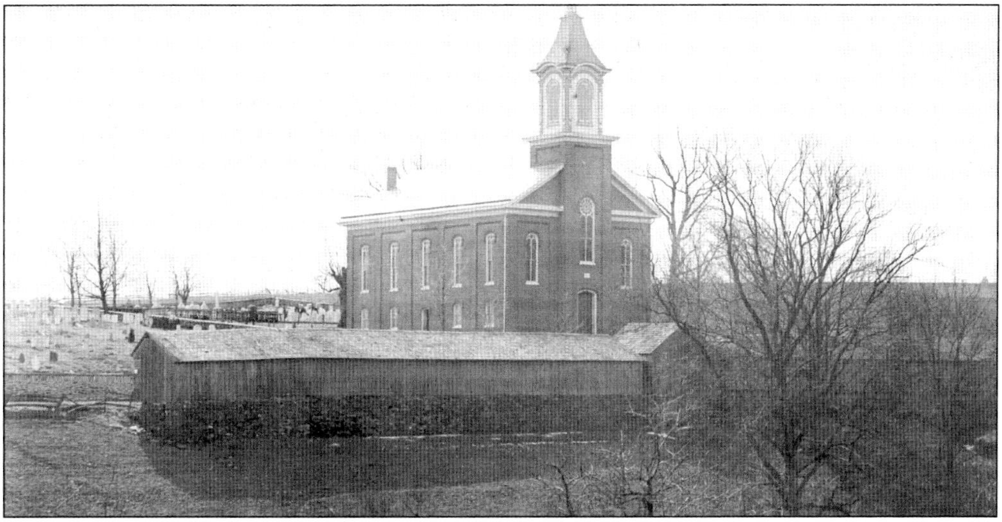

St. Luke's Lutheran Church in Ferndale, the offspring of the Springfield congregation, was organized in 1752. The original house of worship was a 1761 log structure near Center Hill School when Rev. John M. Enderlein was called in 1766. In 1804, the Lutheran congregation worshiped with Reformed brethren at the Church Hill Road building, thus Union Church was formed. The cornerstone of the new church, shared by the two congregations, was laid in 1813, and the building was completed in 1814. Services were conducted solely in German until 1828. (NHS.)

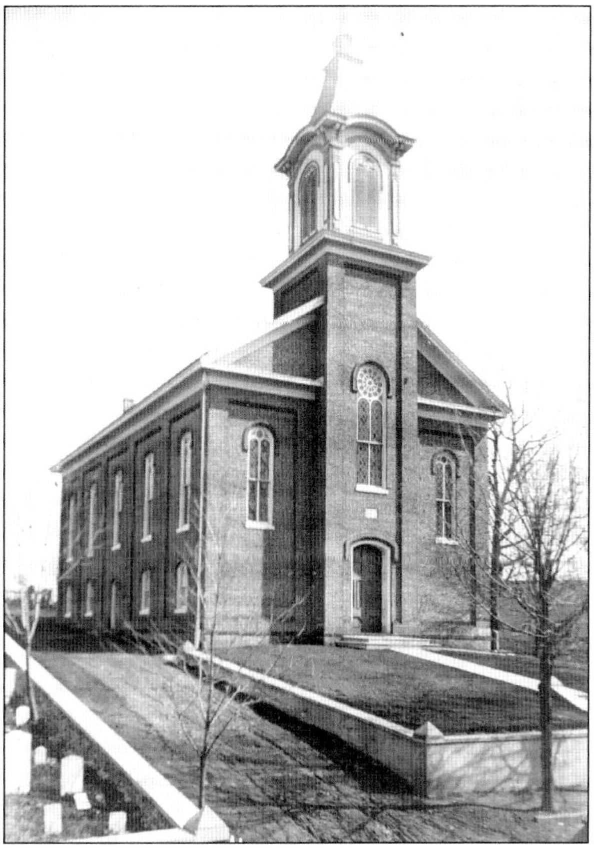

The fourth building, and present one, for St. Luke's Lutheran Church remains a handsome edifice. The cornerstone was laid on July 3, 1875, and dedicated on May 20, 1877, by Rev. William S. Emery. The congregation's membership was over 500. The church had a flourishing Sunday school, an active missionary society, and a regular evening bible class. The Lutheran congregation retained sole possession of the church in 1976 when the Reformed church relocated to Ottsville. (NHS.)

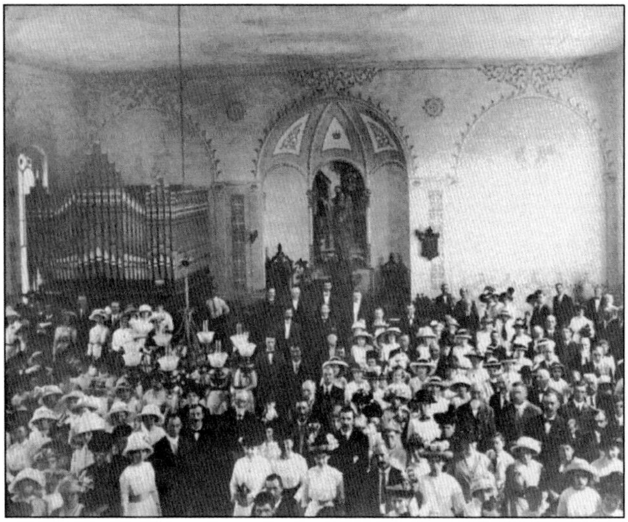

The centennial of St. Luke's Union Church Nockamixon in Ferndale was held Sunday, August 10, 1913. Rev. Samuel S. Diehl of the Lutheran church and Rev. Charles B. Weaver of the Reformed Church presided over the centennial service and celebration. This photograph includes both congregations. Standing in the rear center, second from the left, is Rev. C.B. Weaver; third from the left is Rev. S.S. Diehl. Both ministers were called to congregations in 1892. Diehl served until 1924. (NHS.)

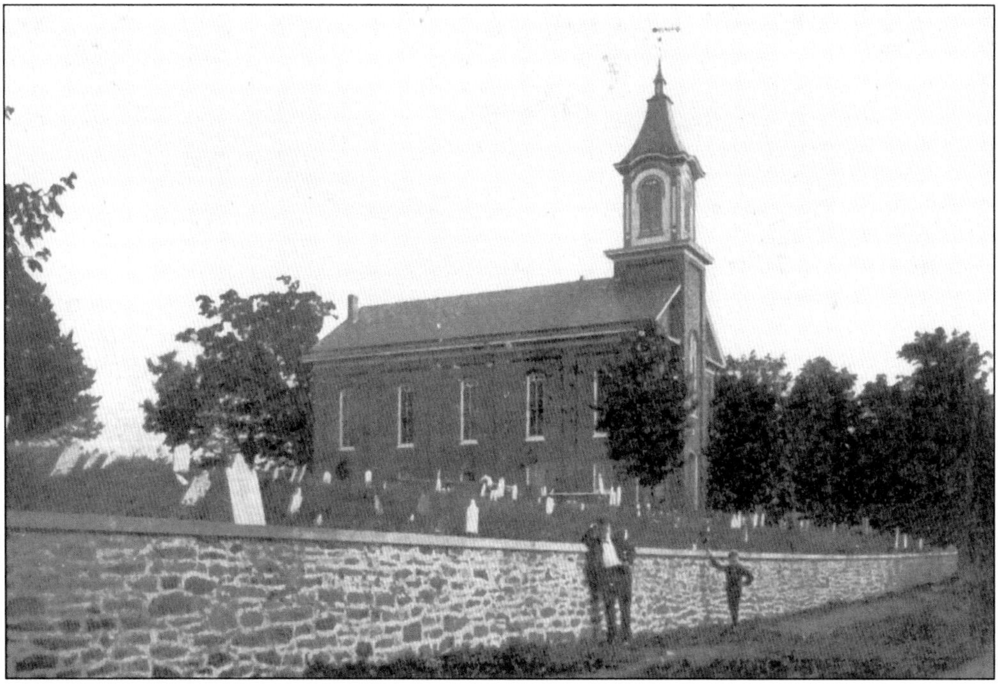

Nockamixon settlers brought the religion of their native land, seeking a place where they could live and worship in freedom. The church ledger records the first baptism as John Frederick Krause, son Michael and Barbara Krause, born August 12, 1766. Many of St. Luke's members served their country, and the cemetery contains veterans' graves. Rev. Jacob Frederick Miller's son was killed in the Battle of Gettysburg and is buried with his father and mother in the Lutheran cemetery. (NHS.)

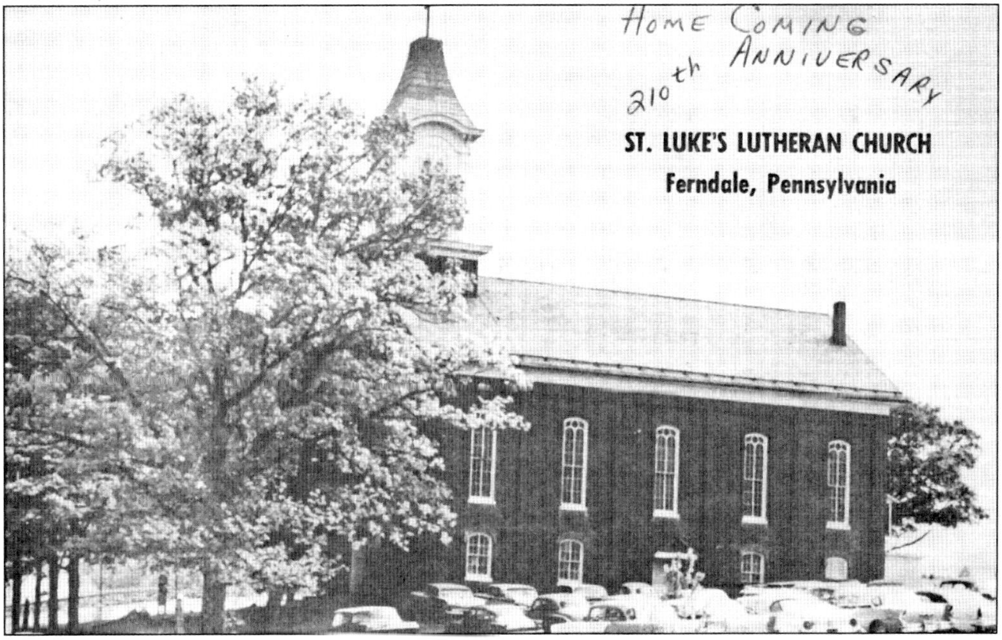

St. Luke's Lutheran Church celebrated its 210th anniversary on August 26, 1973. The brochure listed information for this special occasion. Sunday worship was held in the morning, a luncheon was served early afternoon, and an informal reunion service took place afterwards. Many clergy members were in attendance, including previous pastors along with sons of the congregation who entered the ministry. St. Luke's Lutheran Church in Ferndale celebrated its 248th anniversary in 2011. (NHS.)

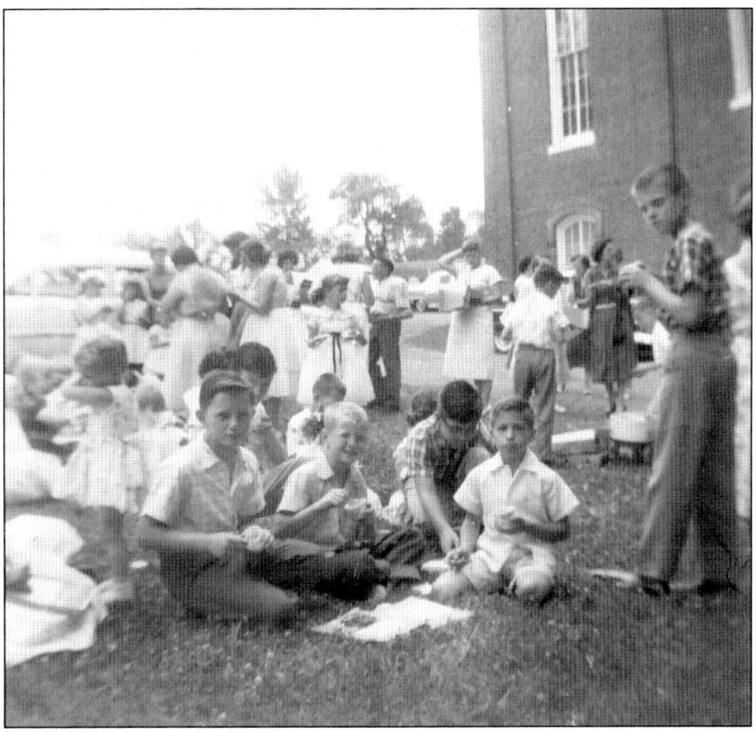

Children from the area are seen participating in Devotional Vacation Bible School held at St. Luke's Lutheran Church during the summer. In this July 1957 photograph are, from left to right, Robert Seifert, James Overpeck, Barry Seifert, Benjamin Naska, and John Jolly enjoying a recess break before getting back to a project they were working on. (BNB.)

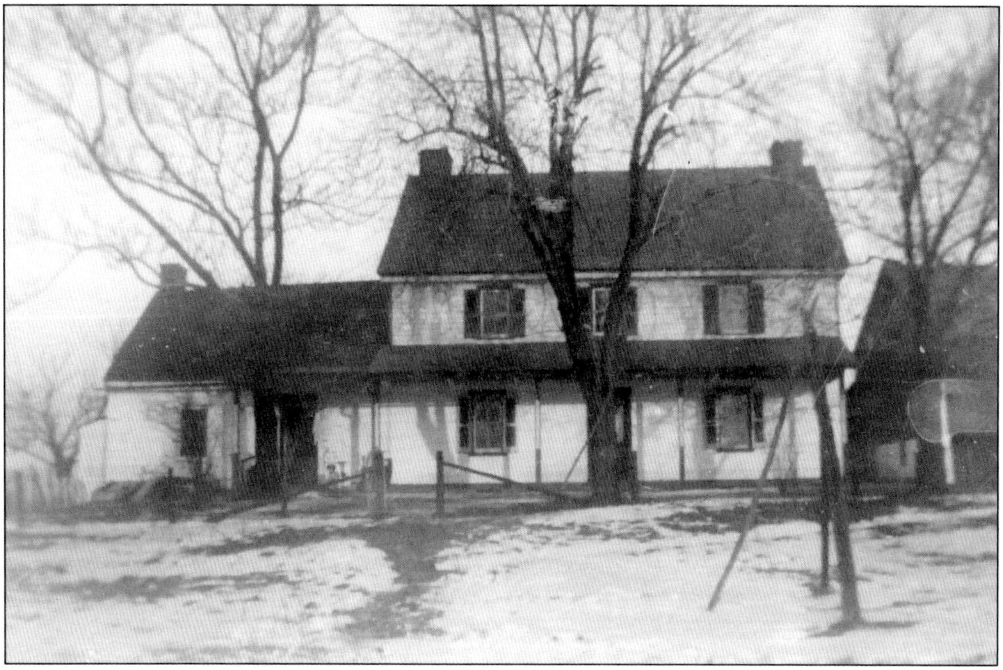

Mass was first read at the home of Edward McCarty (second generation), who emigrated from Ireland in 1737 seeking religious freedom. Later, Nicholas (third generation) and Albertina (Kohl) McCarty built a new family home in 1776 with a large room for Catholics to attend Mass and a small second-floor room that accommodated a missionary priest. Bonfires on surrounding hills notified residents of services. The Thomas Roscoe McCarty (seventh generation) farm on Church Lane in Bucksville is now a private home. (RMC.)

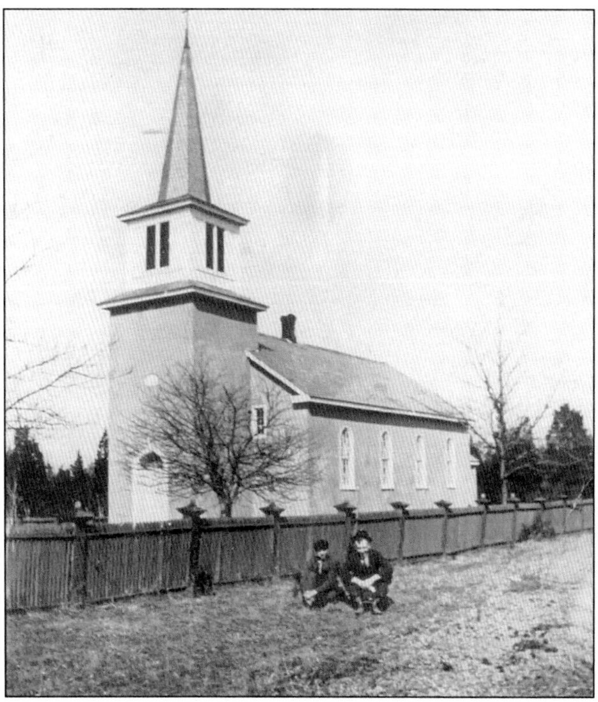

St. Joseph's Mission Church in Marienstein was built due to the efforts of Fr. Henry Stommel, pastor of St. John the Baptist Church in Haycock. He ministered to families of boatmen employed by the Delaware division of the Lehigh Canal. Ground for the chapel was broken in August 1872; the cornerstone was laid the following day, with a dedication in December. Located along the road from Revere to Upper Black Eddy, the young men pictured here in 1873 may have been workers. (MGS.)

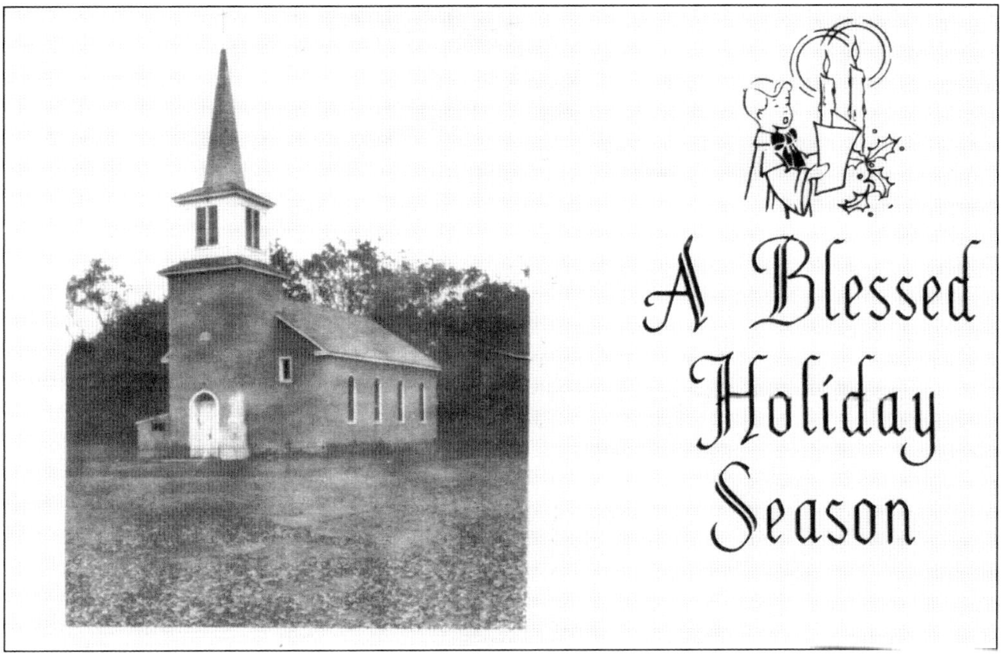

Seen here is a c. 1940 holiday message sent St. Joseph's Marienstein parishioners. The church, built at the request of Irish-German-English immigrant boatmen and their families, was a necessity when harsh winters kept them home. Built by the Schwar family of stonemasons, its Roman-style architecture is often admired. The altars were built and furnished by Josiah Shuman, and carpentry work was done by Thomas Kohl. Recently restored, St. Joseph's is now a private home. (MVD.)

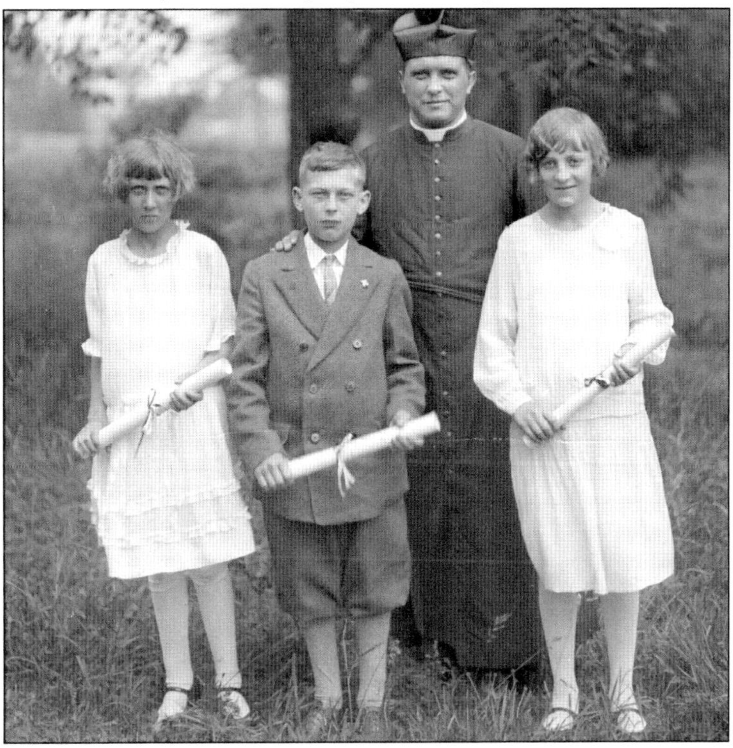

The first graduation at St. John the Baptist School is celebrated in this 1927 photograph. From left to right are Nockamixon residents Elizabeth (Reitter) Pearman, Joseph Kimenhour, and Anna (Balbirer) McCarty (Rosanne McCarty's mother), with Rev. John Schillo. They graduated from a two-room elementary school built in 1925 across the road from the church. Two additional classrooms were added in the 1940s, and the present school was built in 1959 on Durham Road. (RMC.)

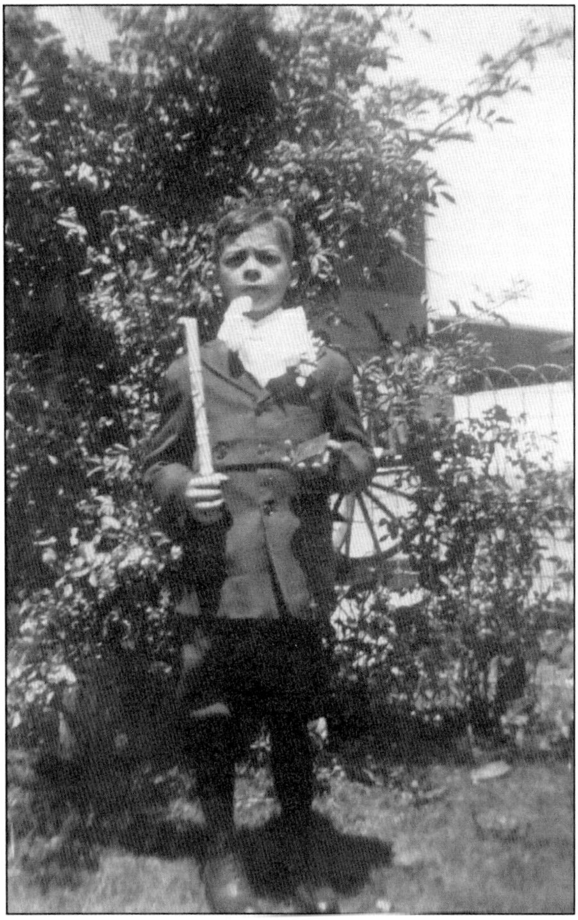

Rosanne McCarty's father, Charles Paul McCarty, the eldest son Thomas Roscoe and Mary (Fleck) McCarty, celebrated his first Communion at St. John the Baptist Church in 1920. The McCarty family, from Ireland, was among the first to arrive in the late 1730s and began the formation of the parish community. They warranted land from William Penn's sons, which was deeded to them in 1739. St. John the Baptist, founded in 1743, is Bucks County's oldest Catholic parish. (RMC.)

This 1928 photograph shows St. John the Baptist's first school bus, driven by John Kresh. Early records from the 1780s indicate a schoolhouse, built on the property of Thomas D. McCarty's homestead, served until Haycock Church was built in 1798 with an attached schoolroom. This early school was probably built in accordance with John McCarty's 1766 will designating a portion of his inheritance be used for the education of his three sons: Nicholas, Thomas, and John. (EMH.)

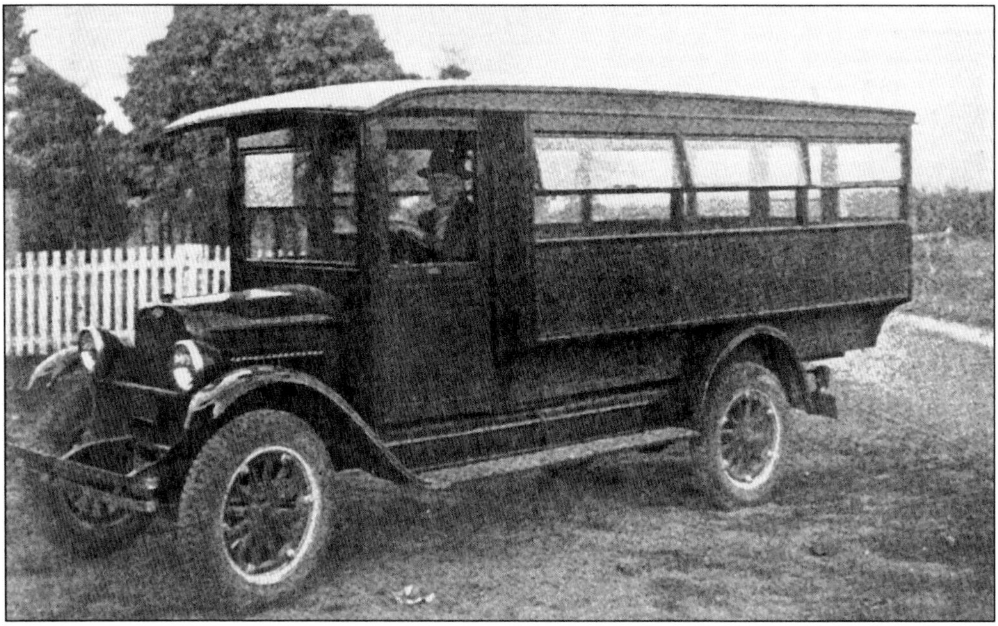

Sr. Mary M.S.C. (Ethel McCarty), seen at Holy Family Parish in Nazareth in 1940, celebrated her first Communion at St. John the Baptist Church in 1932. On her 21st birthday, Sr. Mary went to convent, and her family did not see her for 10 years. She was later allowed home infrequently; however, she stayed at the Haycock convent. The family would have a large reunion with relatives attending to visit with Sr. Mary. Eventually, she was allowed to stay in the family home. (RMC.)

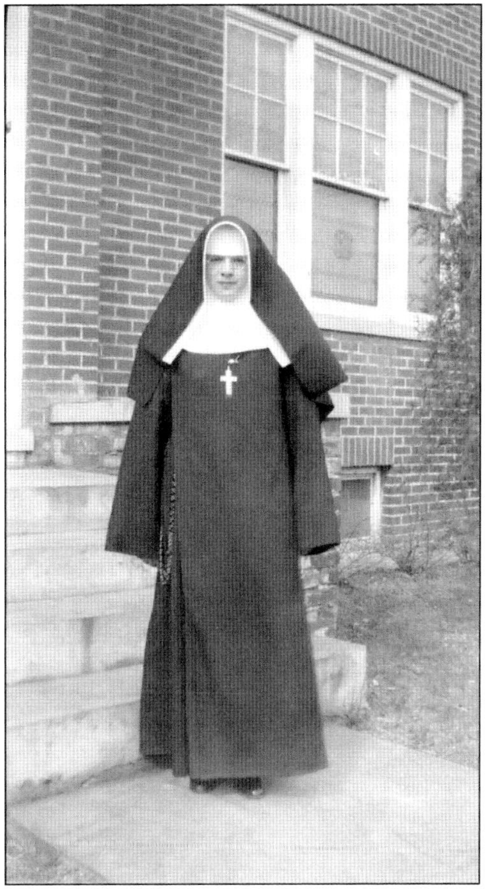

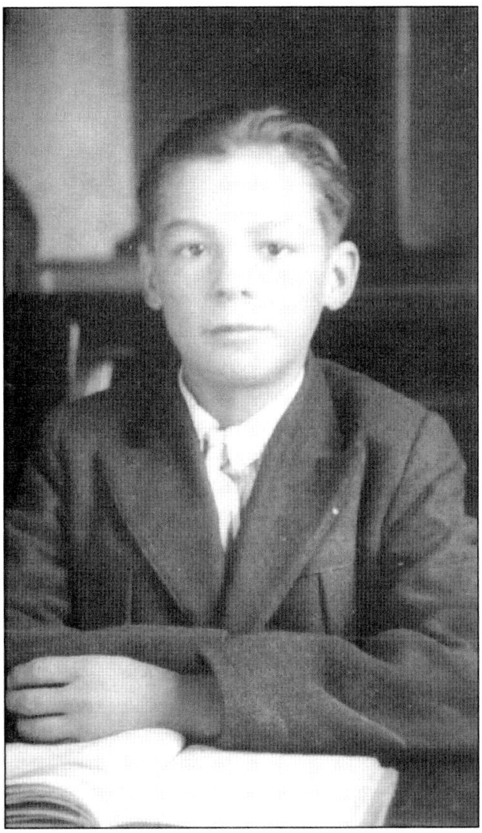

Charles Paul McCarty, born on December 1, 1912, attended St. John the Baptist School. He and siblings Vincent, Ethel, Helen and Herman are in the school's first photograph dated 1925, along with many friends. Fifty-four students attended the new school, and some of them were cousins of the McCarty children. The nuns would often remind the girls and boys to be nice to fellow students since they may be related to one other. (RMC.)

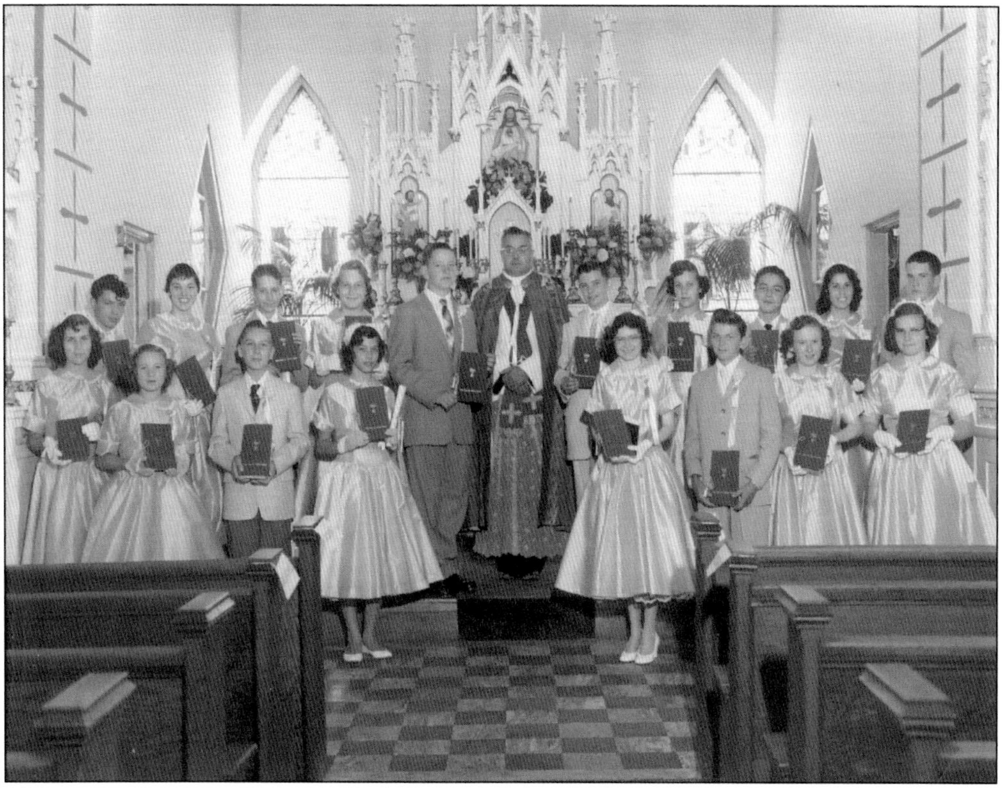

This Notre Dame graduation took place in June 1957. Students pictured are, from left to right, (first row) Gloria Roberts, Barbara Fleck, William Stahley, Joan Carney, Erica Mattern, Anthony Jucewicz, Maryann Balbirer, and Joanne McNichol; (second row) Thomas Kocsis, Rosemarie Kramer, Robert de Groot, Elizabeth Moninghoff, Thomas Sienkowski, Rev. Martin G. Swayne, Thomas Gaughan, Joan Proca, Richard Kocsis, Mary Grace Ferris, and Richard Johnson. Nockamixon children attended Notre Dame, as St. John the Baptist did not have a high school. (RMC.)

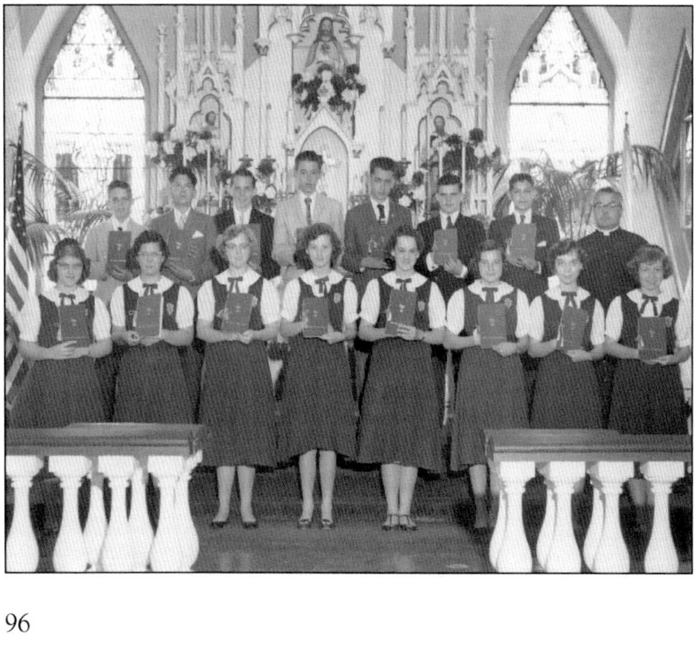

This class photograph is from the June 1958 Notre Dame graduation. From left to right are, (girls) Maryann Gerhart, Pauline Hoper, Rosanne McCarty, Pat Brennan, Charlotte de Groot, Cathy Zalesak, Janet Kocsis, and Rita Van Emmerik; (boys) Philip Lapsley, John Nostadt, Larry Wismer, Ron Kita, John Stevens, Gerry Johnson, Joseph Thaler, and Rev. Martin G. Swayne. (RMC.)

Four

LEISURE ACTIVITIES

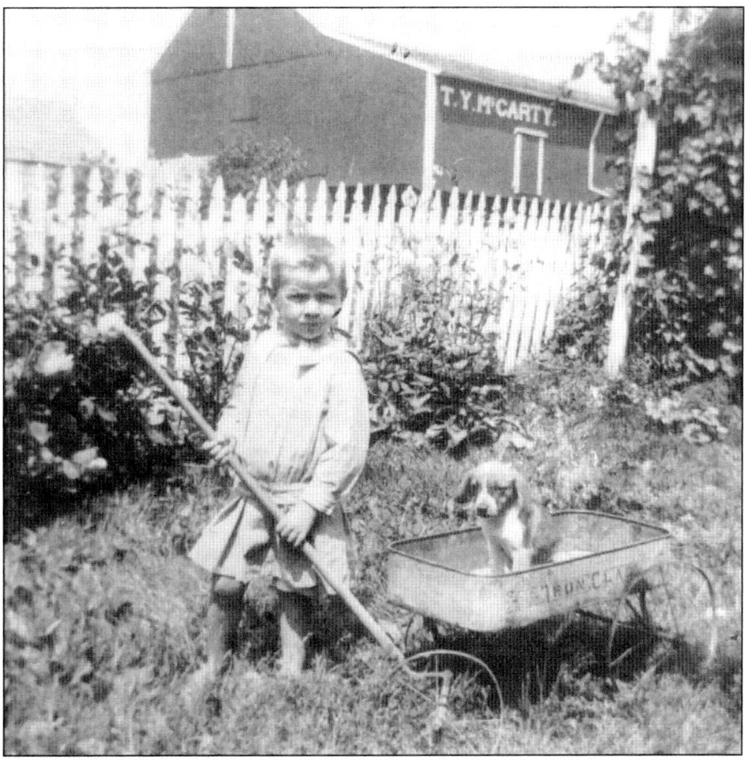

Charles McCarty, the young son of Thomas Y. and Isabella McCarty, is shown in this 1901 photograph. Born in 1899, he was a typical boy and liked anything mechanical. Only about two years old at the time, Charles enjoyed taking his puppy for a ride in his wagon while playing on the front lawn of the family's farm. (RMC.)

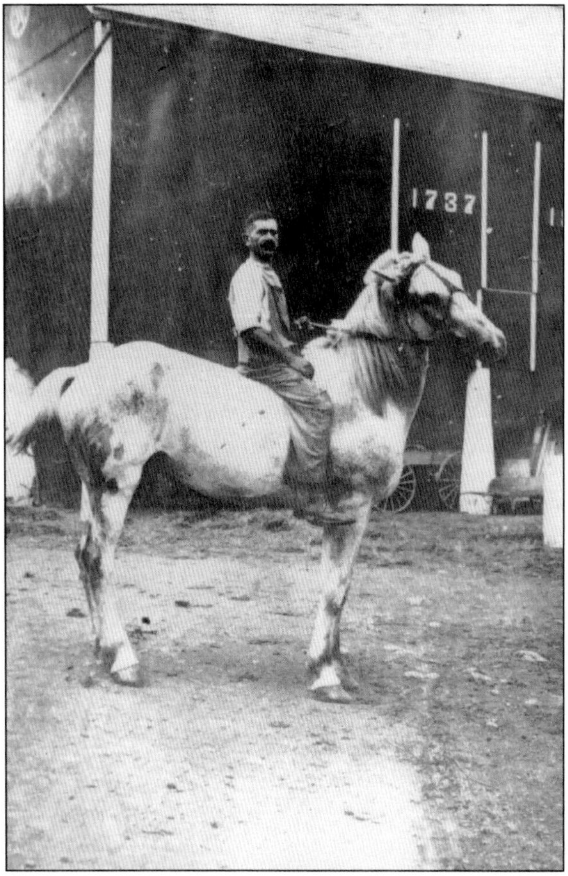

Thomas "Roscoe" McCarty, son of Thomas Y. and Isabella McCarty, is seen in this 1920 photograph in front of the 1737 McCarty barn. Born in 1883, he was known as Roscoe since his father's name was also Thomas. An amiable gentlemen, he was also a skilled horseman, often riding bareback overseeing the McCarty property as well as his farm. (RMC.)

Before leaving for a Sunday drive in their four-door Phaeton automobile, the McCarty family stops in front of the barn in 1920. Father Roscoe McCarty is in the driver's seat, and mother Mary is holding young Herman; the older children, (from left to right) Vincent, Ethel, Helen (McCarty) Thaler, and Charles P. are ready to go, seated in the back with Catherine Schaefer. (RMC.)

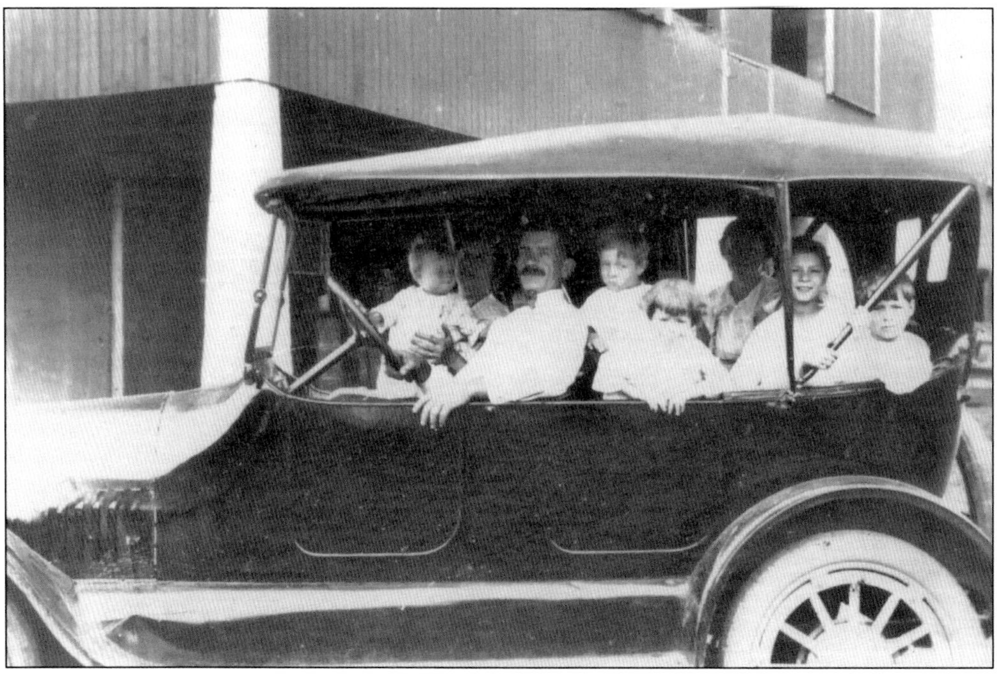

Pictured from left to right are (first row) Robert Balbirer and Anna (Balbirer) McCarty; (second row) Betty Kamena, John Olinick, and Victoria (Balbirer) Damjanits. The group is pausing before enjoying a ride in an old-fashioned glider in 1925. This type of swing was often seen in backyards during the 1920s through the 1950s. It looks like the Balbirer family and friends were trying to see how many people could fit in one. (RMC.)

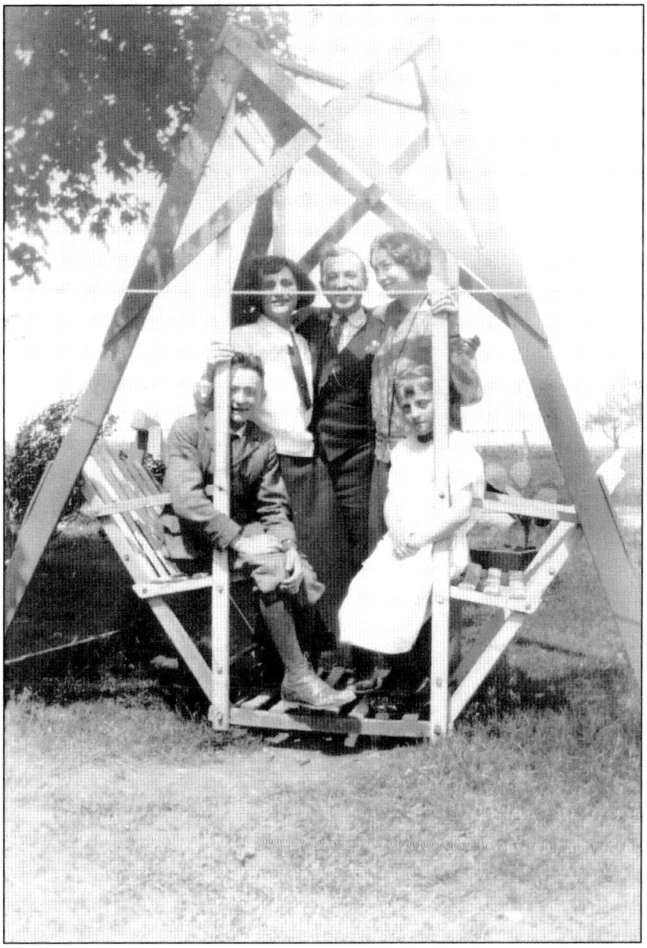

A group of young friends get together at the Tumble Inn, owned by Ottilia and Andrew Balbirer, in 1933. Typical of the antics at the time, they are forming a pyramid. From left to right they are (first row) Lawrence Courtney, Vincent McCarty, Charles McCarty, Robert Balbirer, and Harry Wessner; (second row) Isabel (McCarty) Ebner, Anna (Balbirer) McCarty, Helen (McCarty) Thaler, and Myrtle Courtney. (RMC.)

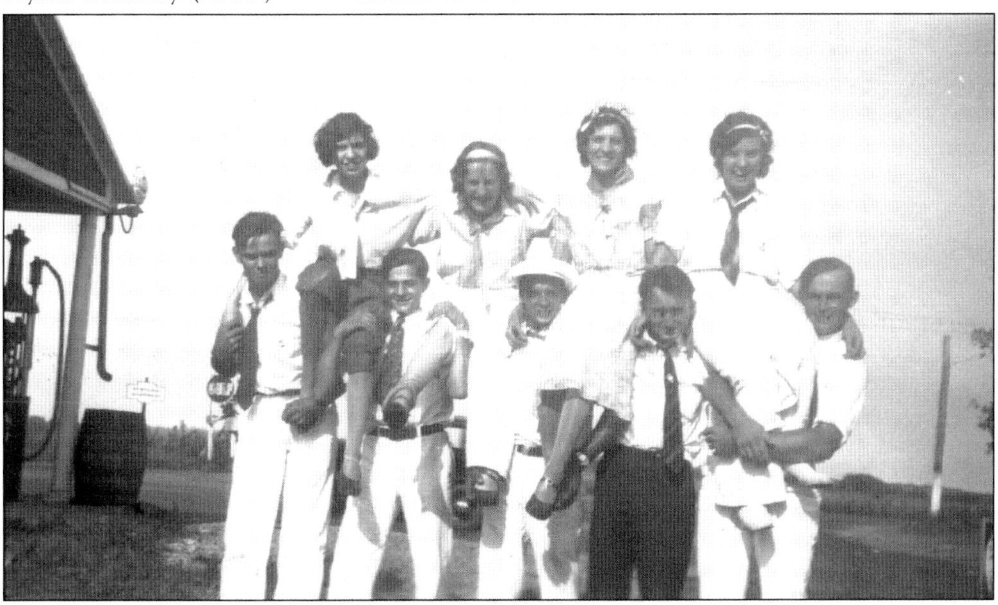

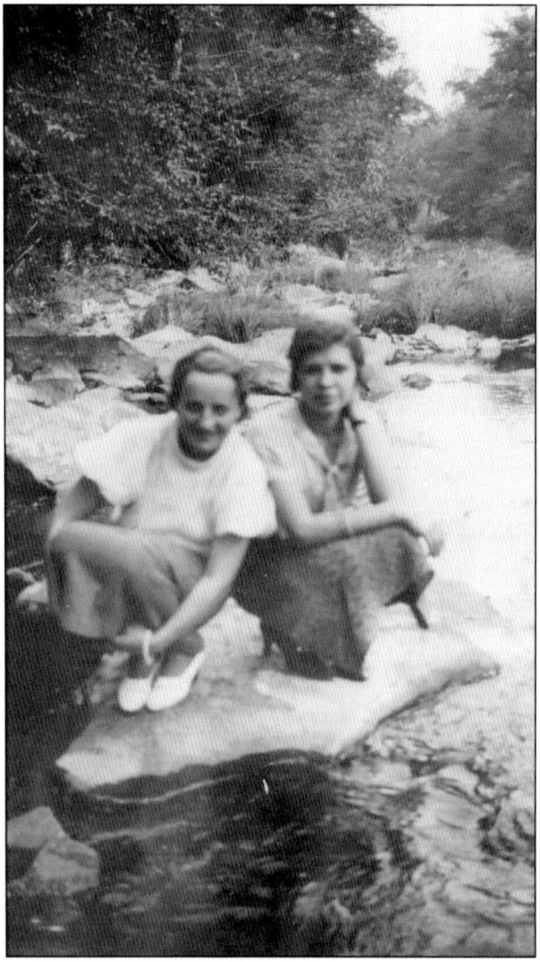

Best friends Anna Balbirer (left) and Isabella (McCarty) Ebner enjoy the cool water of the creek in 1934 by the McCarty homestead on Church Lane. Rosanne McCarty remembers her mother, Anna (Balbirer) McCarty, saying children always made sure to have fun at the creek during weekends since the nuns would not allow them to cross the creek while attending St. John the Baptist school. (RMC.)

Cousins Charles McCarty (left), John Thaler (center), and Robert Balbirer were probably at a family function and decided to get away from the grown-ups and walk down the road. In this 1935 photograph, the three friends are posing on the bank of the creek just behind the old school on Church Lane near the original McCarty home. (RMC.)

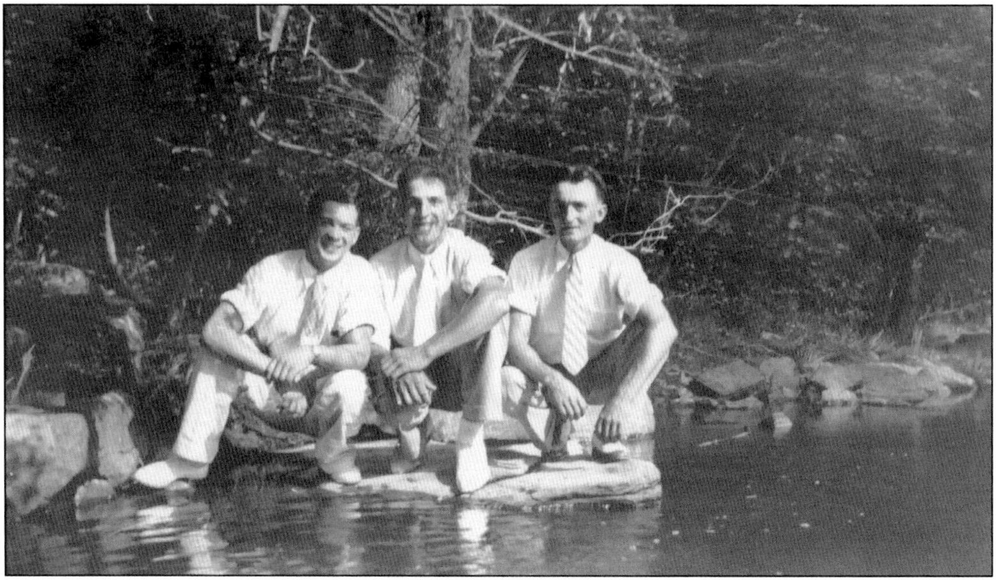

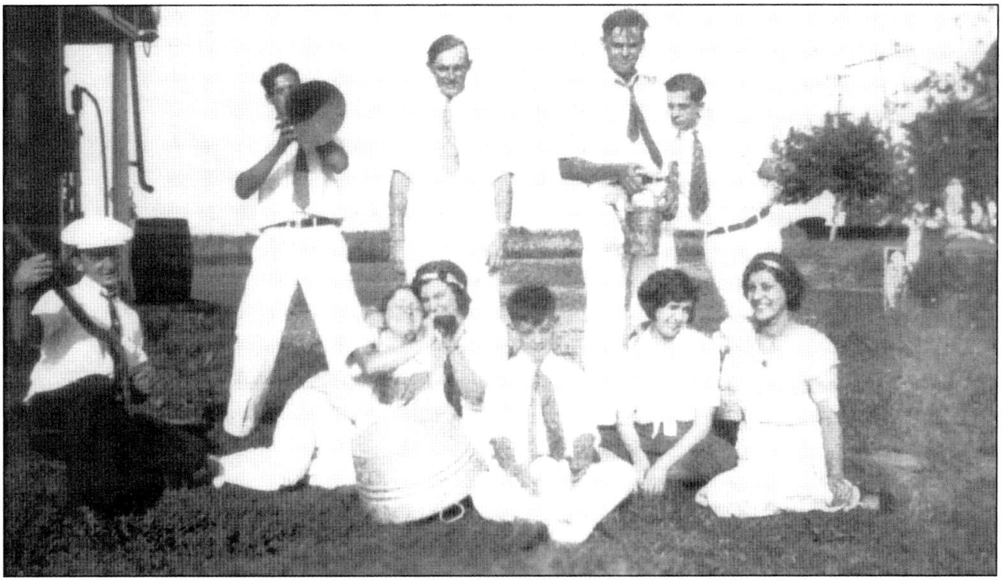

It looks like these young adults are enjoying themselves at Balbirer's Tumble Inn in 1933, a local spot for ice cream and food. Several of them are playing instruments, one is singing into a megaphone, and others are doing impersonations to entertain everyone. From left to right are (first row) Robert Balbirer, Anna (Balbirer) McCarty, Myrtle Courtney, Bernard Courtney, Isabel (McCarty) Ebner, and Helen (McCarty) Thaler; (second row) Charles McCarty, Harry Wessner, Lawrence Courtney, and Vincent McCarty. (RMC.)

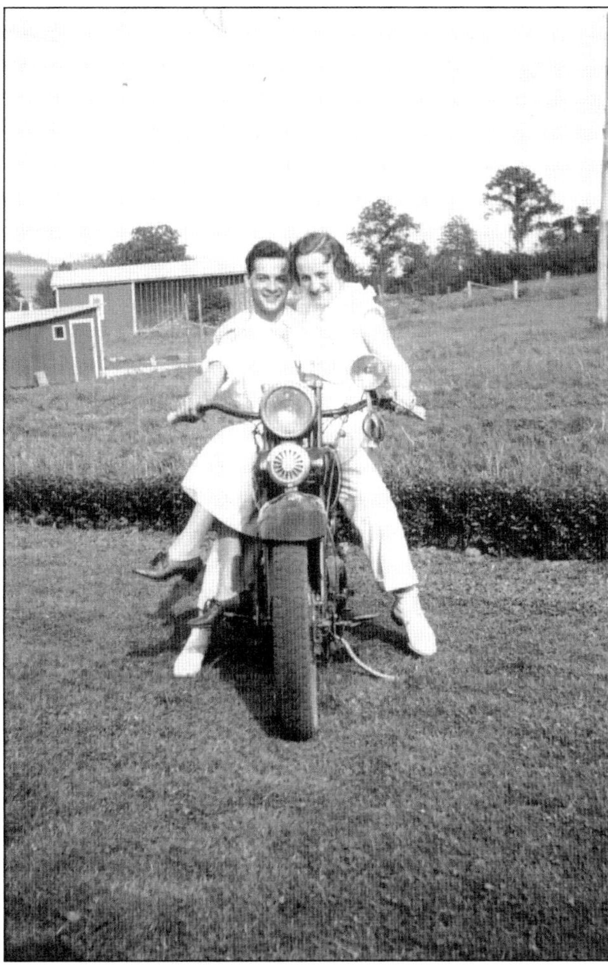

Charles P. McCarty, seen here at age 23, and girlfriend Anna H. Balbirer, age 20, pose for this photograph in July 1935 after taking a ride on his motorcycle. Charles, the oldest son of Roscoe and Mary McCarty, and Anna, the youngest daughter of Ottilia and Andrew Balbirer, met in grammar school. Wanting to get Anna's attention, Charles would stick her pigtails in the inkwell on her desk. They were married in September 1936. (RMC.)

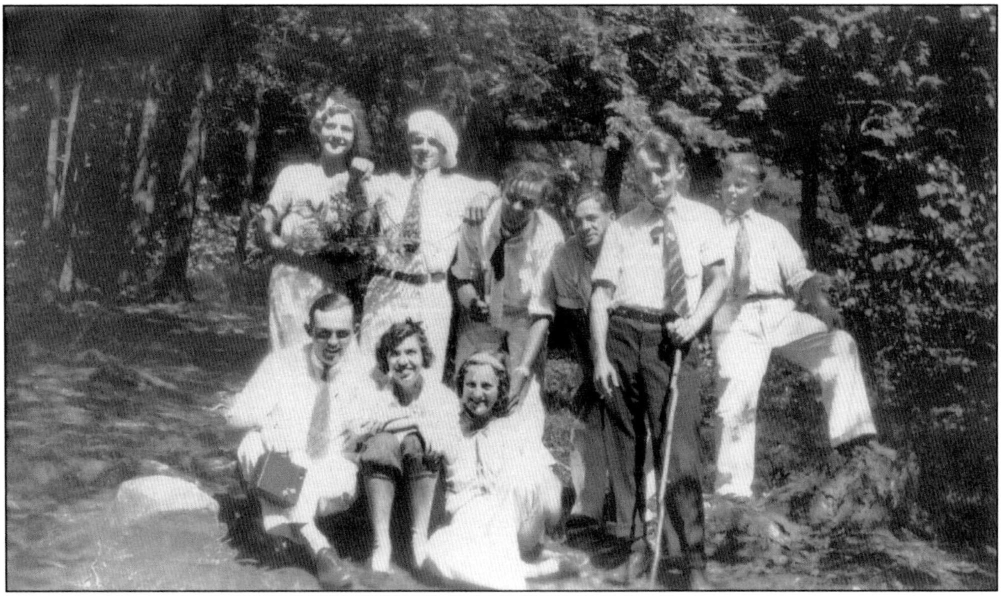

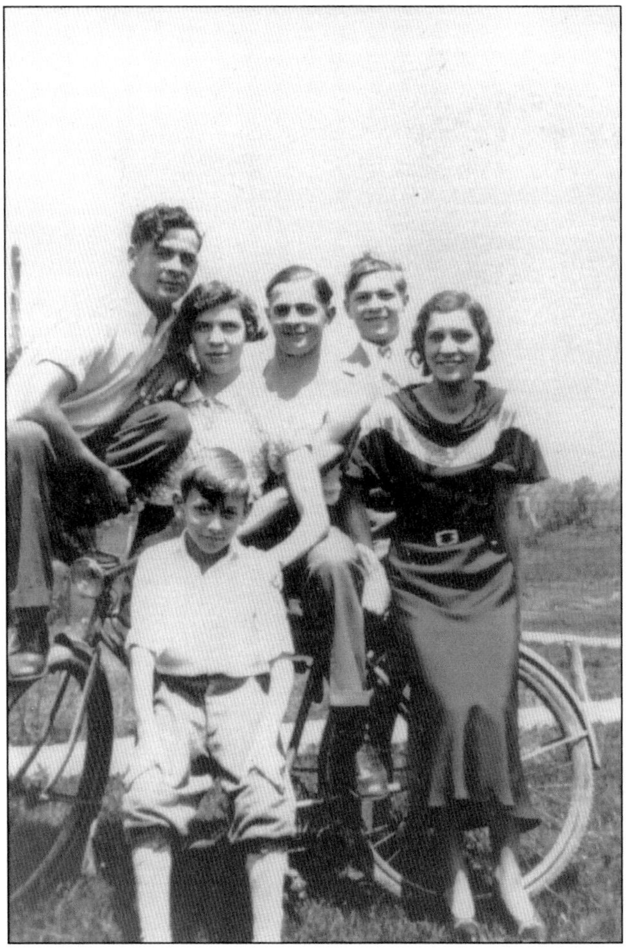

Always ready for something different, this active group climbed to the pinnacle of Top Rock in 1933. After seeing the great panoramic view of the Delaware River along River Road, friends and relatives posed for this photograph. From left to right are (first row) Harry Wessner, Isabel (McCarty) Ebner, Anna (Balbirer) McCarty, and Robert Balbirer; (second row) Helen (McCarty) Thaler, Vincent McCarty, Lawrence Courtney, Charles McCarty, and Bernard Courtney. (RMC.)

Young members of the McCarty family pose for a 1935 photograph using Raymond Haney's bike as a prop. Raymond, son of Russell and Ethel (McCarty) Haney, is in front; the rest are, from left to right, Charles P. McCarty, Isabella (McCarty) Ebner, Vincent McCarty, Herman McCarty, and Helen (McCarty) Thaler. (RMC.)

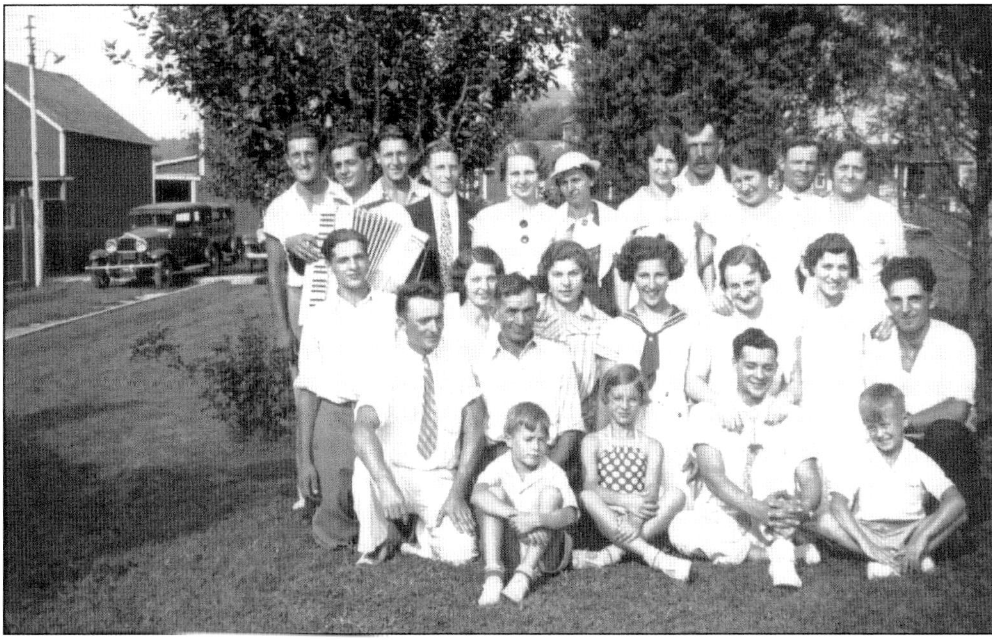

Roscoe and Mary McCarty enjoyed the camaraderie of family, friends, and children Charles, Helen, Vince, and Herman and extended the welcome to their Bucksville farm in July 1935. Vince entertained, playing accordion when visited by youngsters Robert and Theresa Wakely and Joseph Schrader and their parents, along with Robert and Anna Balbirer, Mary, Clara, Anna, and John Thaler, John Biresch, John Zalesak, Simon and Sadie Zellin, and Marian Zellin and husband. (RMC.)

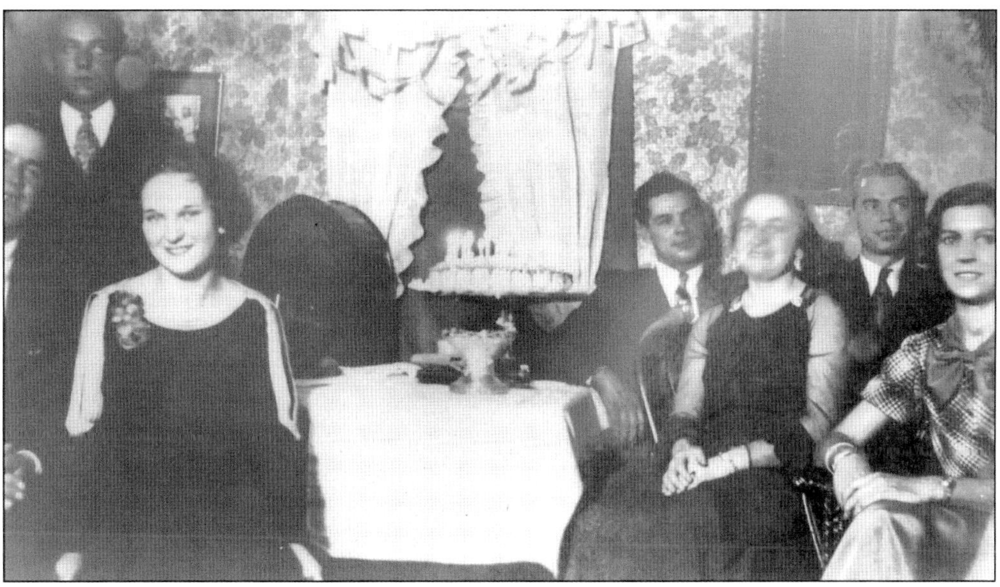

Anna Balbirer celebrated her 21st birthday at this October 6, 1935, party. Some of the friends in attendance are, from left to right, Norman Wessner, Albert Rausch, Anna Schwechtje, Charles McCarty, Anna (Balbirer) McCarty, Fred Lindmeier, and Helen (McCarty) Thaler. Anna, the youngest child of Ottilia and Andrew Balbirer, was the only one born in the United States. She married Charles P. McCarty on September 26, 1936. (RMC.)

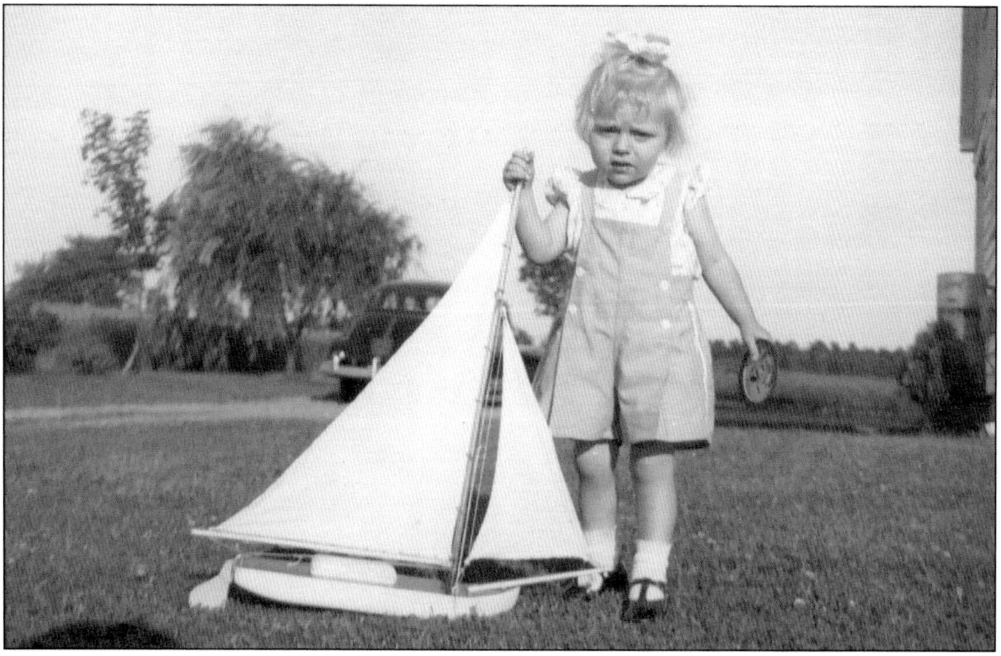

Rosanne M. McCarty, seen here at age 2, the oldest daughter of Charles P. McCarty and Anna (Balbirer) McCarty, is playing with her toys in the family's yard. Holding up her sailboat in spring of 1946, it looks almost as tall as she is. Cute as a button, dressed in bib overall shorts and top with a bow in her hair, she is holding on tight to her favorite toy top in her other hand. (RMC.)

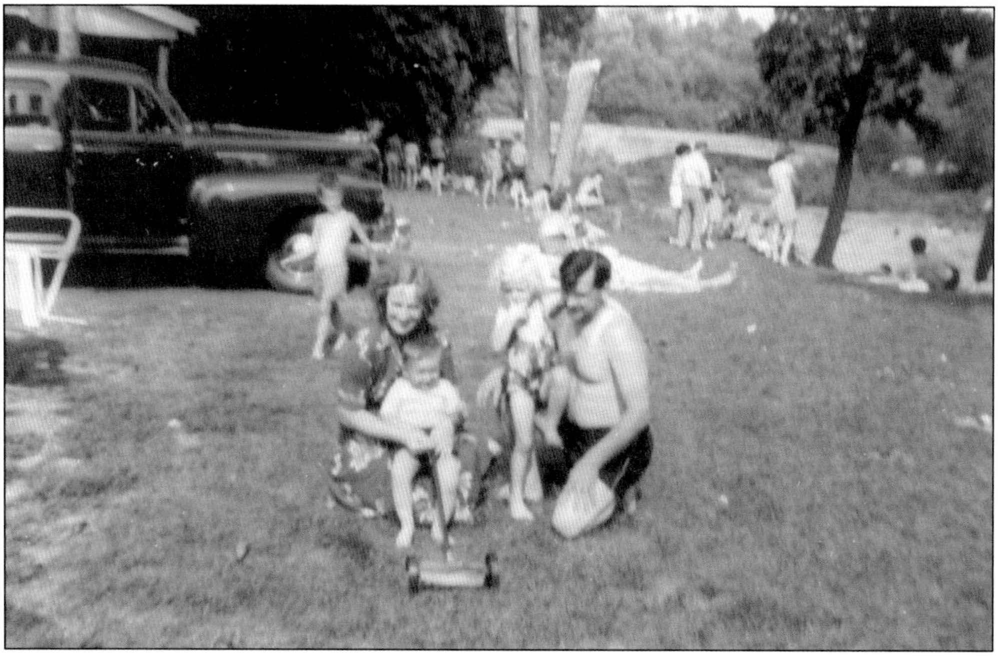

Charles P. McCarty family members are enjoying a summer day by Tohickon Creek in 1948. Posing for a photograph, Anna (Balbirer) McCarty is holding her young son Charles G. on her lap while he is playing with a toy lawn mower. At the same time, Charles P. McCarty balances daughter Rosanne, who also has her eye on the mower, on his knee. (RMC.)

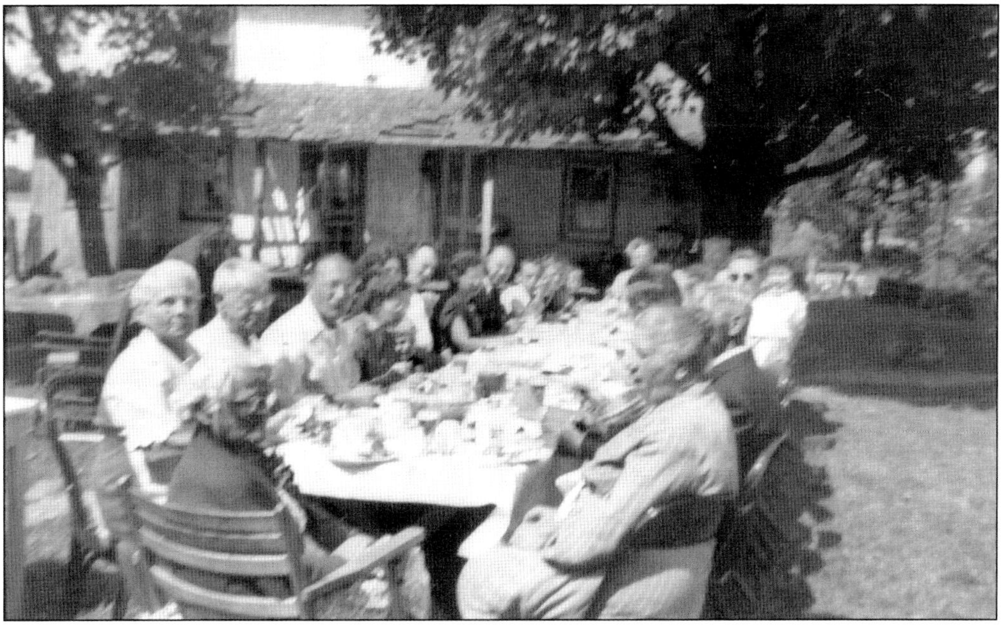

Family members celebrated Ottilia (Loeffelman) Balbirer's 70th birthday in 1949 at the Balbirer residence. Her children and their families attended with many friends. Ottilia, seated at the head of the table, enjoyed this special day with Robert and Mary (Miketta) Balbirer, Arthur and Emma (Balbirer) Bahnck, Andrew and Regina (Balbirer) Snyder Sr., Charles and Anna (Balbirer) McCarty, Joseph and Victoria (Balbirer) Damjanits, and Ann Meyers. (RMC.)

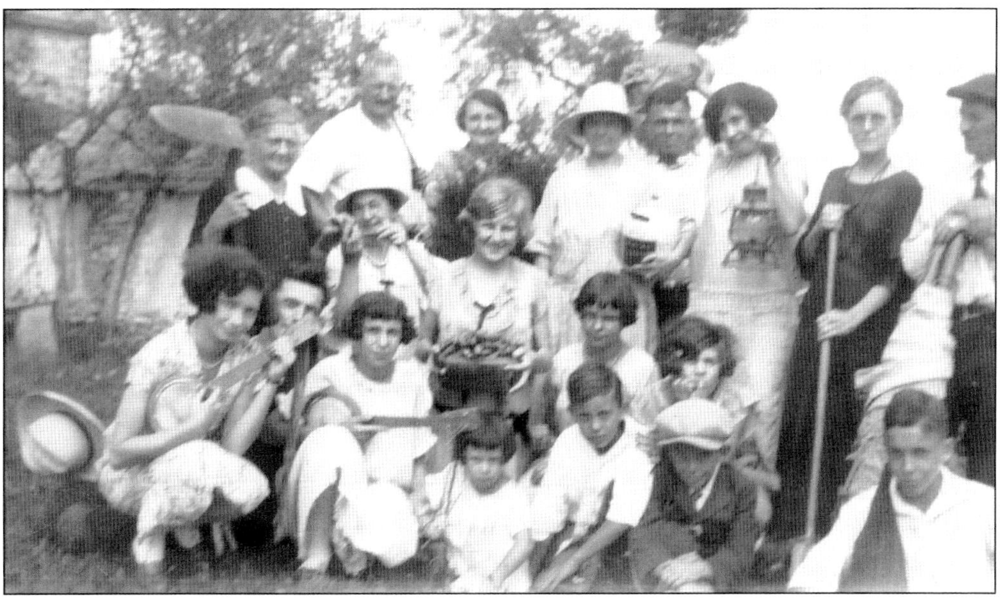

Philip and Bessie Strott and guests sing along as children play ukuleles at the Ferndale farm in 1925. From left to right are (first row) Thelma Matter, unidentified, Helen Romberger, Laverne Romberger, Norman Romberger, Mervin Matter, and Charles Matter; (second row) Mame Schlimm, Lorraine Schlimm, Laura Matter, and Roxie Schlimm; (third row) Amelia Schlimm, Herman Schlimm, Ethel Matter, Bertha Romberger, Herb Matter, Florence Romberger, Bessie Strott, and William Romberger. (CJF.)

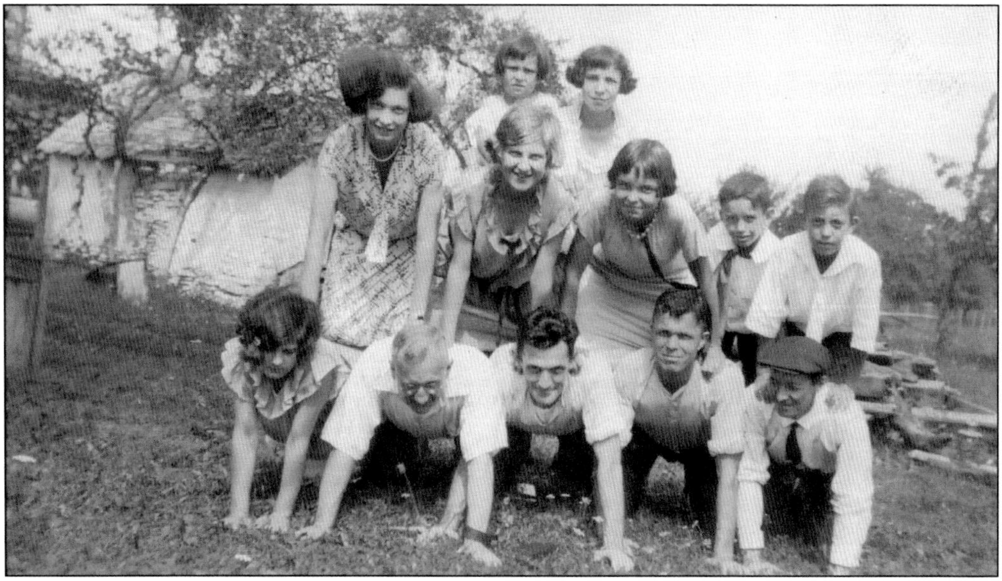

Young Strott farm visitors form a pyramid in 1925, a popular pose for photographs of that era. From left to right are (first row) Roxie Schlimm, Herman Schlimm, unidentified, Herb Matter, and William Romberger; (second row) Thelma Matter, Mervin Matter, Charles Matter, Laverne Romberger, and Helen Romberger; (third row) Laura Matter and Lorraine Schlimm. Charles, seen here at age 15, is now 100 years old and remembers the children sleeping in the barn's hayloft. (CJF.)

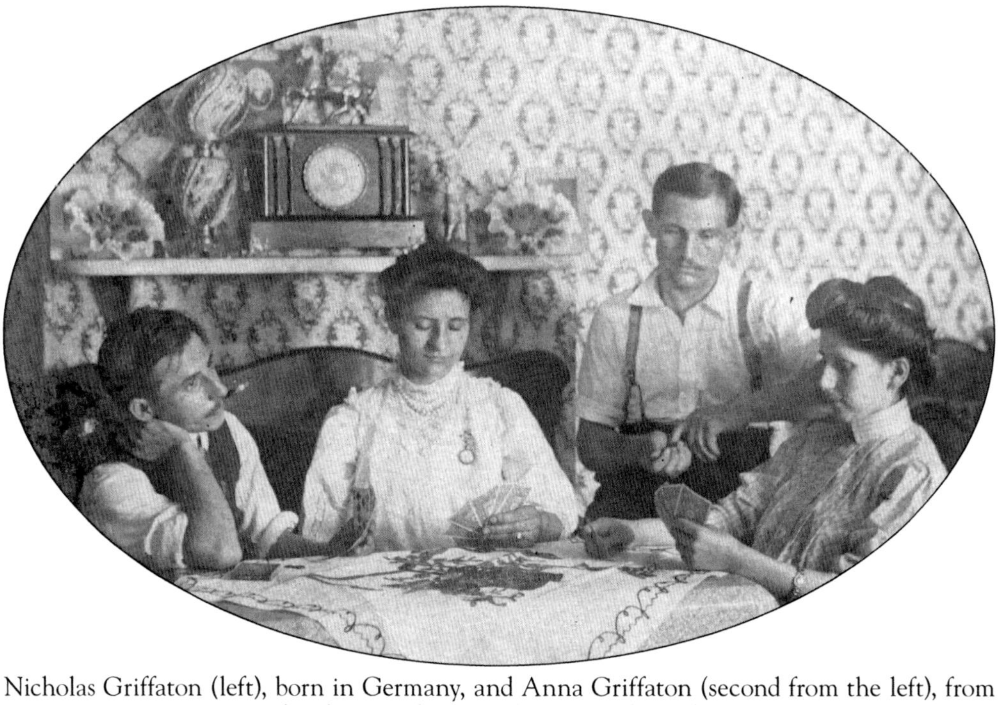

Nicholas Griffaton (left), born in Germany, and Anna Griffaton (second from the left), from Austria-Hungary, emigrated and met in the United States in the early 1900s. This old photograph shows them playing cards with relatives, enjoying a relaxing evening. Nicholas worked as a tailor in Philadelphia and later Doylestown, while Anna owned a candy store in the city. They purchased a Ferndale farm in the 1920s. (CGG.)

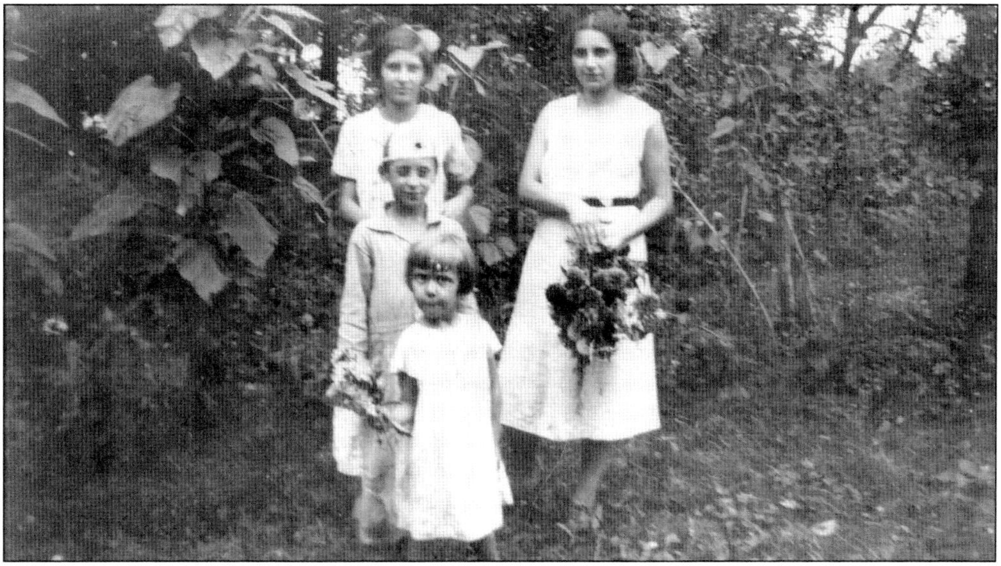

Gathering wildflowers in the fields of their Ferndale farm in the 1920s, four of the Griffaton children pose. From front to back are Ann, Edward, and Joan, with Elizabeth to the right. Walking to the one-room schoolhouse as a child, Elizabeth would bring a variety of the flowers home to her mother. Wild daisies, trailing arbutus, lavender blue hepaticas, Queen Anne's lace, and wild roses blooming in the fencerows were her favorites. (CGG.)

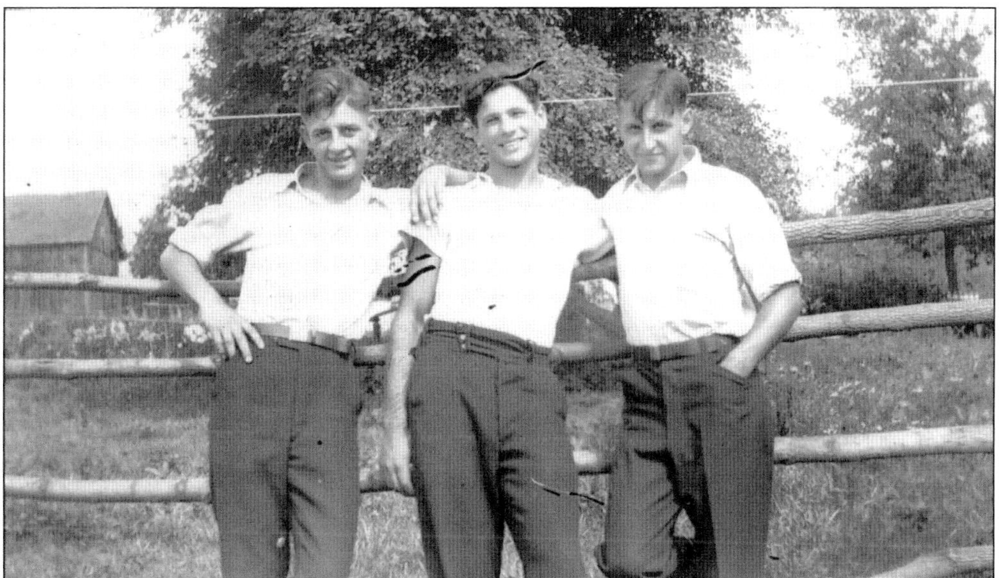

Leaning against a fence, Conrad Mattes is standing between brothers Nicholas Griffaton Jr. and Charles Griffaton on their family farm. These teenagers seem to be contemplating what to do next on a beautiful spring day in 1930. Neighbors in Ferndale, the three friends attended school together. Nicholas would later marry Elizabeth Mattes, Conrad's sister. (CGG.)

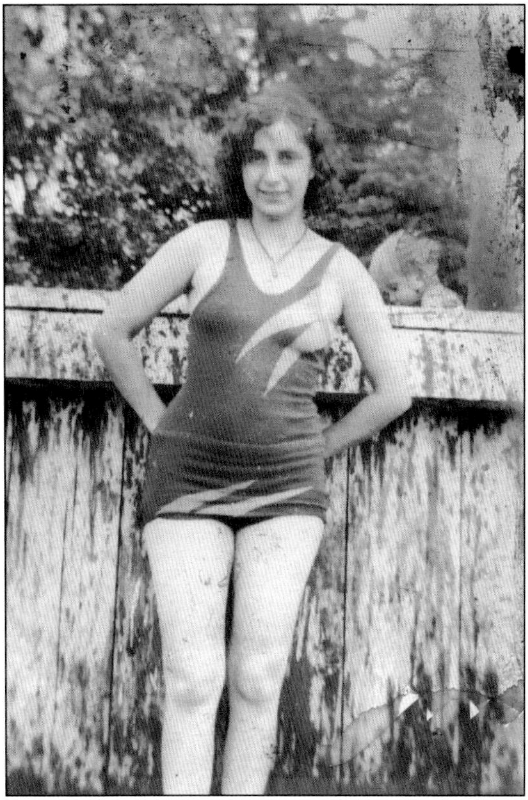

Teenager Elizabeth Griffaton appears in a 1920s-style bathing suit. While working as a cook for a wealthy Philadelphia family, she met Erwin von Hohnen and brought him home to meet her parents. On their first date, he took her to Willow Grove Park to see John Philip Sousa's band. They were married two years later and settled in Philadelphia. (CGG.)

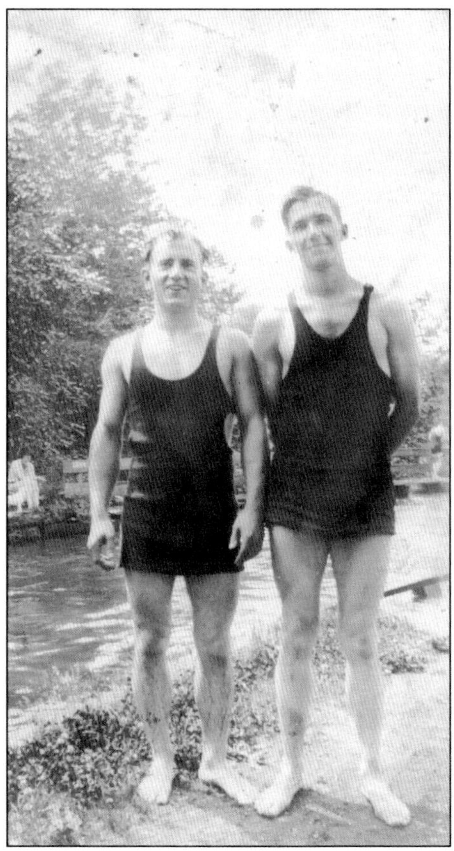

Taking a break from swimming in the Delaware Canal, Erwin von Hohnen (right) and his friend ? Reiber enjoy their visit with the Nicholas Griffaton family in late 1920s. The area was busy with visitors during the summer as seen in this photograph. Two people and their dog are relaxing on the other side of the canal. (CGG.)

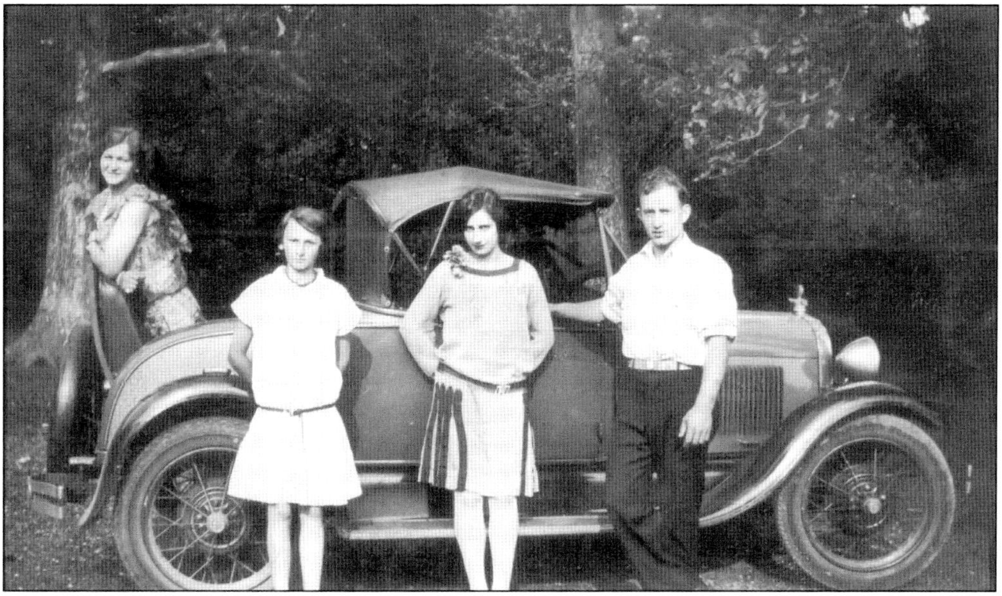

Elizabeth Griffaton's best friend and neighbor, Olga Plickta, sits in the rumble seat while Olga's younger sister, Elizabeth, and ? Reiber pose in front of Reiber's 1929 Ford Model A Roadster. Erwin von Hohnen was most likely the photographer. His friend Reiber drove Elizabeth and Erwin to visit her family in Ferndale. (CGG.)

Sisters Carol (left) and Joan von Hohnen, children of Erwin and Elizabeth Rose (Griffaton) von Hohen, sit on the front lawn of grandparents Nicholas and Anna Griffaton's home in the mid-1940s. They experienced many happy summers there growing up with their young uncles. The Griffaton family was very close and spent special holidays together at the farm. (CGG.)

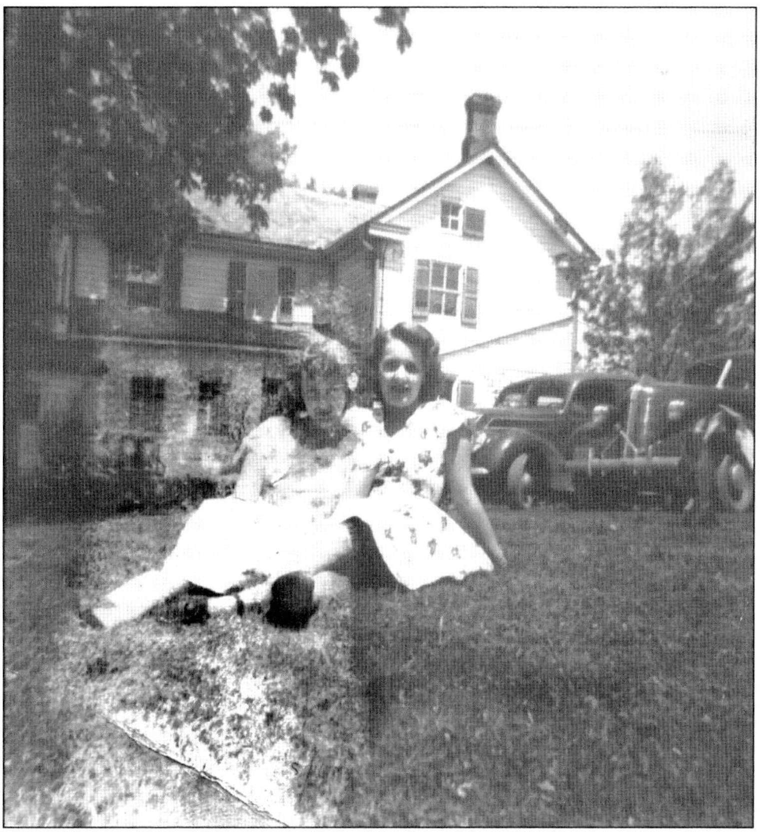

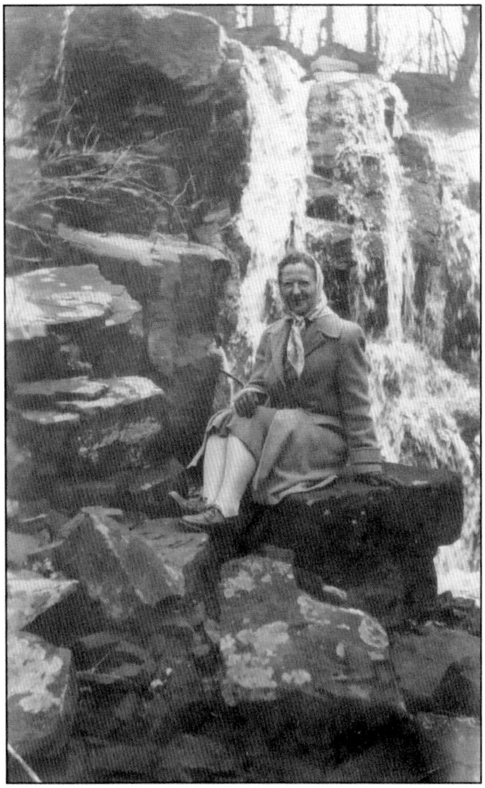

In the spring of 1943, Mabel Foellner sits at the foot of the Nockamixon Falls by Rapp Creek enjoying the peacefulness. The falls are located on state game lands between Marienstein and Beaver Run Roads in the village of Revere. Mabel, a long time township historian, researched and issued *The History of Nockamixon Township*, excluding the Kintnersville area, for the 1976 bicentennial. (NHS.)

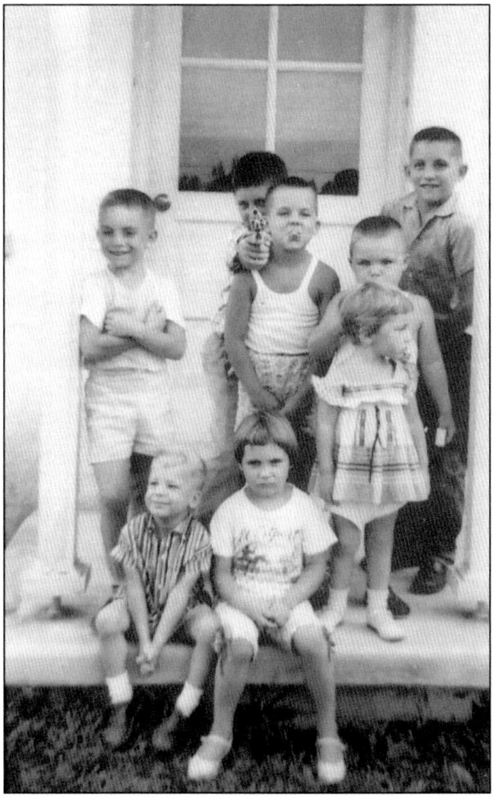

Pictured from left to right are (front) Dennis Trouts and Sally Zheltonoga; (middle) John Trouts, Michael Trouts, and Noreen Pursell; (back) Rodney Pursell, Thomas Durborow, and James Zheltonoga. They are patiently posing for a 1962 photograph. During a busy day playing at Robert and Margaret Trouts home, this active group tried to stand and sit still on the porch while this picture was taken. Typical children, one is sticking his tongue out and another shooting a toy cap pistol at the photographer. (STZ.)

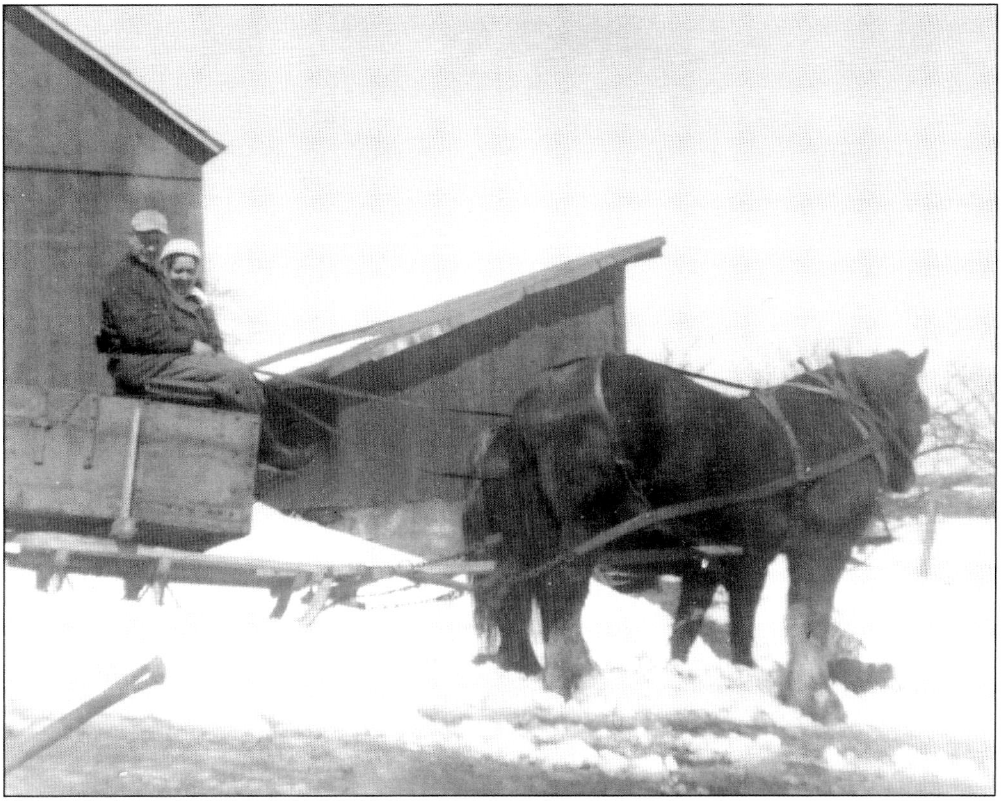

Clarence Berger and wife Mabel (Sames) Berger take their horse-drawn sleigh out of the barn during the winter of 1957. After hitching their two horses to the sleigh, they were ready to enjoy a ride in the Nockamixon countryside with the Harold Berger family. The correct amount of snow was on the ground, so the sleigh blades would glide smoothly over the snow, thus giving an enjoyable ride. (CMB.)

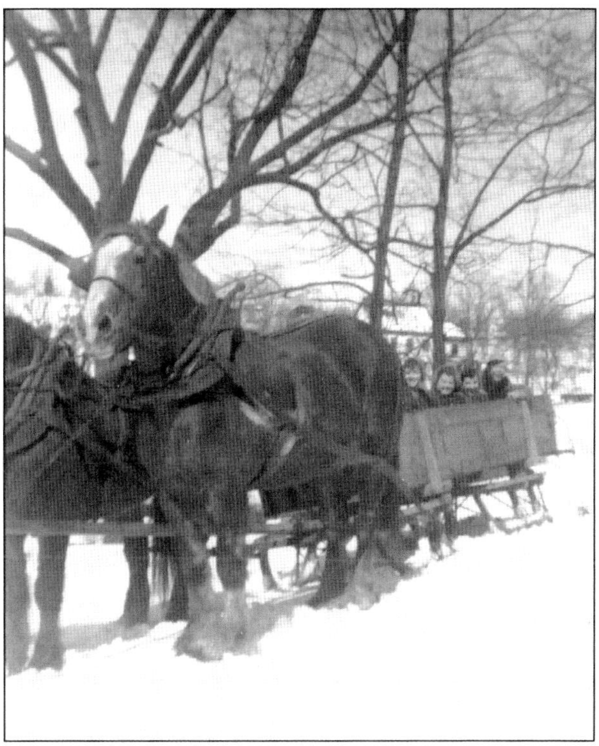

Clarence Berger told his cousin Harold's family that it was a perfect day for a sleigh ride. If they wanted to go along, it had to be that day since the right amount of snow was on the ground; and it might begin to melt in the next day or two. Harold Berger took the photograph of his family—Marie, Arlene, Janette, Jean, and Meryl—bundled up and ready to enjoy the invigorating winter ride. (CMB.)

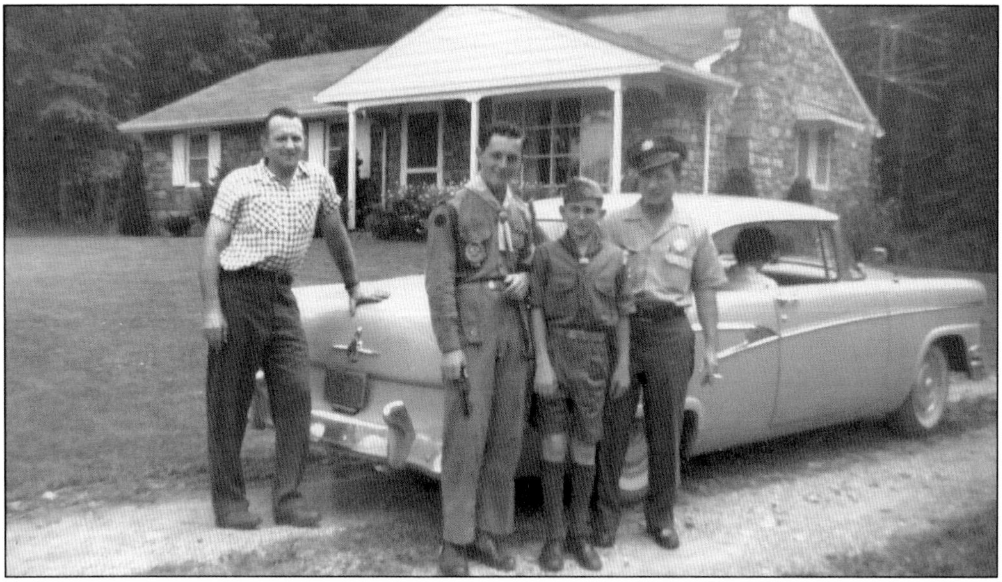

Boy Scout Troop No. 27 members and their parents meet at scoutmaster Fred Fischer's home on Park Road East in Bucksville in August 1961. From left to right are Alex (Babe) Zheltonoga, Benjamin Naska, James Zheltonoga, and Frank Naska. The scouts will be off soon for Camp Ockanickon in Tinicum to take part in the many activities there. (BNB.)

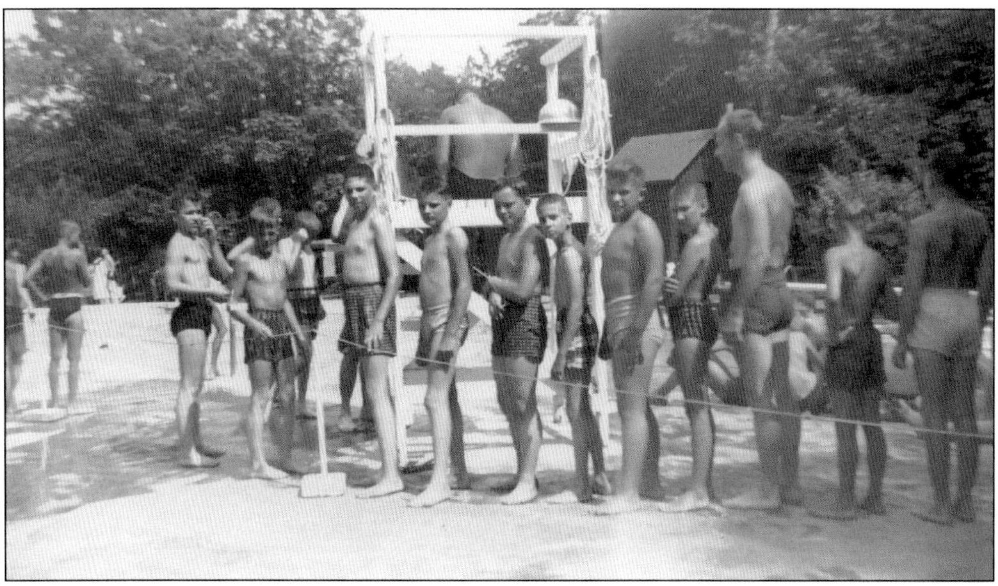

Nockamixon Boy Scouts line up for swimming tests held at Camp Ockanickon in August 1958, along with other participants. Troop members anxiously awaiting their turn to participate are, from left to right, James Eccher, Kurt Nicholas, Lee Freeh, Neil White, Benjamin Naska, William Bean, Darryl Whitman, Ronnie Houseworth, and Donald Ward, along with scoutmaster Fred Fischer. (BNB.)

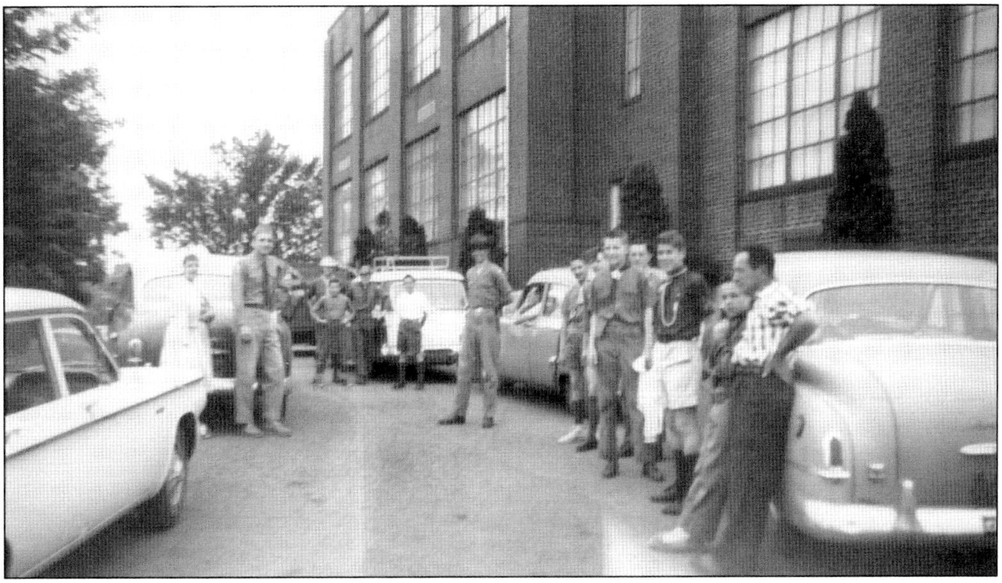

Cars line up in front of the Nockamixon Consolidated School in Revere. The Boy Scouts and their families meet before caravanning to Quakertown for Camparree in July 1961. From left to right are scoutmaster Fred Fischer, Gerald Miller, ? Jesiolowski, Lee Freeh, an Australian exchange student, Ronald Houseworth, Benjamin Naska, John Westbrook, Charles Freeh, and committee member Frank Naska. (BNB.)

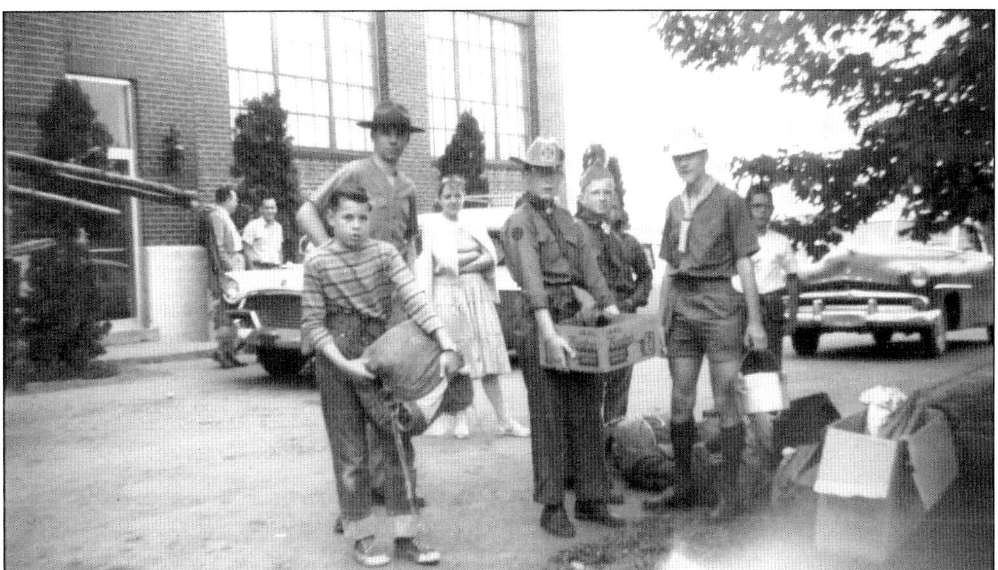

Other scout troop members are seen with loaded boxes and bags, waiting impatiently to leave for Camparree in Quakertown in the summer of 1961. It looks like the question they kept asking each other was, "Do you think we brought everything we need?" Ready to go are, from left to right, scouts ? Jesiolowski, Lee Freeh, Eric Teichman, and Gerald Miller. (BNB.)

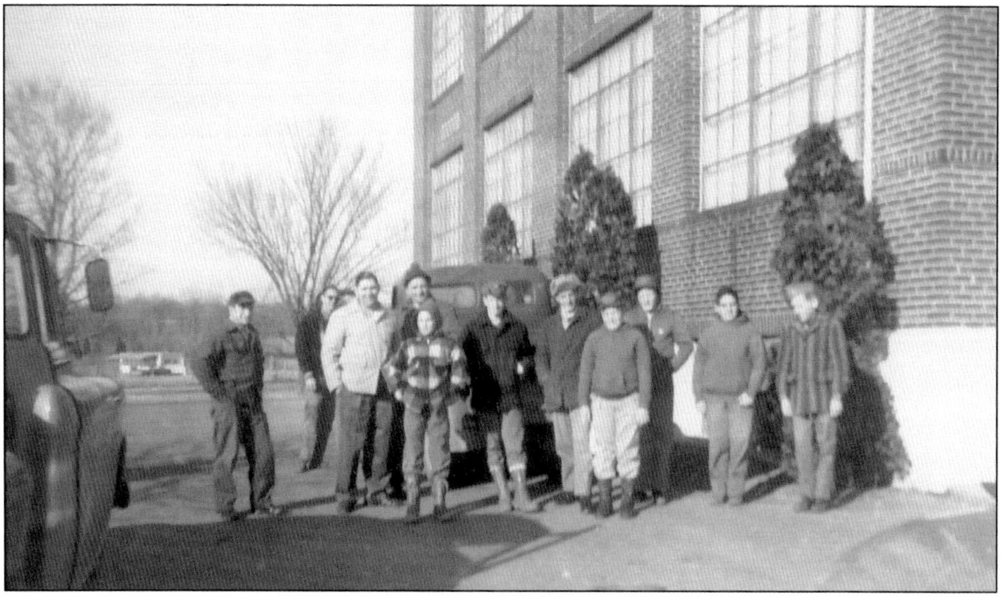

This March 1962 photograph shows everyone dressed warmly as they meet at Nockamixon School. Boy Scout Troop No. 27 scouts and parents are off for the weekend. From left to right are Frank Naska, John Westbrook, Harmon Wright Sr., Alex "Babe" Zheltonoga, James Zheltonoga, Thomas Jesiolowski, Benjamin Naska, Harmon Wright Jr., scoutmaster Fred Fischer, James Fischer, Walter Gaibler, and John Schmidt. (BNB.)

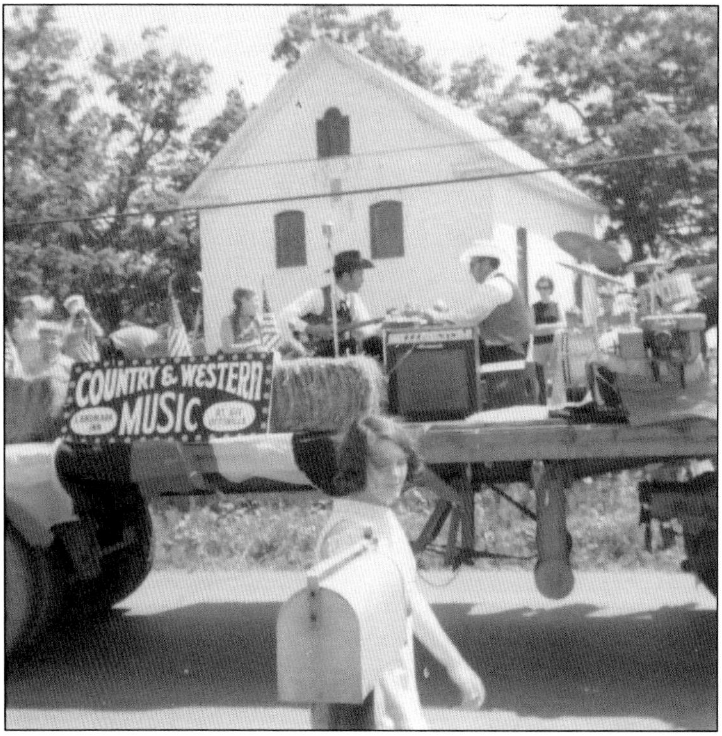

R. Woolston and Edith Rapp, owners of the Landmark Inn, participate in the 1970 Memorial Day parade with their float traveling from St. Luke's United Church of Christ in Ottsville to the Ferndale Inn. Friends and relatives enjoyed riding on the float. Tommy Sinkowski's flatbed truck provided the transportation, while Ray Allen and Gordon Botsford entertained with country and western music as Edie Rapp sang. (ERR.)

Edith and R. Woolston Rapp owned the Landmark Inn on Easton Road from 1969 to 1978. The hotel was very busy during that time with Nockamixon State Park being built on Mountain View Road. Workers took lodging and ate their meals at the hotel from Monday through Thursday each week. The Rapps enjoyed meeting the workers and listening to their interesting stories. (ERR.)

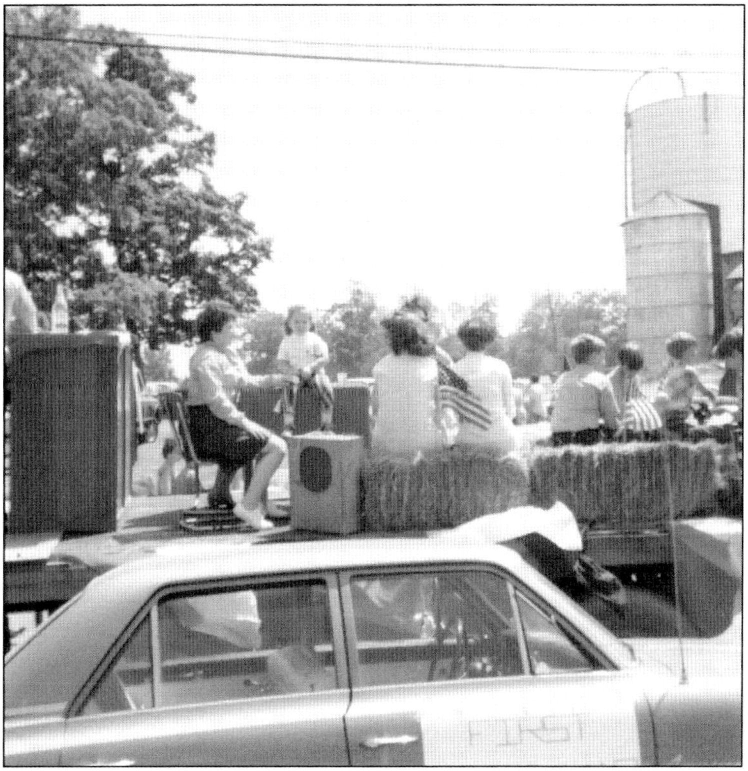

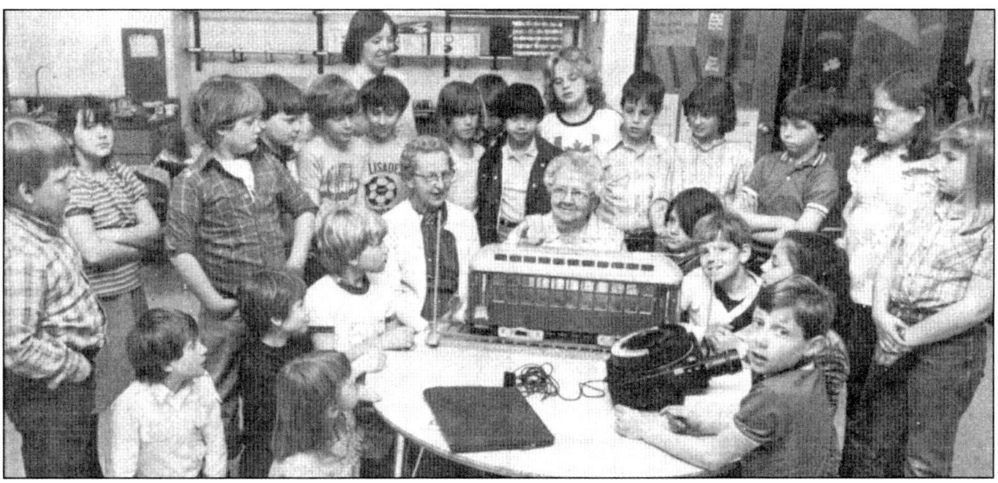

Two senior citizens, Mabel Foellner (left) of Ferndale and Emma Landis of Pipersville, display a model of a trolley made by the late Roy Fair of Ferndale. He was a conductor on the Doylestown to Easton trolley that once ran through Nockamixon Township. The women, members of Eastern Upper Bucks Seniors, were attempting to bring history alive for Durham Nockamixon Elementary School students in 1982. (NHS.)

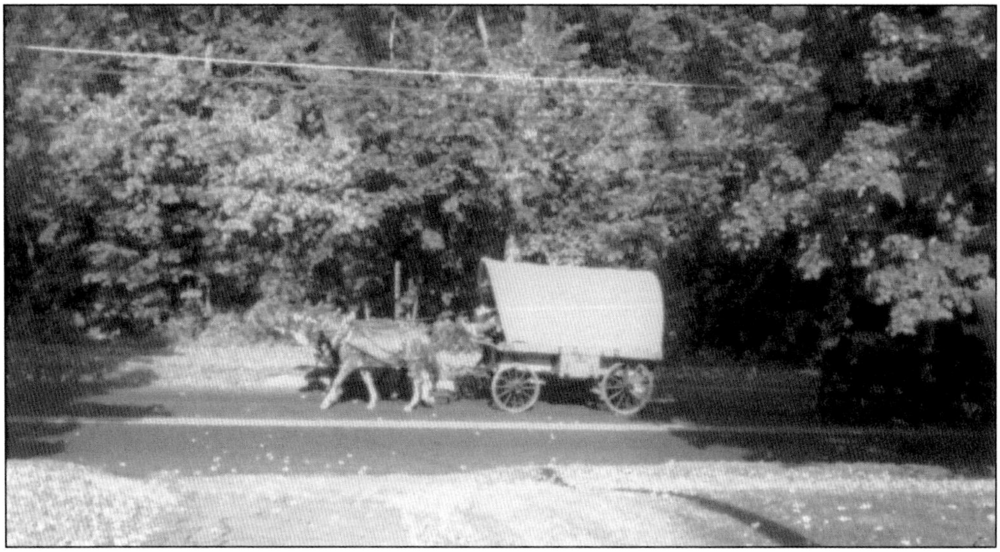

More than 25 Conestoga wagons from the Bicentennial Wagon Train Pilgrimage traveled down Route 611 in Kintnersville in early July 1976. The group was on their way to Valley Forge to celebrate the bicentennial, joining other wagons carrying close to 2,000 persons from all 50 states. Seven separate caravans of official states' wagons and modern pioneering families from rural America were participating in this historic event. (MRW.)

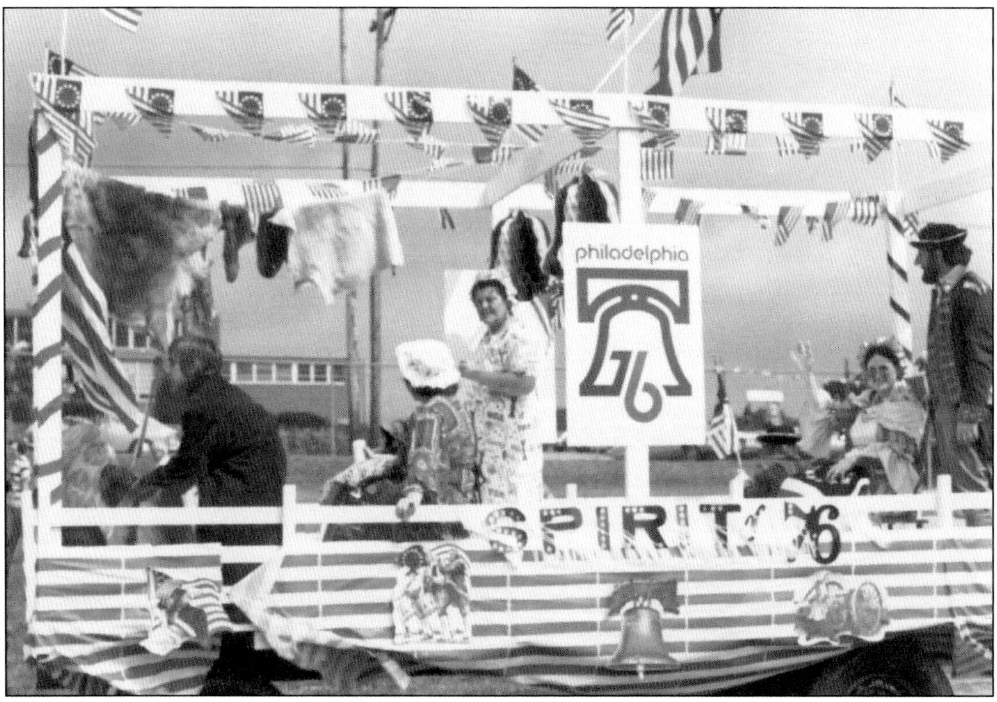

Many Nockamixon residents participated in the Spirit of 76 bicentennial celebration. About 500 people watched the June 19 parade that started at St. John's School and proceeded to Palisades High School athletic field with marchers, floats, and bands. Farm tractors pulled decorated hay wagons made into bicentennial floats. From left to right, residents Michael Olimpo, Julia Bizon, Julia Naska, and Barbara and Benjamin Naska ride in this Spirit of 76 float. (BNB.)

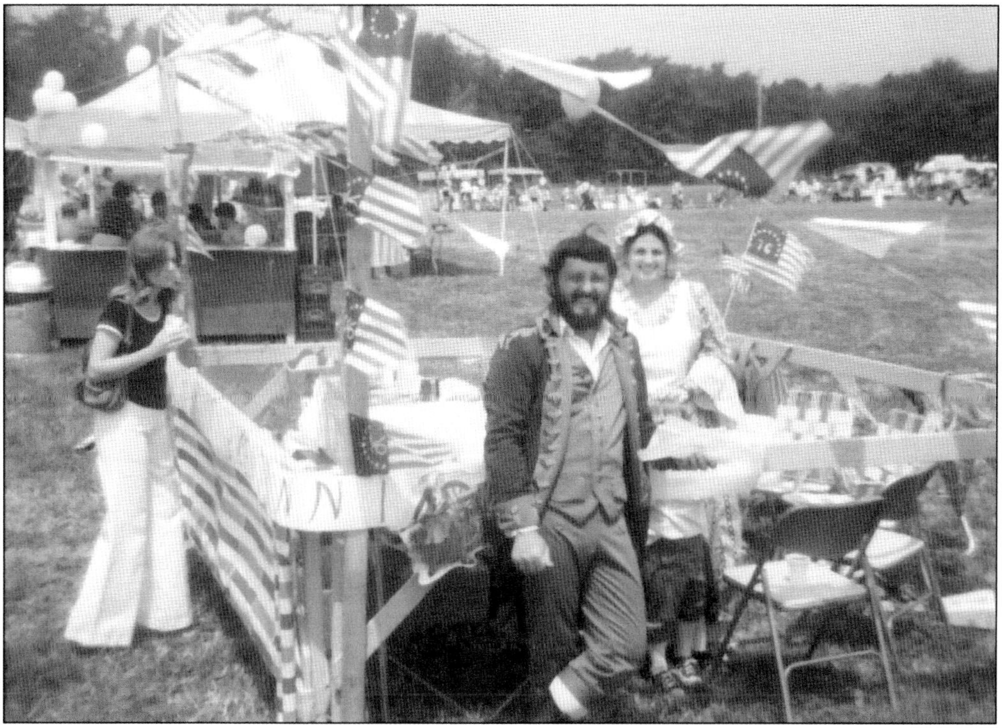

The bicentennial fair, held after the parade, provided fun and games, special events, exhibits, displays, arts and crafts, and refreshments. Barbara and Benjamin Naska are manning a booth. Residents, churches, and community organizations participated, and Ferndale resident Mabel Foellner presented her book, *The History of Nockamixon Township*. The Bucks County Rifleman of Pennsylvania Militia staged a demonstration to show how soldiers in 1776 participated in a skirmish. (BNB.)

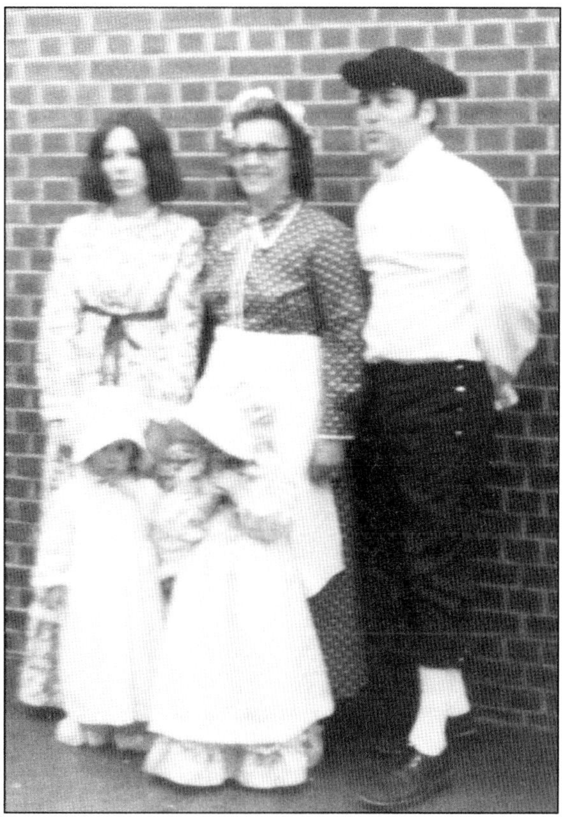

Nockamixon residents were encouraged to dress in period costume for bicentennial activities. Many people in attendance made their own era clothing, which they enjoyed wearing. Dressed as Ben Franklin for a special bicentennial Memorial Day service, Palisades High School assistant principal Thomas Free has a family portrait taken with wife Joan (Custer) Free, their two young daughters, and Evelyn Custer, Joan's mother. (BNB.)

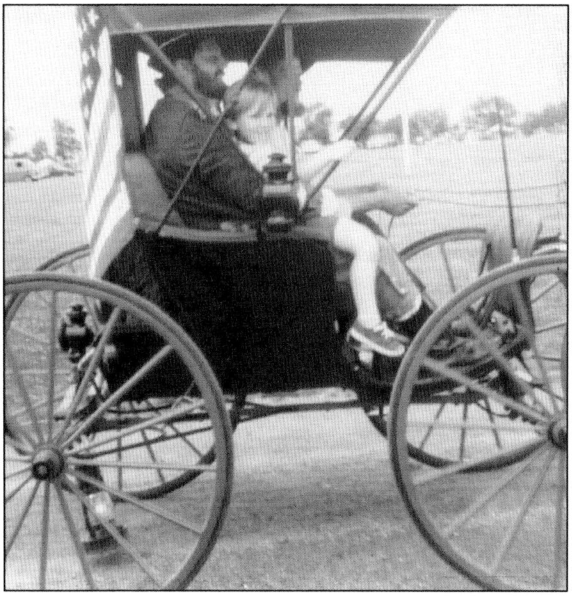

A local resident provided rides in his antique open carriage during the 1976 bicentennial celebration, which provided a special moment for those in attendance. Going back in time, Benjamin and Barbara Naska enjoy an old fashioned horse-and-buggy ride with their young son Benjamin Jr. before the day's festivities. (BNB.)

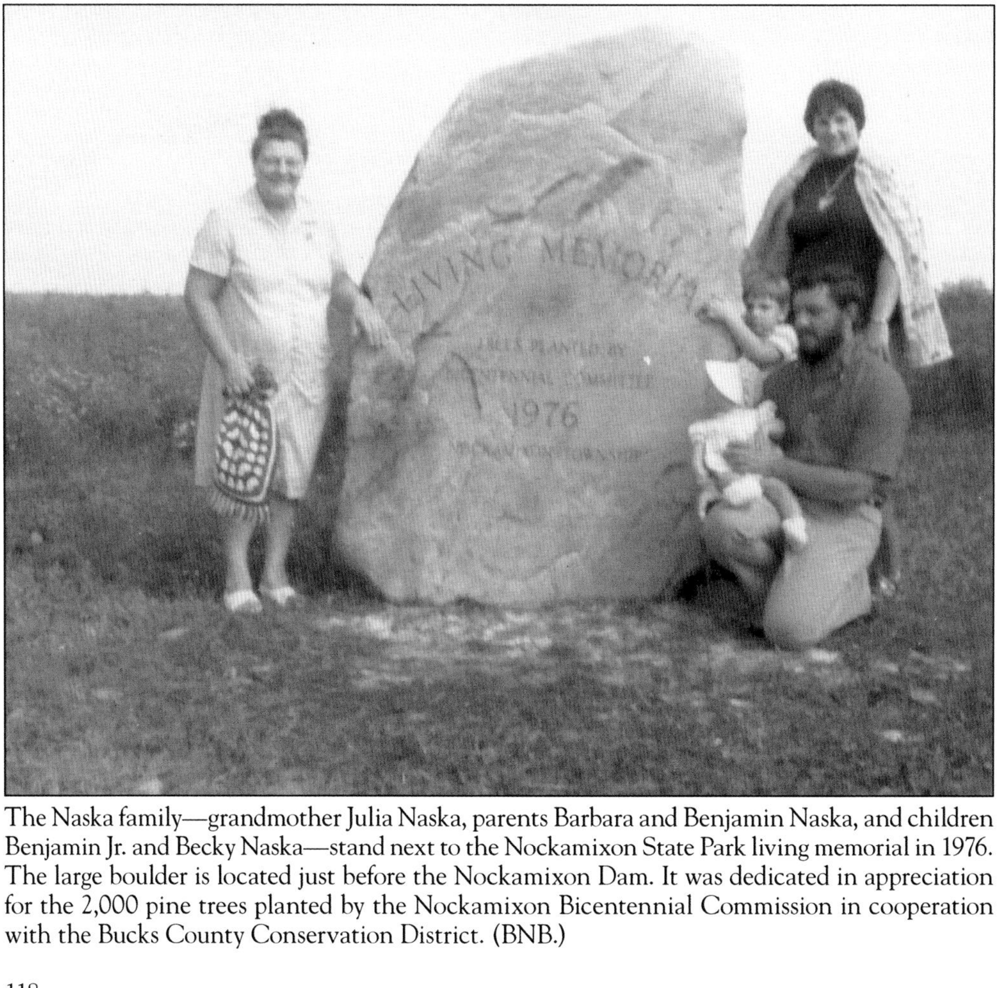

The Naska family—grandmother Julia Naska, parents Barbara and Benjamin Naska, and children Benjamin Jr. and Becky Naska—stand next to the Nockamixon State Park living memorial in 1976. The large boulder is located just before the Nockamixon Dam. It was dedicated in appreciation for the 2,000 pine trees planted by the Nockamixon Bicentennial Commission in cooperation with the Bucks County Conservation District. (BNB.)

Five

Service to Our Country

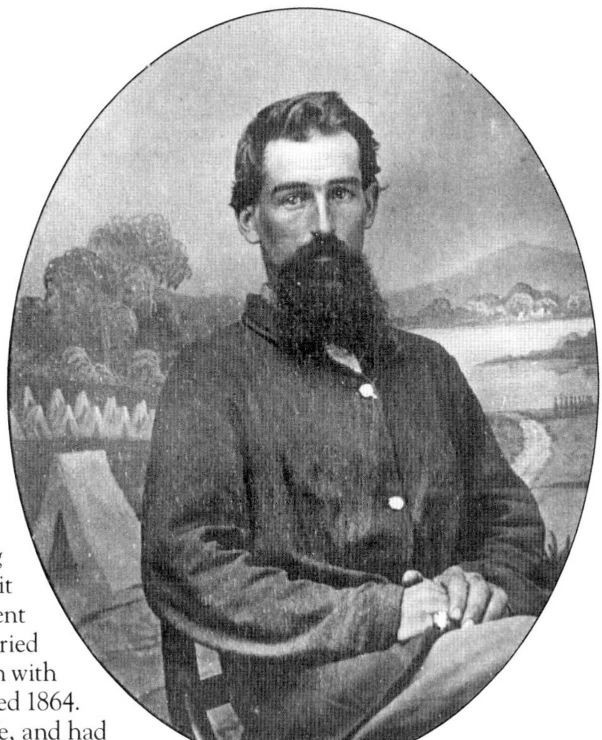

Born in 1834, Franklin D. Trauger of Kintnersville served in the 174th Regiment, Pennsylvania Volunteers, Company F, during the Civil War, from November 1, 1862, until company mustered out on August 7, 1863. Wearing an infantry sack coat, the formal portrait mural depicts the Sibley tent encampment and marching regiment. Franklin, married twice, died in 1920. He had five children with wife Catherine (Rufe) Trauger, who died 1864. Later, he married her sister, Mary Rufe, and had 10 children. (CLK.)

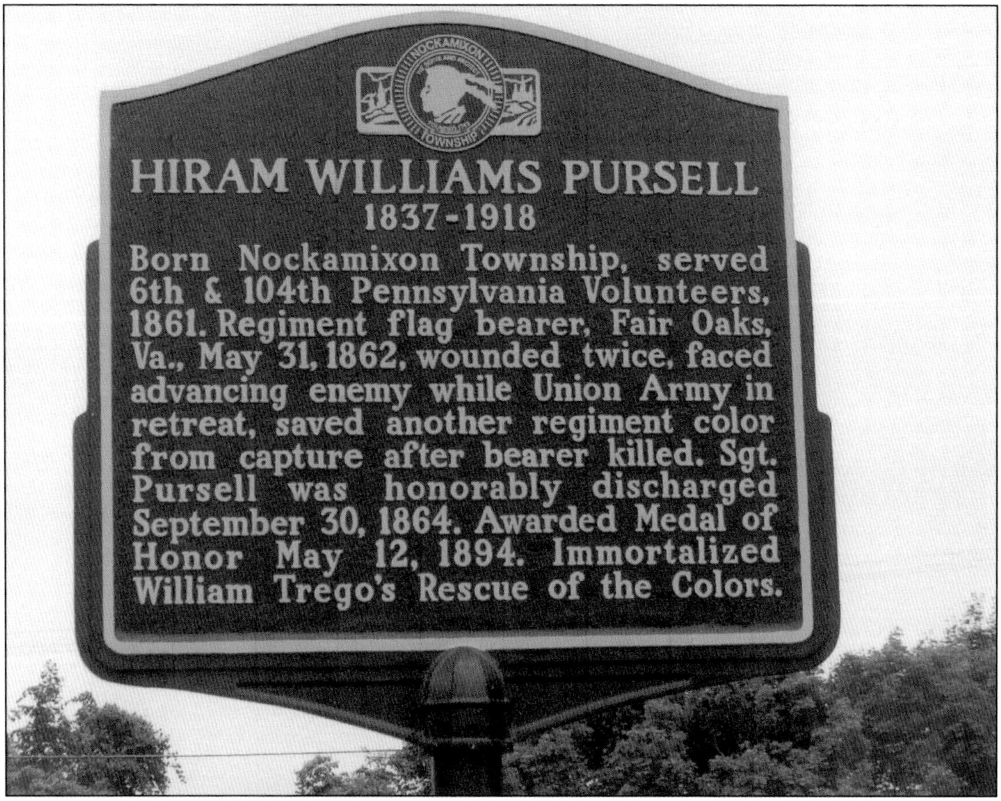

Hiram Williams Pursell was born in 1837 in Nockamixon Township. A canal boatman, he went on to serve in both the 6th and 104th Pennsylvania Volunteers. As a regiment flag bearer in the Civil War battle at Fair Oaks, Virginia, on May 31, 1862, he was wounded twice. When the Union Army was in retreat, Hiram faced the advancing enemy. He saved another regiment color from capture after the bearer was killed, and Sgt. Pursell was awarded the Medal of Honor in May 1894. Pursell died in 1918. A Nockamixon Historical Society marker was dedicated in April 2007 at the Veterans Memorial Park in Revere. (NHS.)

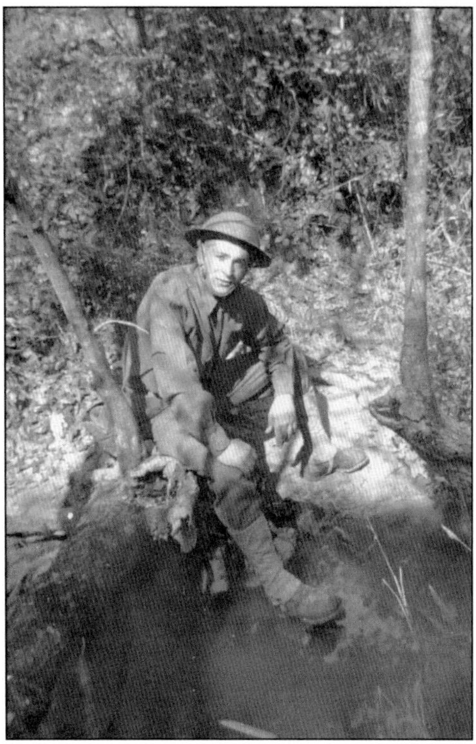

Herman McCarty, the youngest son of Roscoe and Mary (Fleck) McCarty of Bucksville, takes a break from US Army military training on May 5, 1941, prior to going overseas during World War II. He served in the 2nd Armored Division at Normandy, at the Battle of the Bulge, and the long campaign across Africa under Gen. George S. Patton. Returning home, Herman married Helen Somp in November 1945. (RMC.)

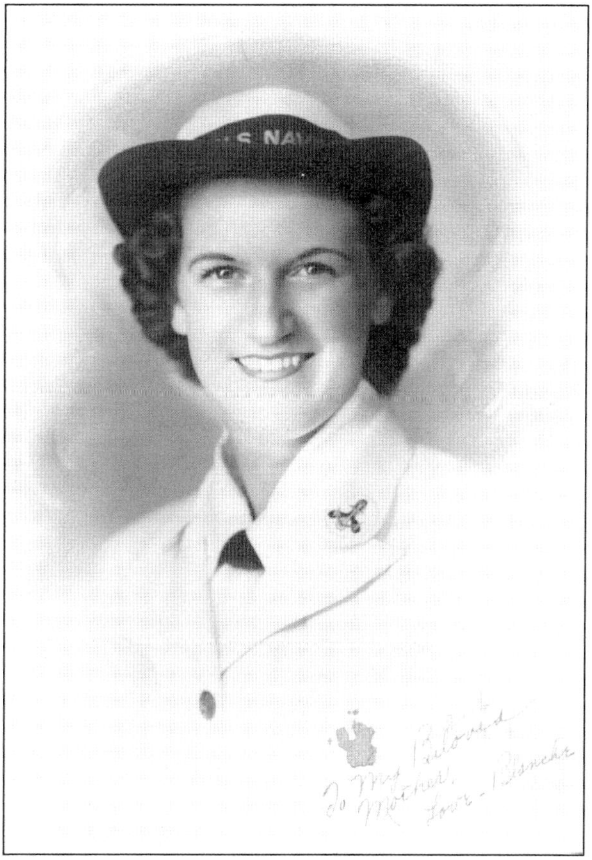

Blanche (Bartman) Wehrung of Ferndale served in naval aviation during World War II, from 1943 to 1945. One of two waves among a 50-member inspection department for radio radar repair at Alameda, California Naval Air Station, she made in-flight checks on radar sets that had been repaired for carrier-based Navy planes. Blanche was put in communications when they were short-handed. She worked on planes and would fly them to check out instruments. (BBW.)

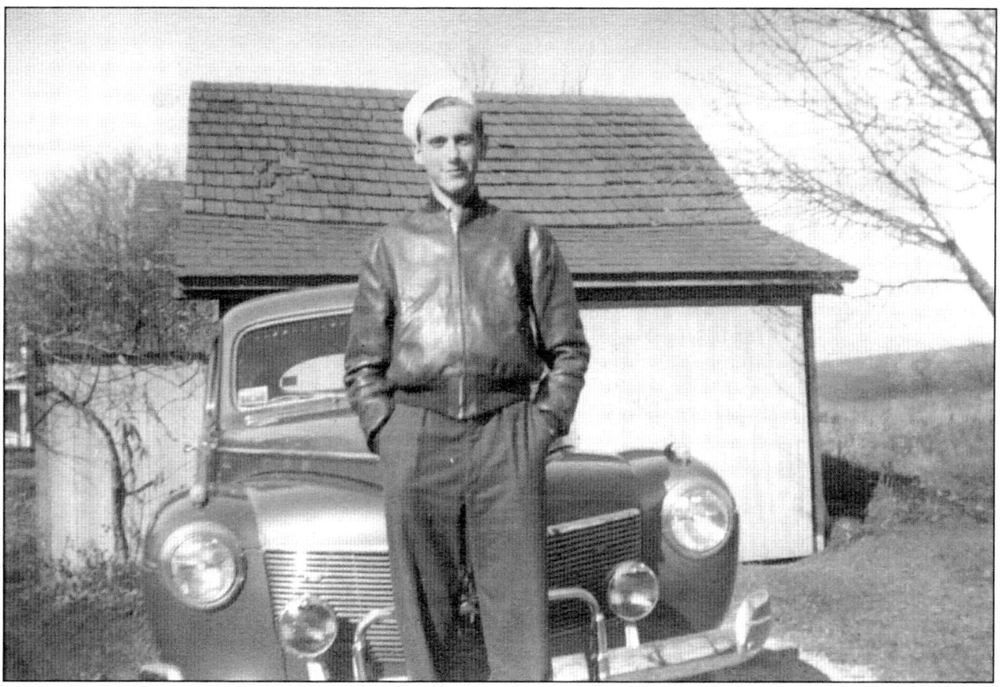

Prior to entering the military in 1942, Lloyd Keller of Ferndale is pictured with his 1941 Mercury, which was a rare sight due to the wartime production halt. Wearing a sailor hat and leather jacket, Lloyd served with 786th Tank Battalion attached to the Army 99th Infantry Division in World War II. Discharged in 1945, he returned to Keller Glove Factory, working there for a total of 27 years. (LHK.)

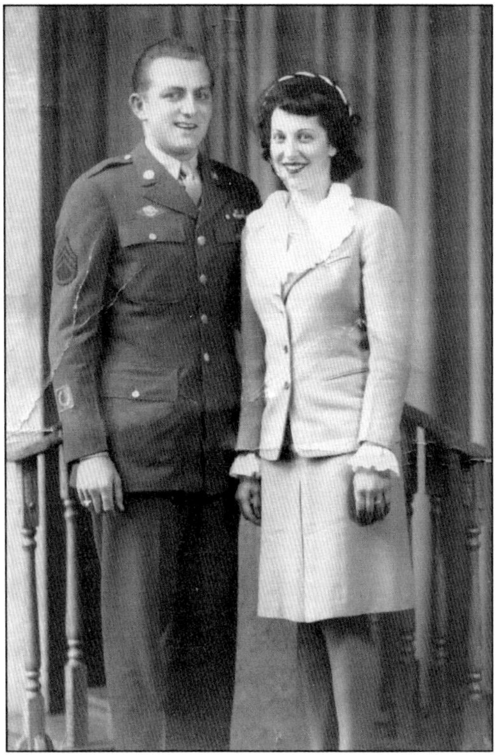

Alex "Babe" Zheltonoga, son of Alex and Mary Zheltonoga of Pleasant Valley, served in the Army Air Force during World War II, from 1942 to 1945. Upon returning home, he married Salome Trouts, daughter of Harry Sr. and Madeline Trouts, from Harrow. Their wedding took place in Quakertown on January 26, 1946. They celebrated their 65th wedding anniversary in 2011. (STZ.)

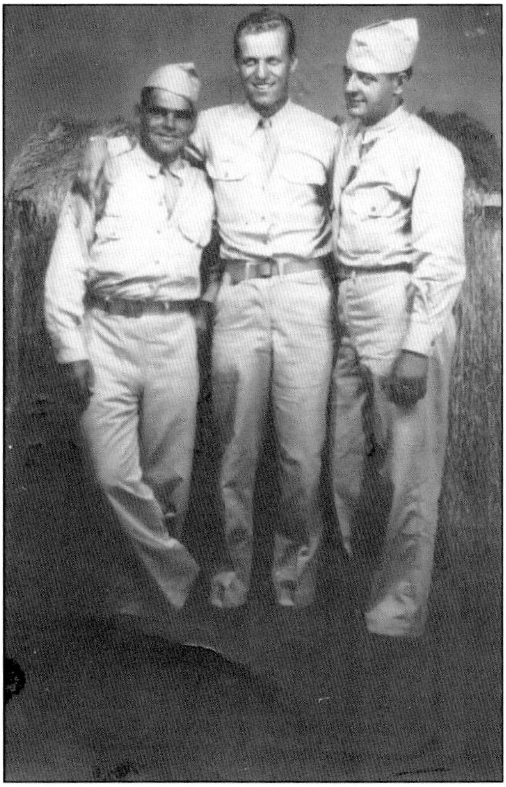

Nicholas Griffaton Jr., on the right, the oldest son of Nicholas and Anna Griffaton, is seen with two Army buddies in this July 15, 1944, photograph. His mother, Anna Griffaton, was honored when the Nockamixon War Memorial was commemorated since five of her six sons served in the military during World War II—one son was allowed to remain home. Nicholas later married Elizabeth Mattes, his next-door neighbor growing up in Ferndale. (CGG.)

Nockamixon Boy Scout Troop No. 27 is marching in the 1962 Memorial Day parade as the procession snakes through village of Ferndale. From left to right, assistant scoutmaster Christopher Hampton gives commands while scout Gerald Miller carries the American Flag, Benjamin Naska bears the Troop 27 Scout flag, and honor guard Ronald Houseworth keeps pace. Residents are lined up on both sides of Easton Road as the Ottsville Volunteer Fire Company truck approaches. (BNB.)

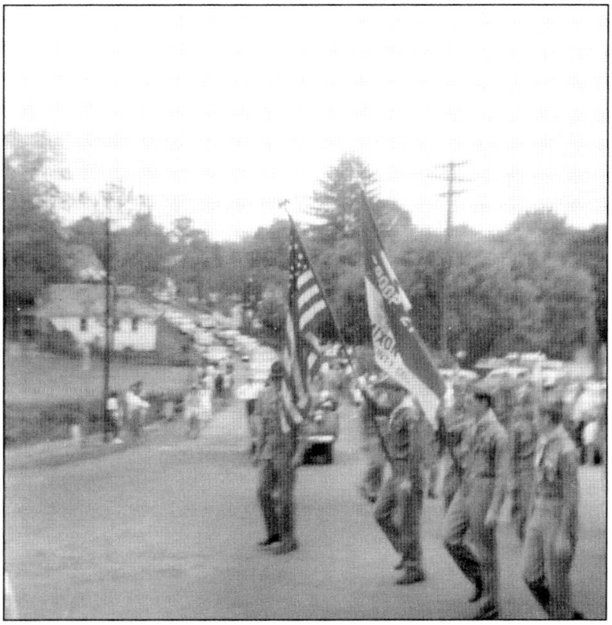

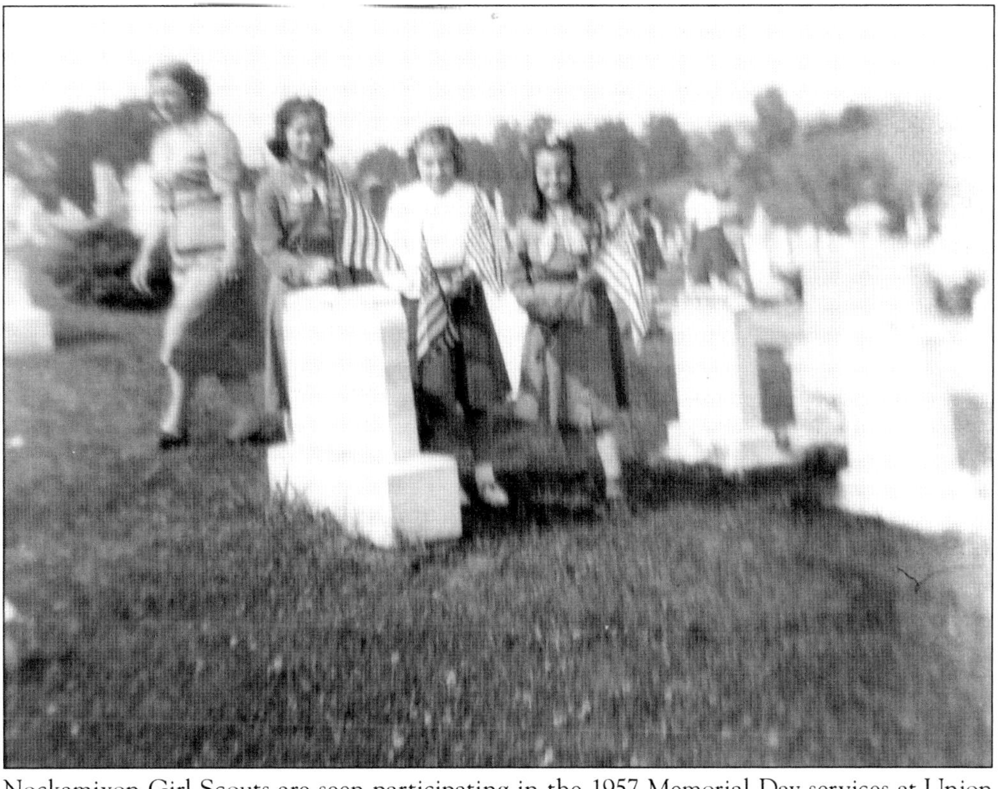

Nockamixon Girl Scouts are seen participating in the 1957 Memorial Day services at Union Cemetery on Church Hill Road in Ferndale. Troop leader Alberta Freeh and Girl Scout troop members place American flags on the graves of all members of the military to honor their sacrifice. Services were also observed at other cemeteries in the area to acknowledge residents' dedication to the country. (BNB.)

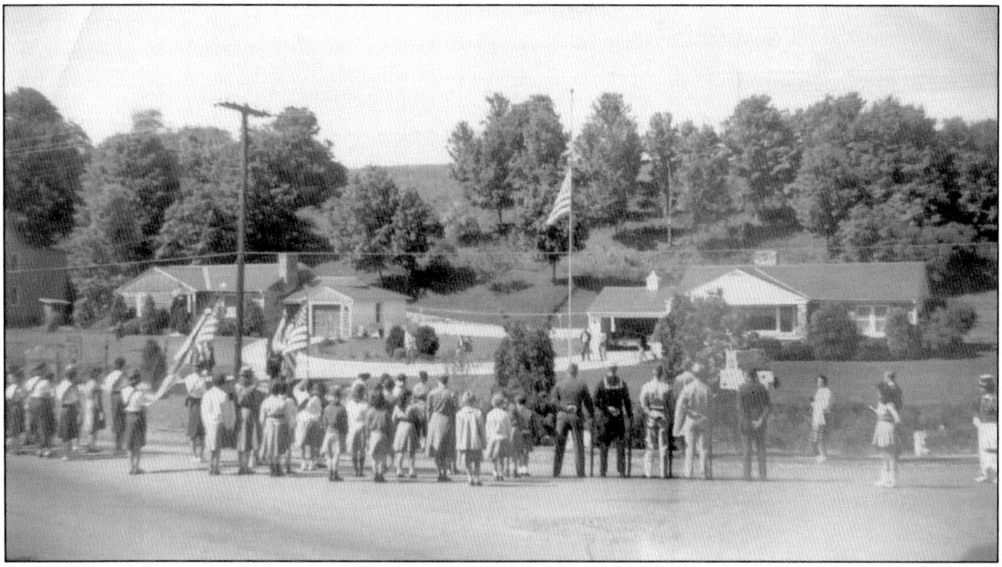

Members of the US Military, American Legion, Girl Scouts, Boy Scouts, Brownies, and Cub Scouts assembled at Veterans Memorial Park on Easton Road for Memorial Day services in 1961. Participants paid homage to all those who have fought bravely for this country so that everyone could enjoy the freedom they had protected. The Nockamixon High School band played "Taps" during the flag-raising ceremony. (BNB.)

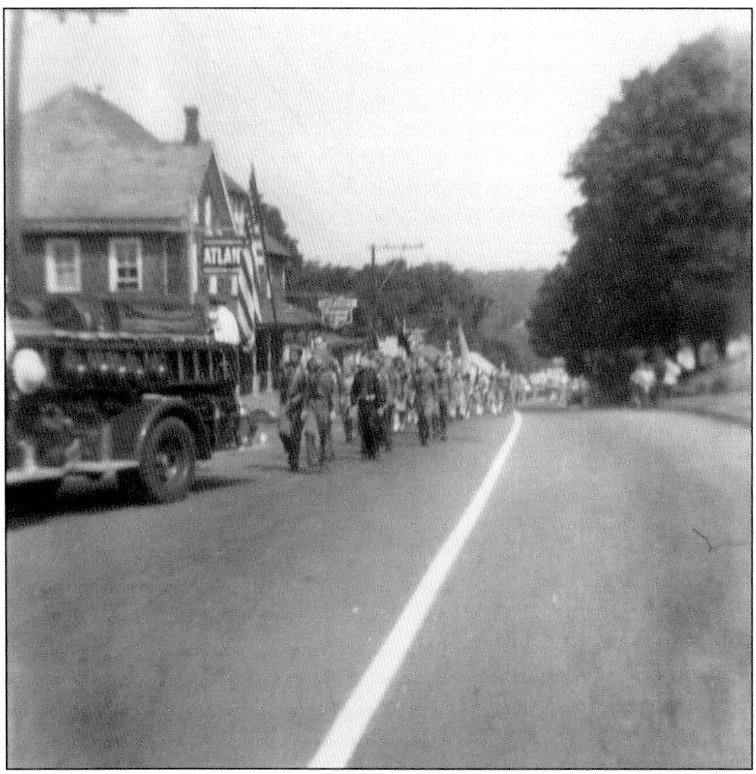

Ottsville Volunteer Fire Company members lead the 1957 Memorial Day parade, travelling south on Easton Road following the old Doylestown and Easton trolley run. Marching past Moyer's store, the creamery, and other businesses before stopping at the Revere Ferndale Hunting Club, the many organizations and participants followed the parade route to Ottsville Cemetery. (BNB.)

Comdr. Coloman Balogh stands at attention after raising the flag at the original home of American Legion Palisades District Memorial Post No. 399 on Anawanda Road in Ottsville in 1976. The legion started Memorial Day observance in the early 1970s, honoring those who served in the military. Services start at St. John Baptist Church and Cemetery in Haycock before moving on to St. Luke's Church Cemetery and Union Cemetery in Ferndale, Red Hill Cemetery in Ottsville, and then concluding at Veterans Memorial Park in Revere. (ALP.)

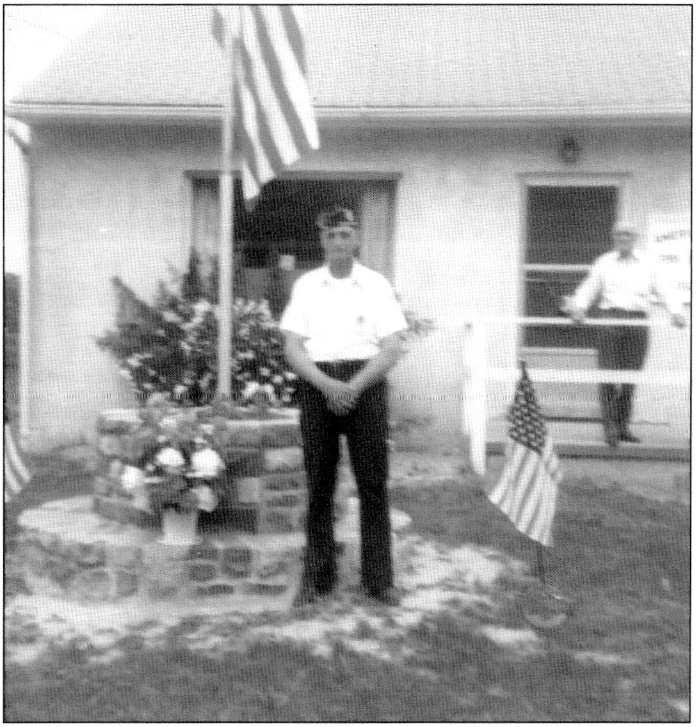

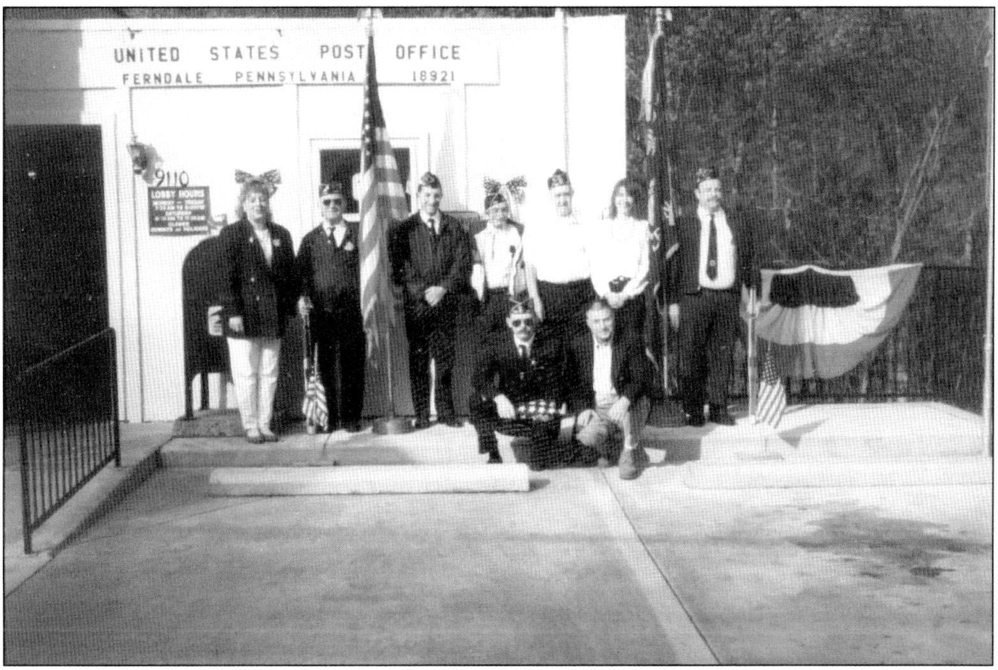

Palisades Memorial American Legion Post No. 399 members participate in a dedication ceremony of Ferndale Post Office's new handicapped parking area in May 1995. Ferndale postmaster Nancy Dilliplance, Comdr. Rodney Pursell, and Second Vice Comdr. Barry Smith officiated the flag-raising ceremony for the much-needed handicap-accessible ramp. Other legion members participating were Edward Litschauer, Robert Parash, and Henry Gawronski. (ALP.)

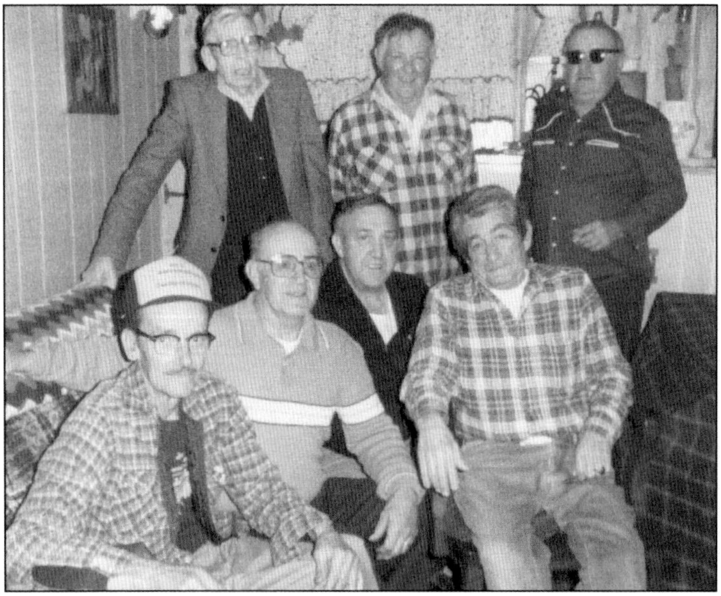

The annual picnic held by American Legion Palisades Memorial District always brings together many members and their families. This May 1989 photograph shows many longtime members, some of whom have passed away. From left to right are (first row) John Carney, Edward Litschauer, Jack Schmidt, and Earl (Squirrely) Pursell; (second row) Louis McNichol and the Donchez brothers. (ALP.)

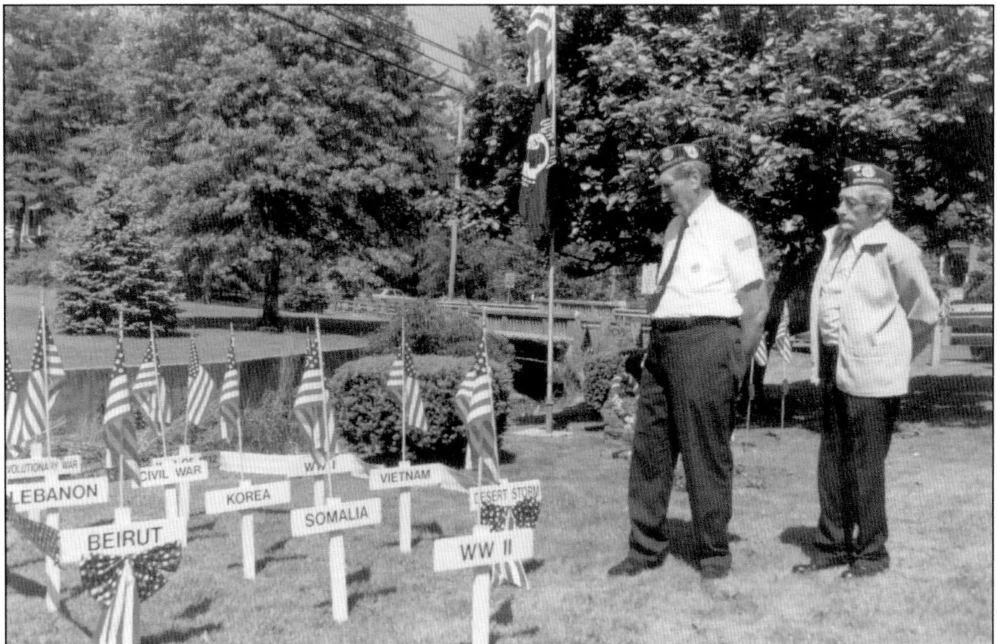

Continuing a Memorial Day tradition, post No. 399 members Coloman Balogh and Earl Pursell pay their respects in May 1994 to their fallen comrades in the various branches of the military. This site, located on corner of Easton and Church Hill Roads, was later renamed and dedicated as Coloman Balogh Memorial Veterans Park. (ALP.)

About the Nockamixon Historical Society

The Nockamixon Historical Society was founded in 1991 to encourage preservation of the township's history. Our purpose is to collect, preserve, research, and interpret objects, properties, historical and documentary records or materials, and oral traditions that illustrate the civil, cultural, political, and religious history of the township, as well as the promotion of the study of that history.

Our organization assisted with Nockamixon Township's 250th anniversary celebration in 1992 and published a commemorative book. Starting in 1994, we have sponsored old-time concerts, bringing back family entertainment reminiscent of Bucksville where music was an important part of community life. We have also commissioned pottery and redware tiles comparable to items that were made during a thriving industry in the township years ago.

The Nockamixon Historical Society is proud to have received the "Preserving Our Communities" award from the Heritage Conservancy for a pictorial survey of older township dwellings. Most recently, a historical marker was erected at Veterans Memorial Park in Revere to commemorate resident Hiram W. Pursell. It was a privilege to honor this Congressional Medal of Honor recipient for his valor during the Civil War battle in Fair Oaks, Virginia.

The Nockamixon Historical Society celebrated its 20th anniversary in May 2011. We appreciate the community's support of our many endeavors over the years. Our thanks to the many residents who have attended our reminisce sessions and shared their memories about growing up in Nockamixon Township. One of our most popular activities, we will continue hosting them in the spring and look forward to seeing many of you. We hope you enjoy the Nockamixon Township book, our latest project.

Consistent with our mission to preserve history on a local level, this book was printed in South Carolina on American-made paper and manufactured entirely in the United States. Products carrying the accredited Forest Stewardship Council (FSC) label are printed on 100 percent FSC-certified paper.

MADE IN THE USA